Scribe Publications
KEVIN RUDD

Nicholas Stuart joined the ABC in 1985, worked in Radio News, ABC Radio Current Affairs, and ABC TV, and was the ABC's Indochina correspondent. He went on to research the factors influencing ABC News for a PhD, and taught broadcast journalism at the University of Canberra until the lure of political journalism became too strong. He is now a regular columnist for the *Canberra Times*. He is married to Catherine McGrath, formerly chief political correspondent for the *AM* program, and now political editor of *Australia Network*. They live in Canberra and have three children.

Thanks to all those who have supported me,
especially in this project,
and Catherine, without whom nothing would be possible

KEVIN RUDD

an unauthorised political biography

NICHOLAS STUART

SCRIBE
Melbourne

Scribe Publications Pty Ltd
PO Box 523
Carlton North, Victoria, Australia 3054
Email: info@scribepub.com.au

First published by Scribe 2007

Typeset in 12.5/16 pt Granjon by the publishers
Printed and bound in Australia by Griffin Press

National Library of Australia
Cataloguing-in-Publication data

Stuart, Nicholas.
Kevin Rudd : an unauthorised political biography.

ISBN 9781921215582 (pbk.).

1. Rudd, Kevin, 1957- . 2. Australian Labor Party - Biography.
3. Political leadership - Australia. 4. Politicians - Australia - Biography. 5. Australia - Politics and government - 2001- . I. Title.

324.29407092

www.scribepublications.com.au

Contents

Introduction

I had been chatting easily with a senior Labor figure about Kevin Rudd for about an hour when she suddenly leaned forward and fixed me with her hazel eyes. 'The problem with political biographies is that you can't get the whole story. I can't be frank with you. Kevin won't be frank with you. You can't attribute stuff; you don't know how accurate it is. History hasn't shaken it down yet. It's premature.'

Unfortunately, we cannot wait for a complete biography of Kevin Rudd. He is standing for election today, asking us to trust him with our hopes for the future. We need to know about Rudd now. That's why this book has been written. It is an attempt to reveal more about the person who may soon become the next prime minister of Australia.

Kevin Rudd did not cooperate with the preparation of this book. Initially, he told a number of people not to speak with me. Just before publication, his attitude changed.

Fortunately, other people have been far more forthcoming about the events that are described here. Perhaps that is because this is a serious attempt to understand the man and something of his remarkable drive. I have made no attempt to wipe away the blemishes, but neither is this some sort of 'demolition job', trying to spotlight his flaws. This book simply attempts to capture an accurate portrait of him.

As recently as 2004, Rudd was simply one of a number people who aspired to lead Labor. He hadn't progressed much further by the end of 2005. It was only in the winter of 2006 that he finally pulled ahead of the pack of other potential leaders. How and why the Labor Party went through this process as it attempted to find a new direction is the other important subject of this book. Unlike the other candidates, Rudd managed to transform his desires into reality. To reveal how this has happened is a simple tale. But to comprehend *why* it has happened, it's necessary to understand Rudd. Not just the man, but also his ambition—an ambition not simply for himself, but also for his party.

An average person doesn't seek to become prime minister. This extraordinary ambition has been made realisable for Rudd because of the vital support he's received along the way from his wife, family, and colleagues. Unfortunately, limitations of space and the necessity to complete this book before the coming election have curtailed further exploration of some of these issues. I've sought instead to concentrate my focus on the story of his political rise from being a fatherless eleven-year-old on the Sunshine Coast to becoming Labor's leader.

This is Rudd's story as told by the key people who have watched and interacted with him during his rise. Not everyone agrees about exactly what happened. Not everyone I have spoken to is his friend. He has asked some people not to cooperate with the preparation of this biography. As a result, this can only provide one part of his story.

In his *Diaries*, Mark Latham writes, 'If a journalist makes out he is your mate, he is lying to you.' I do not pretend to be anyone's mate, but I hope people will find this account accurate. Some will disagree with my judgements, but the account is as exact as I can make it, considering limitations of time and space.

Wherever possible, I have attributed direct quotations to individuals. However, some sources have insisted on anonymity. So that the reader can determine which perspective any such comment comes from, I have tried to include general identification of the position held by that person at the relevant time. But sometimes even these general descriptions would have been enough to reveal exactly who provided the information. Other people, initially willing to be quoted, later asked for their names to be disguised. There would have been no way to write this book except by agreeing that some things would be on an anonymous or background-only basis. I have respected the desires of my informants.

I'd like to thank the many people who were generous with their time and insights. Some had different recollections or interpretations of the same events. I have tried to include both versions in order to allow readers to come to their own conclusions wherever possible.

Finally, this is a portrait of someone who is still moving and developing—both as an individual and in his political views. In that sense it is a snapshot, because the evolution will continue. A willingness to transform and accept change is a mark of great strength.

***

The hazel-eyed politician referred to above is correct. It is too soon to form a judgement about Rudd's personality. We do not know enough about this man to form a final verdict.

Lindsay Tanner puts the same idea in another way. 'I'm in favour of political biographies being written after, not before, people have been in power. What are far more interesting to me are their ideas and whether they've been able to fundamentally change the political landscape. That's the really interesting question: what's underneath all this?'

In December 2006, the Labor caucus decided to back Rudd in his claim for political leadership of the nation. This book tries to explain why.

PROLOGUE

Challenge

January 2005

> 'About three or four years ago there were five or six of us, all positioning ourselves with leadership ambitions. Gradually, we fell away. In 2005 there was a kind of phoney contest for the leadership. By that time I'd begun to think that he might be the right person to lead the party.'
>
> –Labor parliamentarian Lindsay Tanner

Surrounded by the detritus of cold party pies and tomato sauce, plastic tablecloths and drooping streamers, Labor supporters were left in despair by the 2004 election result.

'I was absolutely furious at the time,' says one frontbencher. 'Whenever anyone telephoned me for the next couple of days I bit their head off.' He did, too. First he outlined some electoral history. He said it was necessary to go back to the Great Depression to find an election where the party had suffered a swing *against* the leader at his first election. But that wasn't the real problem. There was something else far more significant for his party's future prospects.

'Mate,' he'd then ask callers, 'can you name for me a leader—any leader—who managed to get a better swing in their second election campaign than they managed in the first?' There'd be a pause for a moment as people tried to think. No one came to mind. Then the frontbencher would cut in.

'Nobody! That's right—nobody!'

Mark Latham's days as leader were numbered from that moment on.

In the days following the result, telephone conversations ricocheted around the nation as individuals considered the options for change and for dragging the party out of the deep quarry it had fallen into. Vitriol dripped from people's lips as they discussed the extent of the electoral debacle. But, in the short term, nothing happened. No overwhelming consensus for change built up after all the phone discussions. Perhaps things would be different when everyone got together in Canberra. It seemed as if no one had an immediate answer.

The party's primary vote had collapsed to just 37.64 per cent. This was the lowest percentage share of the primary vote that Labor had received since 1931. Every analyst insisted the party needed to win a minimum of 40 per cent of first-preference votes if it was to have any hope of forming government. Without this vital base, even minor-party preferences wouldn't be enough to slip Labor into government. The situation was dire.

The disaster that engulfed the party after the election was even worse than after the Keating debacle in 1996. The next leader would face a massive task because, instead of falling away at successive elections, the government's vote was defying electoral gravity. Despite nearly a decade in office, John Howard had once again been re-elected with an increased majority in the House of Representatives.

The fingers of blame all pointed at one person—Latham. There was no mood for forgiveness. But the problem was that there was no one else to turn to. Bitterness still divided the party after Kim Beazley's backers had launched two earlier, abortive attempts to overthrow the then leader, Simon Crean in 2003. Although Latham had been Crean's surrogate candidate, many in the party still felt intense anger at the campaign of destabilisation that was wrecking Labor.

The party licked its wounds, waiting for a new leader to emerge naturally from the ashes of the Latham experiment. But at that stage he was not in any mood to depart. He dug in, directly confronting one of the frontbenchers who'd been bagging him. In his *Diaries*, Latham wrote, 'All he could do was stutter. He's one of the big men on the blower, but not so courageous in person.'

As parliament met for the first time after the election, the Labor members coalesced into small, sullen camps. Nearly half of the opposition was ready to dispatch their leader immediately, but one less than half was not enough. And there was certainly no consensus about any alternative. The anger erupted at the first caucus meeting following the election.

'Each caucus meeting takes on its own dynamic, but that can change very quickly,' says a Labor member. 'These meetings are just for the parliamentarians, and very little of what happens is reported by media. This provides an effective way of working through the various policy and personal tensions.'

Those who'd felt excluded and frustrated by Latham began by giving vent to their spleen. 'Then,' says the MP, 'Beazley stood up and defended the man who had fought against him for the leadership. It was an extraordinary performance, and a particularly statesmanlike one.'

Beazley had been speaking when he suddenly stopped and looked around the caucus. 'He said, "None of you have got any idea", pausing for a second before repeating, "*any* idea, of the pressures involved in being leader". Basically, he just protected Latham,' says the same parliamentarian. 'People were all over the place. Kim was basically left just trying to herd the party together.'

Another observer has a more sceptical take on the same incident. 'Yes, of course,' he says. 'Beazley supported Latham—then. But he always had one eye out for his own future chance of resuming the leadership, even at that time.'

The question of actual leadership hadn't really come up, but Beazley found himself increasingly being treated as an older statesman who could take the party forward. Immediately after he'd lost to Latham, colleagues say the former leader appeared resigned to the fact that he'd abandoned his last chance to become prime minister. But, in the wake of the defeat, people noticed that something was beginning to change. The parliamentarian quoted earlier says, 'Suddenly, he started to realise that there would be another chance to lead the party, and that it was up to him to grab it.'

Flickeringly at first, but more brightly later on, Beazley's leadership aspirations were rekindled. Today Beazley says, 'I think, at that time, they thought I was the only person hard enough to take it up.'

The leader certainly faced a Herculean task. In the depths of despair after the loss, it seemed almost impossible to believe that the party would ever be able to win the next election. Surely the only hope would be to position Labor within striking distance of winning around 2010. The assignment seemed next to impossible. But, perhaps surprisingly, there was no shortage of aspirants. Or perhaps no politician could resist the challenge.

People may have been positioning themselves, but no one was counting openly. In the last leadership contest, which Latham had won, both Wayne Swan and Stephen Smith had supported Beazley. Latham labelled the pair 'roosters', and few politicians doubted that they harboured their own ambitions. Lindsay Tanner was carving out a new intellectual direction for the party, but this hadn't translated into caucus votes. Julia Gillard was still valiantly supporting Mark Latham.

Then there was always Kevin Rudd. Views of him were far from unanimous. 'A tad too arrogant,' was one colleague's comment at the time, focusing on personal qualities that he didn't like. 'Aloof and full of himself,' he continued. But others concentrated on the positive aspects of these same features of a remarkable personality. 'If Kevin knows he's correct,' says a supporter, 'well, of course, that might come over as arrogance, but that doesn't mean he's not right. He is a thinking person. As well as that, he's always been prepared to do the hard work that is necessary for victory. I've never known anyone to work as hard as he does.'

But at this time Latham hadn't resigned, and the leadership wasn't vacant. No one was prepared to bring on a spill. To do so risked uniting the party—against any new contender. This was the mood as parliament broke up at Christmas 2004. It was not a festive season for Labor. Some were even beginning to wonder if Labor could ever return to power.

Eventually Latham did decide to walk out, but two key events occurred first.

Just before Christmas, Latham's family had been relaxing on Fremantle beach when a journalist and photographer from *The West Australian* newspaper approached. They were both fully dressed, even wearing shoes as they walked across the sand. Latham realised his life was no longer his own. 'Sick puppies,' he thought, later writing, 'It's voyeurism at its worst. It is not natural to be on the *Truman Show*.' Then came another attack of pancreatitis.

Latham claims he had earlier promised his wife he'd leave politics if he suffered from any renewed bouts of this painful illness. This relapse spelt the end of his political career.

***

Latham had been scheduled to attend a cricket test in Sydney with Howard on New Year's Day. He didn't show—he was still too sick. At first no one noticed his absence. The media was absorbed with the terrible tsunami that had devastated countries on the rim of the Indian Ocean.

His friend and senior Labor figure Laurie Brereton telephoned Latham to encourage him to at least issue a statement about the disaster. Latham didn't. He later wrote in his *Diaries* that it was about this time he decided to resign and leave public life altogether. There was no canvassing of colleagues about the decision. For the next few days the media spotlight remained elsewhere.

But soon it focused on Latham again. Towards the end of the first week in January, news of Latham's painful illness was released to the media, but by then the disaster had begun to engulf him in a tsunami of his own. When the wave had swept away the firmament, Howard had responded immediately. Latham had failed to do so, and it wasn't long before the media storm turned in upon him.

Together with his family, Latham had spent the week on holiday in Terrigal. Reports of him relaxing by a pool in luxury apartments appeared in the press, leading some people people to think that he didn't look sick. Soon, any chance that Latham had of retaining the leadership was blown away by his failure to react as a public person to the news of the disaster. By spending time with his family and nurturing himself through his illness, he had effectively pulled the pin on his career. It was a long, slow, termination that would drag on for weeks.

Latham appeared to be in a foul mood. 'Who cares what the opposition has got to say (at a time like this),' he later told his biographer Bernard Lagan. 'None of my verbiage could make any practical difference—bring back the dead, reverse the waves, organise the relief effort.'

That may have been true, but it wasn't what people expected

from a leader. The situation moved rapidly to a crisis.

Hallinan Park is a shabby, defiant-feeling patch of ground behind the Ingleburn Library. The occasional scrap of plastic wrapping lies where it's been dropped. It's not the sort of place that gives much indication of being loved. On the warm early afternoon of Tuesday 18 January 2005, this stretch of dirt, clumps of grass, and weeds became the setting for one of the most extraordinary press conferences in Australian political history.

The emails and faxes announcing that Latham would be holding a press conference had been sent out less than an hour before. But it's a long trip from the skyscrapers surrounding the harbour, or the television studios of the city, out to the forsaken west. Everyone who hurried there that day knew roughly what Latham was going to say. But no one could anticipate exactly how he'd say it. Or what he might do.

Just after three o'clock, a beige Mitsubishi Magna drove up and parked. The door opened quickly and Latham got out, wearing a dark-blue shirt. His hair was closely cropped. He appeared more like the movie character Colonel Kurtz out of *Apocalypse Now* than the alternative leader of the nation. Some of the waiting reporters thought he looked dishevelled and aggressive as he pushed up to them. It had all happened so quickly that some journalists were still getting out of their cars and rushing into the sucking dry heat as he began speaking.

Photographers jostled each other, kicking up the dust as they searched for the best angle. Latham grasped a piece of paper tightly in his hand. His press secretary stood nearby, distributing the statement. This was a considerably shortened version of the original that Latham had written. When his staff had seen what he initially intended to say, they desperately begged him to redraft his announcement. The original had included a bitter tirade against the media. After some discussion, Latham agreed to take out the vitriolic attack, although a flicker of contempt still appeared to creep across his face as he announced he wouldn't be taking any questions.

'A number of colleagues have asked me to address the uncertainty concerning the Labor leadership,' Latham began. Twenty-three sentences later, it was all over.

***

Labor parliamentarians watched in horror as Latham self-destructed in slow motion across the television news that night. Most were on holidays. Some were overseas. Rudd was in Indonesia, watching the relief efforts after the tsunami. As the political situation lurched towards a crisis, Rudd kept working.

Journalists tried hard to pin him down before Latham resigned. Rudd had tried to ignore what was happening at home. 'The question,' he suggested to reporters in Indonesia at the time, 'the question, which all Australians have focused on since Boxing Day, is how to respond effectively, as a nation, to the tsunami disaster.' The journalists weren't put off. 'Does Mr Latham retain your full support?' one asked. 'Absolutely,' replied Rudd.

Within seconds that answer had become irrelevant.

The media storm quickly rippled back to Rudd. He was not only known to aspire to lead the party; he was also engaging with the media at virtually every moment. One colleague telephoned straight away, begging Rudd to come back. His message was obvious. If Rudd really wanted to have a chance of achieving his dream of leading the party, he needed to be back in Australia, trying to make it happen—lobbying colleagues and getting out in the media, demonstrating that he had a clear plan to take Labor forward.

Rudd must have been tempted, but he didn't return. Instead, Beazley was the first to declare his candidacy for the top job, the day after Latham resigned. He wanted another chance to do what he had done in 1998—make the party competitive again—but Beazley hoped this time there'd be one significant difference. This time he would win. He so desperately wanted to taste victory. He was infused with new determination.

While Rudd remained in Indonesia one of his supporters hit the phones to canvass votes. He advanced three particular arguments for making the transition to his candidate. First, he insisted it was time to move to a new generation. Second, Labor needed urgently to win votes in Queensland and New South Wales. The implication was that only a local from the sunshine state could achieve this. Finally, he pointed to Rudd's policy performance and tireless work ethic.

A person working the numbers for someone else said, 'Kevin thought we'd see him on the TV acting leader-like in Indonesia and that this would be enough. Well, quite frankly, it wasn't.' Latham had resigned on the Tuesday, but Rudd didn't return from Indonesia until Friday. When he was finally back on Australian soil, Rudd said he was interested in the leadership. But he still didn't declare, simply saying he had support 'in the high 20s', with many others still uncommitted. How they broke would decide the result.

Barely off the plane, Rudd was only admitting the truth when he said, 'Plainly, Kim's got the jump on me by a couple of days.' It was ground he would never make up.

Rudd was in Indonesia at the vital time that his personal touch was needed to impress upon the waverers that he was the right person for the job. But there was more to it than just that. Things might have been different if he'd flown over to Perth and told Beazley, right at the beginning, that he was definitely in the race. This would have meant putting his future on the line. He might, just, have been able to persuade the former leader that it was the right time to hand over to a new generation.

Did Rudd have any alternatives? One colleague has thought about this a great deal. 'Right at the beginning, he could have gone out. He could have said the party's been through a very difficult time and there's a need to have an internal debate about where we want to go and who we want to lead us there. But that's a debate that we need to have inside the caucus and not in the media. I'm committed to having that debate, but that's between my colleagues and me. I will not be making any further public comment. What I will be doing is committing to stay in this ballot until the end so that people have a choice. I want to make it clear that whoever wins will have my full support. But as a party we need to have that discussion and take that vote.'

This person feels a statement like this would have emphasised Labor's commitment to the ballot as a means to decide the future. Doing so would have been an endorsement of the democratic process as sound and robust. But it would also have plunged Rudd into a do-or-die contest—a game of dare, where both contenders drove their cars at one another until someone pulled away at the last moment. And Rudd's car was just not powerful enough to risk a collision.

But perhaps the most important factor in determining the leadership was that Beazley declared early and then didn't give up. He knew this would be his last chance, and he was determined to take it. He had nothing to lose. 'He wanted so desperately to win,' said one colleague. 'He wasn't listening to anyone who told him not to go for it again.' This explains the strategy from Beazley's camp. 'It was pretty much to blow alternatives out of the water, by declaring early and establishing a strong position. That way, it was pretty much "catch me if you can," but the message was also that "if you can't, then you've got to get behind us".'

Without Latham, there were 87 votes up for grabs in the caucus. Any serious contestant needed to muster 20 supporters just to get a seat at the table. They needed 30 to bluff their way through to reach the end of the first round. But—and this would be the key to emerging from the process with credibility intact—any candidate would require close to 40 firm commitments before entering the ballot.

Beazley was first to declare, but a number of others were counting quickly. Gradually it became obvious that it was a three-way race between Beazley, Rudd, and Gillard.

As soon as anyone could guarantee that they had the magic number of 40 supporters they could show their hand and hope that they'd get the few extra votes falling in behind. It might be enough to secure the leadership. Momentum was vital. Candidates had to announce before potential supporters had already committed their votes to a rival. Nevertheless, there was a significant danger in declaring too early. If anyone did this and then backed down—or, worse still, received a derisory number of votes—they'd never be taken seriously again. This could deny them the chance to ever have another tilt at the leadership. No one was in the mood for a continuation of the sort of destabilisation that had characterised Crean's period at the helm of the party.

'First, the phones start to ring,' says one of those who were counting the numbers at the time. 'People ask, what's going to happen, who's going to stand? And then there's a flurry for the first couple of days.' Slowly, people firm in their decisions. 'You get a pretty rough idea of which way people are going to vote. Then you make the calls, and check. We had votes switch once, sometimes twice, over a couple of days. Then you have to decide. You might have, say, fifteen people saying yes, and they mean it. You've got these seven people saying they'll "think about it," but you're pretty sure they'll come down on your side. Then you've got three people saying "yes," but you are certain they actually mean "no". You are always in the process of trying to establish what the reality is so that you can then make a decision. Then you've also got to make sure that no one else is firming up their support ahead of yours.'

Even now, simply discussing what went on is draining for participants. 'Leadership choices are always ... well ... most people in a leadership ballot have a view about what they think is best,' says one of those doing the numbers. 'Sometimes it will be held in an evangelical sense. But a lot of the time, people have a good deal of respect for more than one of the alternatives on offer, and they'll be trying to weigh up who is the right person to lead the party forward. People waiver and take time to make decisions, not necessarily because they're indecisive, but because they want to get it right. In this sort of situation it's a matter of getting out there and convincing people.'

Rudd wasn't the only parliamentarian who'd been out of the country. Gillard had been on holidays in Vietnam, only returning a day before Rudd. She hadn't yet declared her hand, but the minute she got back Gillard began corralling her own support base. If she could garner enough votes, no one had any doubt that she would be the third contender. Some of her supporters saw no reason why she should be forced to become the deputy, rather than leader, just because she was from the party's left.

Rudd worked the phone hard over the weekend. There was significant backing for him, but Gillard's base was growing faster. It became obvious that people were switching their support. The person counting Rudd's numbers says, 'We would have benefited from most of her preferences, based on the stated views of individuals about who they were going to vote for'. But to get these preferences, Rudd had to beat Gillard and get into the second round.

One parliamentarian still asserts, 'My reading of the situation was that Kevin was comfortably in front of Julia.' Others aren't so sure. 'Kevin began bleeding the moment that Julia started looking around for support,' says another.

'Gradually, over that weekend, the votes began to seep away.'

Gillard's refusal to fold her support in behind Rudd at this time made it impossible for him to stand. One of his backers had earlier optimistically hoped that, 'If Kevin stood, Smith and Swan would probably have backed him. And then Beazley might have folded, too. But she would not withdraw.'

This same person couldn't understand why Gillard wouldn't just pull out and back Rudd. 'She never had the numbers to win, but she split the non-Kim vote. She wasn't even close.' This wasn't true. She was doing better than Rudd.

One of those counting for her says, 'He was never going to get there.'

An analyst who remained somewhat detached from the contest says, 'No matter how you looked at the numbers, if you turned them upside down or moved them side on, there was no way he could win without a big defection from the other camp.' One of Rudd's backers said, 'The view I expressed to Kevin at the end of it was, look, you've got a chance here. You can still go for it and, if you do, I will stick by you. But chances are, you won't win.' In fact, it was looking as if Rudd would come third in any leadership contest.

By saying that he would consult with colleagues, Rudd had accidentally handed a potent weapon to his competitors. It put the pressure back on him, because if he didn't have the numbers to win, just running for the sake of it would make him look like a spoiler.

There was one other alternative: do a deal with Gillard and become the deputy. Yet if Rudd ever, even momentarily, flirted with this idea, there is no record of it. Neither of the younger candidates was going to relinquish their own demands on the leadership. But they were also unable, as individuals, to muster enough support to make a challenge credible. Before the weekend was out, Rudd folded, although he delayed his announcement. He had decided to back Beazley.

'There's no point being Don Quixote tilting against the windmill,' he said in Brisbane on the Monday, announcing his withdrawal from the race. 'The level of support I've received from the community is unfortunately not reflected in the caucus. To contest this ballot knowing that I'd have no real chance of winning would be a monumental act of political self-indulgence.'

He stated the obvious. 'I did not have enough votes to win, it's as simple as that,' he said.

Rudd had decided to wait. Beazley appeared the logical choice to lead the party back from defeat. Quite soon he became the only choice. Latham left parliament, taking with him all the baggage and responsibility for the election loss. Beazley tried to engineer a new start.

'Would it have been better,' asks Tanner, 'if Kevin had become leader at the beginning of this term? Well,' he pauses, 'that's something we'll never know.'

CHAPTER ONE

Formation

1957–1975

'Let the past serve the present … We can learn what we did not know. We are not only good at destroying the old world, we are also good at building the new.'

–chairman Mao Zedong

Rudd has no doubt about his own life story. It is the narrative that has powered his existence, impelling him from humble obscurity in a small Queensland town to the gates of the Lodge. As far as he is concerned, no lingering questions remain about his past. He remembers it; he tells it with clarity and conviction.

Other people have different and contradictory recollections. Part of this variance is perhaps explained by the fact that Rudd was a child at the time the events occurred. Perhaps an element of the discrepancy might also be explained by what he was told as a child. Family narratives are very powerful exactly because they purport to explain why things are the way they happen to be.

The key to understanding Rudd appears to be the fact that there is nothing imaginary or fabricated about his relentless drive. It seems indisputable that he implicitly believes—or perhaps, believed—his version of the story of his childhood.

How else can we explain the man?

***

Kevin Rudd's father, Albert—known as Bert—was born in the tiny hamlet of Uranquinty on 18 November 1918. The Armistice had ended the bloodbath of World War I a week before, but even important news like this took a long time to reach half-way across the world and travel down to the little railway siding sitting halfway between Wagga and The Rock in southern New South Wales.

The Riverina was still being cleared at this time. Mechanisation had just opened the area. Bert's dad was a railway fettler at the small station. The fading sepia pictures show workers wearing shabby clothing standing proudly around a truck, or bags of wheat ready to be loaded into trains for export, but little else. There was nothing to spare for a working-class family. Life was a struggle, and you just had to get on with things. Immediate needs always took priority over any plans for the future.

While Bert was a child, a massive flood completely inundated the area, ruining crops and destroying property. Then, when he was a teenager, the Great Depression hit. There were more important things for a young boy to do than spend time at school, so Bert was hauled out to work at home, although he'd already learned to write with a beautiful copperplate hand. Life was hard.

By 1939, Bert was turning twenty-one. He was a good-looking young man, 5' 9" tall, strong and fit, and he'd spent some time working in the big smoke of Sydney. He was there long enough to spend time serving in a militia battalion in the lead-up to war. But his lack of education meant that he was working with his hands to earn a livelihood. Although the worst effects of the Depression had lifted, prosperity hadn't returned to Australia.

Then another war with Germany came around. Bert didn't sign up immediately but, even before the rapid fall of France in 1940, he made a decision to enlist. After a trip back to Uranquinty he went up to Wagga, where they were recruiting for the 2nd Australian Imperial Force. He enlisted on 15 July and reported for duty on 26 August. Bert was given the army number NX 36658 and became a private.

He then spent the next 1,958 days in the army. He became a sapper in a field-engineering company, eventually—over a five-year period—being promoted to the rank of lance sergeant. This was quite an achievement for a poorly educated kid from the bush. It shows he had ability and determination. With good schooling, he might have really been able to make something of himself, but even the army wouldn't commission someone who hadn't finished primary school.

Bert had spent nearly two years abroad on active service in the Middle East and Borneo. The only blot on his record had been a single night in 1941 before he left for North Africa, when he was fined 20 shillings for being absent without leave. The army trained him as a driver/mechanic. Bert initially stayed on as demobilisation began because he was unmarried and not in a vital industry, and he had no reason to return early. But finally he embarked at Labuan to return to Brisbane. By the first of February 1946 even an enthusiastic worker like Bert was no longer needed. He was discharged and sent to make his own way as best he could.

Bert never returned to live in dry, outback Uranquinty. The 27-year-old had developed a taste for life in the larger world. He stayed in Queensland.

It was while he was doing itinerant work up there that he met a young girl who offered him not just a relationship but also a future. Margaret De Vere hadn't finished high school, which wasn't unusual in those days. She was training to be a nurse, but perhaps finding a career wasn't really too important for the daughter of Joe De Vere. Joe owned the pub in Nambour, 100 kilometres north of Brisbane in the area that's now called—to attract tourists—the 'Sunshine Coast'. But the verdant green hinterland didn't need a fancy name to convince Bert to stay.

He quickly courted Margaret and won her hand. A couple of years after the war had ended, the couple were married. Bert had few possessions, and so he began working at the manual-labouring jobs that were suitable for a young, fit, and energetic man. Although he was qualified as a mechanic, hard physical work seems to have suited Bert. He was determined and energetic. He began cane cutting, and later he tried growing bananas.

A year later, the couple had their first child—a boy, Malcolm. The following year, a girl, Loree, was born. Another boy, Greg, followed three years later. There was soon a need for the growing family to settle down and find some security.

Joe De Vere had five sons—in fact, Kevin was named after his eldest uncle on his mother's side—and the pub business wasn't doing quite so well. Drinking with the patrons was expected, and Joe had a reputation of liking a drink. 'And it didn't have to be a hot day, either,' a former customer still remembers. So there was not a lot of family money to help the young couple. They had to pretty much make their own way in the world.

In 1956, Bert took up running a share farm on the edge of a pretty little town called Eumundi, a short distance up the road from Nambour. Eumundi—which had a population of 500 at the time—is exactly the sort of country town that is today described as 'idyllic'. About 20 kilometres south of Noosa, and

118 kilometres north of Brisbane, it's slightly inland from the coast. The rambling houses are set in the midst of forested greenery. It is an attractive area. Here, there might be a mass of purple flowers; over there, brilliant orange leaves suddenly erupt to split the lush foliage of emerald-green apart.

A prominent local bearing the imposing name of Aubrey Low owned the 400-acre dairy farm. According to a former neighbour, this was easily 'the biggest and best farm on the coast side of the Kenilworth Road'. Nestled deep in a lush flourishing little valley, it sat a short distance behind the town. A small weatherboard house painted white made it an ideal location to settle into for the future. The property ran from a small hill down to a little stream.

Share farming has a mixed reputation, although it's a simple idea: one person owns the land; the other runs the property. The produce is then sold, and the two parties divide the profit after the cost of running the farm is deducted. At its best, it's a win-win arrangement. But there's a downside as well: the worker gets no equity in the land, so any improvements he makes stay with the farm. Similarly, there's a danger for the property owner, because the land can be overworked and the tenant can leave at any time.

But Bert Rudd didn't operate on economists' opinions; he acted, rather, on what he felt was right. And, at the time, becoming a dairy farmer seemed like a good idea. Aubrey Low was happy to find someone good prepared to work his property. Soon after the family had moved in, the Low farm was running 120 cows that required milking every day.

Nearly two years later, on 21 September 1957, Kevin Michael Rudd was born, the youngest and last of the Rudds' four children. He was eight years younger than his oldest brother.

The youngest boy would not have realised it, but at the same time that he was learning to walk and starting at school, the bucolic world surrounding him was feeling the first flickers of a chill wind ushering in a far less-fortunate future.

Broad-acre farming wasn't possible because of the terrain, and so the region had a limited future as a productive rural area. Today there are virtually no substantial farms around Eumundi. Instead, the area is composed of smaller rural/residential blocks or hobby farms. Proximity to Brisbane—only a couple of hours away by car in those days—meant that the area wasn't cut off, but it still wasn't really close enough to become a weekend retreat. The still-undeveloped Gold Coast was the place the wealthy went to relax. Increasingly, the town began to depend on travellers heading north on the highway, who'd stop briefly on their way. For many, existence was pretty much hand to mouth.

Christine Fogg's parents owned the newsagency in the town that catered to the passing trade, while she was two years ahead of Rudd at the little school. She didn't think life was idyllic at all, remembering instead the restrictive atmosphere of country Queensland. 'Life was brutal,' she says, thinking back on her schooldays. 'For example, one little boy shouldn't have been in a normal school at all; he wasn't able to cope. But that was just how things were done. If kids were needed to work, they just stayed home. We simply accepted this sort of stuff. It was the way things were.'

She insists that the division of wealth was very real and apparent. 'Lots of kids came to school barefoot and looking hungry,' Fogg says, 'although others were pretty well-off. My dad ran the newsagency, and we did okay. If you were an owner, you had money. But there were the others in the town, and I was very aware of the social distinctions. Marginalised people, like the railway workers and the share-farmers, did it very hard.'

At least the Bruce Highway brought a steady flow of money into the town. 'There were four garages and two grocery shops,' adds Fogg, 'and the owners were well-off. But the others struggled and couldn't always make ends meet.' Just over the main road from the newsagency there were a couple of empty shopfronts. More were soon to come.

Phillip Borg Smith, the curator at Eumundi Museum, says, 'The area rapidly fell on a downhill slope from the late 1960s. The place was struggling. The Butter Factory closed in '74, and the fruit and vegetable co-op not long afterwards.' By 1976 the Bruce Highway bypass had cut the town off from the people who once stopped to refresh themselves on their journey up the coast road.

Adding to the economic pressures was the repressive social environment, according to Fogg. 'The dynamics of social interactions are hard to explain if you haven't lived in a small country town,' she insists. 'You know things, but you don't say them openly. You speak in a coded language because you know you will be living with these people for the rest of your life. It can be stultifying.' This was the way status worked. 'Money made a big difference to the way someone was treated and the life they led. Facilities were basic. There was no sewerage system. Drinking water came from rainwater tanks. A phone call went through the exchange. It was a very old-fashioned, conservative, rigid, parochial, insular town.'

By the standards of absolute deprivation nearby, the Rudds don't appear to have been too badly off. But those standards were pretty low.

Rudd said later, 'The kids I went to school with—most of them the daughters and sons of good Country Party families—were unable even to begin to realise their potential because of the abysmal levels of funding to the Queensland school system. It made me think that there was something fundamentally crook. If equality of opportunity does not begin in the school system, it begins nowhere at all.'

Ironically, Eumundi Primary has already produced at least two national figures. As well as Rudd, Pat Rafter attended the school. An administrator at the school gushes. 'He came back here just a couple of years ago to present the prizes,' she says. And Rafter has also lent his name to the new suburb. 'We've got the Rafter Estate now,' comments another local. 'There are some really lovely big houses up there,' she adds, with just a slight hint of envy slipping out with her words.

Today Eumundi is thriving. It was reinvigorated by the counter-culture. Young people moved in, captivated by the beauty of the surrounding region. The coast is just a short drive away, and residents are happy to find that the mad rush of development has, like the highway, bypassed the area. The old farms along Sieb Road, where Rudd once lived, are now being subdivided and sold off to the new people who are being attracted to the area. 'No one seems to be doing it too tough these days,' says one of the workers at the school, who's been in the area for about five years.

Rudd returned to the school in January 2007. He'd brought a television crew to film a commercial designed to reveal exactly who the new Labor leader was. He stood beside one of the buildings where he'd first learned how to read and write and, using the idyllic backdrop of the country town, talked about the values he wants to restore to Australia. But, according to another local, 'The headmaster nearly had apoplexy. The first time he knew there'd been a film crew on his property was when he saw the advertisement on TV. Apparently, he was furious. But he was later told that Kevin had checked with the Queensland Department of Education and that they'd approved the filming. No one had got in touch with him about it, though.'

Students at the school got on well with the headmaster when Rudd was a student. 'He taught the class for our final two years,' says Fogg. 'He was a really good guy. One of the other teachers seemed to hate every moment she spent at school, and it was horrible in her class.'

Rudd appears to have worked hard and done well. Even at an early age, he seems to have been very happy reading. His mother apparently encouraged his interest, and neighbours say they had a close relationship. Undoubtedly, she helped stimulate his curiosity. At the age of ten, he remembers being given a book on ancient civilisations, including China. Books seemingly revealed to the young boy that the world was much bigger than the narrow confines of Eumundi.

***

On 14 December 1968, Bert Rudd went to Brisbane. He enjoyed bowling, and later told a policeman he'd been at a bowls meeting at Redcliffe, where he'd had lunch, 'about six 5oz glasses of beer and some whisky.' Later, from eight till midnight, he went to a 'Buffalo Temple' dinner at Fortitude Valley. Drinks accompanying the meal included another six beers with whisky chasers. He then left for the drive home. In those days the Bruce Highway wasn't the fast two-lane route it is today. It seems to have taken him a considerable time to make the 120-kilometre trip.

Around three in the morning, the car suddenly swerved across the centre-line and onto the right-hand side of the road. It plunged off the tarmac, smashing directly into a telegraph pole.

Bert wasn't wearing a seatbelt, and his Rambler didn't have anything like crumple zones to protect the driver. He suffered massive internal injuries from the impact. Some time afterwards he was taken to Nambour General Hospital, where he received initial treatment. The local hospital soon realised it wasn't equipped to look after Bert's injuries, and he was taken to Royal Brisbane Hospital. Almost two months after the accident, on 12 February 1969, Bert died. He was 50 years old. Kevin was eleven.

Nearly 40 years later, Ellen Fanning compiled a profile of Kevin Rudd for the *Sunday* program. In it, Rudd appeared to have no doubt about what had happened to his father. 'His prognosis had been quite good, but he developed pretty bad infections in the hospital system,' Rudd told the cameras.

'It became clearer and clearer to me that the hospital system that I grew up with and that he had to use was, by that stage, pretty well Third World. It was not well funded at all. I'm talking here about the late '60s. It was pretty ropy back then; pretty ropy indeed.'

'There were great concerns about the calibre of the surgeons who were operating on him towards the end of his period in hospital,' said Rudd. 'I'd like to know exactly what their skills were and what happened to them professionally. Because I have heard reports that some of them were subsequently removed from medical practice. I'd like to know the truth of that one day.'

Fanning investigated, eventually unearthing the coroner's report into the death. This didn't back up Rudd's allegations of malpractice; it didn't even hint at anything untoward. The coroner instead determined that Bert had suffered massive internal injuries sustained at the time of the crash. Despite a series of four operations, his condition had continued to deteriorate. The report insists that death came as a result of peritonitis combined with the other injuries to the pancreas, liver, and stomach.

In her subsequent report, Fanning suggested this raised the 'prospect that Kevin Rudd's conversion to the Labor cause may have been motivated, in part, by a misunderstanding of what in fact killed his father'.

The peritonitis may explain the young child's lingering suspicions of malpractice. If not operated on immediately, it can often be fatal. The membrane lining the abdominal cavity becomes inflamed, causing acute pain. If it's properly treated, peritonitis is serious but not life-threatening. But it's vital to act quickly—it's much more difficult to save someone who hasn't been operated on immediately. Perhaps this is how a young child came to believe that inadequate medical treatment was responsible for his father's death.

In the wake of Bert's death, Margaret obviously couldn't continue operating the farm. The Rudd's neighbour, Col Seib, was already helping out by milking the cows. He'd been clearing a firebreak the day after the crash when he'd heard that Bert was in hospital. He jumped straight off the tractor and went to help his neighbour. He continued milking the cows twice a day for the next six weeks. But he couldn't keep up the pace much longer.

Bert may have run the dairy, but Aubrey Low owned it. Just after he became Labor leader, Rudd described to *The Australian Women's Weekly* what, as an 11-year-old boy, he thought had occurred. 'Within two or three weeks of dad's funeral, we were told we had to go. I can remember the terrible discussion between my mother and the fellow who owned the land. I felt the indignity of being treated that way and remember thinking, "This shouldn't happen to anybody",' he said.

When Rudd was elected opposition leader, this story came to play a prominent role in the media. He hadn't highlighted it before, although he had hinted at it in his maiden speech to parliament. Then, he simply said, 'My mother, like thousands of others, was left to rely on the bleak charity of the time.' The story apparently infuriated the Low children, who complained about it to their friends.

Later, Kerry Anne Walsh, a reporter from the Sydney *Sun-Herald*, heard about this very different version of Rudd's 'eviction'. Together with a colleague, Eamonn Duff, she investigated further and found that Low's children angrily disputed the implication that their father had been heartless. His youngest daughter, Jill McCahon, pointed out that 'there was absolutely no reason for them (the Rudd's) to have left until the new farmer arrived in July.'

'Provisions were put in place by our father for Margaret,' says McCahon. 'She could remain up on the farm at no cost whatsoever until such time as the new farmer arrived. What Kevin has always failed to state is that the new farmer didn't even arrive until July—that's almost six months after his father's death.'

'To continuously say he was evicted immediately after his dad's funeral is quite an unbelievable statement,' McCahon insisted. Rudd had 'dragged our father's proud reputation through the mud time and time again'.

Rudd did provide the journalists with a response to their story. 'My mother was told that she had to leave the farm—and that was that,' he said. 'I remember sitting in the next room when my mother was delivered the bad news by Mr Low—and an argument ensuing about how much Mr Low would reimburse my mother for the improvements my dad had made to the farm over the previous thirteen years he had worked it.'

'I also remember clearly a working bee with family and neighbours pitching in to scrub clean the walls and floor of the farmhouse before my mother and I left together by car.'

But it was the unprintable background to this story—the story behind the story—that caused a much greater furore when it was later exposed. The *Sydney Morning Herald* journalist Alan Ramsey later reported that Rudd had attempted to get the paper to kill the story. On 3 March 2007, Walsh had been called by Rudd's young press secretary, who proved himself inexperienced at working at this level. She says a stream of belligerent invective followed. A few hours later, he called again, this time threatening to 'trash you and your paper' if the story was run.

The editor decided to make further checks, and the story was held over that weekend. A week later he was confident enough to run the story. This time, *Sun-Herald* editor Simon Dulhunty received the calls—a succession of them, initially from Rudd's office but finally from the opposition leader himself. 'He went ballistic,' says Dulhunty, 'and kept insisting the story shouldn't run.'

A precise lawyer might, of course, point out that the two stories were not necessarily mutually exclusive. Margaret may have been *told* to leave some months before she actually had to go. But, as Dulhunty certainly realised, this was certainly not the impression that had been created—an impression Rudd did nothing to correct.

What had begun as simply two different interpretations of events nearly 40 years earlier had suddenly developed into a story about ownership of the truth. It seems plausible that a young child might not remember precisely what happened or in which sequence particular events occurred. However, the journalists were astounded at the reaction to their story. Ramsey finished his piece with the proclamation that 'Rudd has a dangerously glass jaw'.

It certainly appears that Rudd continued his schooling at Eumundi for some time, although he may have been staying at a neighbour's place. After carefully trawling through his interviews, I have not been able to find any statement by Rudd definitively stating that his family was booted off the farm immediately; simply that they were told they'd have to leave.

A further assumption has been drawn: that the family was kicked out of the home with nowhere to go. In the *Women's Weekly* article, Rudd referred to being told to go to sleep in the car by his mother. People naturally conjectured this was as a result of being evicted from the farm, although careful reading makes it clear that this was not the case. Rudd said he and his mother 'stayed with relatives a lot. But sometimes it didn't quite match up, so you were left stranded in between. It only happened once.'

It is important to realise that these events were obviously traumatic. Nevertheless, it was the publication of that Ramsey story, all those years later, which took the first gloss off the bright new opposition leader. It was not the discrepancy between the two accounts that caused concern, but rather the way Rudd had treated those questioning his story.

'He has to learn to let go,' said a senior press gallery journalist. 'He had young puppies in his office who weren't experienced enough to actually provide advice; or, if they did, Rudd certainly wasn't listening to it.'

'Rudd has to understand that there are some things you can't control,' he added, 'and it's foolish to even try. It was his failed attempt to bottle things up that ended up causing far more ructions and grief than the original story, which was very balanced.'

Rudd initially refused to provide any further elaboration about any of these events for the preparation of this biography, despite my numerous requests for him to do so.

In his maiden speech to parliament, Rudd insisted that his mother, 'like thousands of others, was left to rely on the bleak charity of the time to raise a family'. In the absence of any hard information, it is difficult to establish the family's exact financial or other circumstances. Margaret had five brothers, at least one of whom was on his way to becoming quite wealthy. Rudd's eldest brother, Malcolm, was in the army at this time, and his sister Loree was in a convent. Greg was at boarding school in Brisbane. Nevertheless, Rudd's mother had just lost her husband, who supported her completely. He was young. Departing the farm was a traumatic experience for the boy.

Margaret also seems to have expected to be paid something to acknowledge the work Bert had put into improving the farm. Apart from (possibly) remaining in the house for a number of months without paying rent, there is no record of this happening.

John Dougherty's sister was a close friend of Margaret at the time, while he later got to know Rudd through the Labor Party. 'Of course Margaret had to leave the farm,' Dougherty says today, 'because she couldn't milk 120 cows. But Kevin realised his mother had been dealt with harshly.'

'Bert had been getting half the cream cheque, and it was a highly productive farm,' Dougherty continues. 'The Rudds were on a good wicket. Well, there was no social security in those days, and Aubrey was a hard man and very wealthy. He could have been a lot more compassionate.'

Aubrey Low was undoubtedly an influential figure. He died a year later and, according to his family, a thousand people came to his funeral. What hasn't previously been revealed is that Aubrey's cousin was David Low, the National Party member for the area in the Queensland parliament.

The year before Bert's death, Margaret's brother Eddie De Vere had stood against David Low in a particularly bitter pre-selection battle. De Vere was successfully wresting political control of the area out of the hands of the Lows.

At that time, Dougherty was the Labor candidate against both Low and De Vere in a three-way tussle for the shire presidency. 'David was very sick with cirrhosis of the liver,' he says. 'His health was shocking. When Eddie challenged David, it left a very bitter taste in the mouth of the Low family. They didn't appreciate watching David getting kicked while he was down. Eddie hadn't exactly ingratiated himself with the Lows.'

Dougherty suspects that the way his family was treated may also, in turn, have contributed to Rudd's motivation for joining the Labor Party. 'It was a way of getting back at them, of saying he was different. It was a protest against the way he, and particularly his mum, had been treated.'

'The Lows could have been a lot more compassionate and given Margaret some compensation for all the work Bert had done over the past thirteen years,' continues Dougherty. He pauses for a second and then quickly adds another thought. 'Of course, later he saw the opportunity to do something more, you know, to make life better for other people.'

Regardless of whether the family was evicted or not, after the sudden death of his father the exact length of time that Rudd actually remained on the farm may not have really mattered to the young child. Dougherty emphasises this. 'It had a tremendous effect on him,' says Dougherty, 'the poor little bugger. He'd experienced at first hand the severe distinctions in wealth between wealthy Australians and others who had nothing.'

The house in which he had been living in since birth was suddenly gone. He had to move schools before finishing. It was a personal catastrophe that made the loss of his father even more difficult. Rudd claims that around March he was 'sent to stay with farmers from a neighbouring farm to live until I finished the remainder of my first term of the 1969 year at the Eumundi State School.' The Seibs don't confirm or deny this account.

Rudd's world was collapsing around him. He appears to have been gripped by a tremendous economic anxiety, as well as concern about the family's future. His father's death may suggest where Rudd's remarkable drive—as well as, possibly, his political leanings—come from.

The key to any understanding of Rudd is the fact that he never seems to stop. He pushes himself and everyone around him hard. He is extremely ambitious, displaying a determination to achieve that appears quite remarkable. In retrospect, it seems difficult to over-estimate the significance of these early events.

***

Margaret had to work. She decided to retrain as a nurse, eventually buying a house a few hundred metres from the hospital in her home-town of Nambour. It was very convenient for a single mother caring for a young boy.

The house still stands at 4 Princess Drive, Nambour, although now it's Rudd's sister Loree who lives there, and the street's name has been changed to Princess Circuit to avoid confusion with the Princess Drive on the other side of town. The monarchy is still writ large across the routes bisecting rural Queensland. Quite naturally, 'Princess' was the name chosen for the street joining Elizabeth Avenue with Alexandra Avenue. There are, of course, a Queen Street and a Kings Place nearby. Dotted around are the natural features that mark out the other routes—Waterfall Road and Spring Myrtle Avenue culminating, somewhat more prosaically, in Hospital Road.

Everything here was in its place. Australia had not yet celebrated its bicentenary, and it is easy to imagine that, for a young boy, life in the self-satisfied town would have been stultifying. The first inklings of political consciousness may have compounded the way he felt.

It's probably no wonder that the young boy used to bury himself in his books. He said later he'd do 'two to three hours' homework a night', claiming this was nothing unusual. Nevertheless, it was probably much more than double what most other children in the country town were doing. It seems Rudd found that books and work provided a way of escaping from the boredom of daily life.

After finishing primary school, Rudd was sent off to board. He attended the Marist Brothers College in Ashgrove, Brisbane. The school is only seven kilometres from the city but, with its eight ovals on 23 hectares of land, it's almost as if it belongs to a different world. Set on the banks of Enoggera Creek, it was established in 1940 before being almost immediately occupied by the military. After the site was resumed at the end of the war, a sporting tradition emerged to completely dominate the school, subsuming other interests within a cult of physical excellence. This, rather than academic prowess, remains the ascendant image portrayed by the school. At the time, rugby and cricket were compulsory. The school had a reputation for winning. It still does.

The school's motto was *viriliter age*, 'act manfully'. Another student later said he hated 'the half, harsh, unforgiving institutional Catholics of the old school'. Sport was so highly extolled it was sometimes difficult to remember that the institution was founded to educate students, rather than to just form them into competitive teams. It's understandable that Rudd did not find the boarding environment congenial. It wasn't that he lacked the desire to succeed; rather, he was searching for intellectual pursuits and not just the physical.

Everything was organised. There was no opportunity for an individual to follow his own interests, particularly academic or intellectual ones. Rudd has not spoken about the time he spent at the college, and it seems plausible to surmise he didn't enjoy it. Instead, he returned to live with his mother and attend the local school back at Nambour.

By one of those strange ironies of life, Labor's future shadow treasurer Wayne Swan was two years ahead of Rudd at Nambour High. They never met at school, because Rudd was in Brisbane when they otherwise might have gotten to know one another. Nevertheless, at that time their interests were different. Swan was one of the 'cool' kids. When he returned to Nambour, Rudd was more associated with academic pursuits.

'I was doing the surfing, football, girls thing,' says Swan today, finishing his sentence with a slightly nervous laugh after mentioning girls. He'd also grown up on the edge of Nambour, and his family lived on one of the old dairy farms. His father, Donnie, had worked during the week in the local RSL. On weekends he delivered oil and petrol. The kids were expected to pitch in, and became expert at transferring fuel from the big 44-gallon drums to 5-gallon cans for deliveries around the town.

Swan's was a typical country lifestyle for those days—lots of sport, including being used as target practice by his brothers throwing cricket balls at him. At that time, the school was filled with football, cricket, and surfing. 'A whole summer would pass between cricket and being down at the beach or the surf club,' says Swan.

'We had a lovely old teacher called Mrs Jones,' he says today. 'The problem was she couldn't hear very well. So while she'd be writing on the blackboard, the people up the back would be moving chairs, desks, and just mucking up generally. People would get away with whatever they could.' Nevertheless, in general the school was run quite formally. Teachers were called 'Sir', 'Mr', or 'Mrs'.

'I was always very serious about school, I wouldn't want you to get the wrong impression,' says Swan. He walked to school along the train lines. Swan's dad's family had established a garage in Nambour in the 1930s. His father worked there after coming back from the Second World War with what was, at that time, called 'nerves'. Today it would be called post-traumatic stress disorder.

Swan was awarded the economics prize in his final year, but was told before the assembly that he wouldn't be receiving it unless he got his hair cut. Swan shrugged. He wasn't going to let a prize get in the way of his life. He received the prize anyway—his bluff worked.

Life was very egalitarian in the small community. 'Nowadays, the dentists' kid might be over at a private school, and the Catholic kids will be at a parish school, or whatever,' says Swan. 'But back then, we all used to knock around together.' The place was a real community. 'These days,' he adds, 'those bonds are fraying. I'm not saying that we can recreate where I came from all those years ago—there are much greater disparities in wealth now—but there shouldn't be any unwritten rule that we've got to grow radically more unequal.'

Later, Swan was to write a book which focused on this issue. In it, he investigates what he describes as the 'fraying Australian patchwork of winners and losers', before putting forward his proposal of a blueprint to stop this 'splintering of the nation'. But while he was at school, Swan had not become politicised. He joined Labor later, when he was at Brisbane University and confronted with conscription and the Vietnam War.

Rudd was quite different. He threw himself into schoolwork. For his Junior exam (as the Year 10 exam was called at that time) Kevin completed six subjects. His best results were in History, where he received a 7 out of 7. English, French, and Geography were all 6s, but his worst subjects were Science and Maths, which he was soon to drop. Nevertheless, even here, he managed to achieve a meritorious 6 in Maths A and Science B; however, Maths B and Science A were both 5s. The difference was that he was interested in the humanities, whereas the sciences didn't kindle any spark of excitement. Two other personal traits also became evident.

He was absorbed by work. This meant he shut himself away, every day, without being told to. He'd simply sit down to study. Once his homework was complete, he'd do some more. Much later, when asked if children were studying too hard, he gave a surprising answer for a politician. Rather than proffering a traditional glib answer such as, 'Yes, it was all so much easier in our day,' he tackled the issue from the basis of real personal belief. He pointed out that he personally used to do plenty of study every day. For him, this was apparently interesting. He could also see that it was necessary to succeed in later life. The question of not working as hard as you could just didn't seem to have occurred to him.

The second feature was that, even with those subjects he was about to drop, he still studied hard and performed far more than just creditably. These results were far better than those received by most of his fellow students who continued on with those subjects. He was determined to apply himself until he mastered issues, even if he didn't necessarily enjoy doing so. He could already find a way of applying himself by reaching deep within to some inexhaustible reserve of application and dedication.

Study was paying off. Rudd realised he was not simply better than anyone else in the school—he was amongst the best in the state. Achieving results like this while in a rural state school was not completely unheard of, and Nambour had done well before, but Rudd certainly demonstrated exceptional ability.

In 1939, the past-Students Association had clubbed together to give the school a prize for public speaking and debating. As a school magazine recalled, the presentation of this 'handsome cup thus launched one of the school's strongest extra-curricular activities'. In fact, debating languished until it was reinvigorated by two teachers, Ron Derrick and Fae Barber, who formed a new debating club in 1974. Rudd captained the just-formed team in his final year, leading it to win the zone debating title later that year. The team was narrowly defeated in the Queensland finals.

'The early years (of debating) were the most successful,' the school's golden jubilee magazine noted a decade later. In fact, the school continued to win the title in four of the next five years, with the 1978 team travelling to Sydney for a competition where 'St George Girls pipped them at the post, taking the title by one point'. Nevertheless, Rudd had undoubtedly become a favourite of Barber's, and was remembered fondly for his contribution to civic participation in the school.

Rudd enjoyed public speaking, and entered 'Youth Speaks for Australia', a similar competition, which required individuals to talk on particular topics. This was 'conducted for high school students to promote confidence and skills in public speaking,' and Rudd revelled in the opportunity to demonstrate how well he could excel in this field. He reached the Australian finals, having first trounced his competitors at the chapter finals and state level, both of which he won. The prizes included books that were donated to the school library, including a lavishly illustrated work on Roman mythology. At this time, Queensland schools felt no need to explore Asia in anything other than a cursory sense. The department's official view was that any attempt to understand the human dimension of the world obviously needed to begin in Europe.

The extra-curricular activities also included entering other competitions, such as the 'Lions Youth of the Year'. The picture that emerges from the photographs of the time is of a polite young boy, hardworking and scholarly, who enthusiastically threw himself into civic activities. It's also possible to imagine others thinking him a nerd.

Nambour was a very conservative town, but this was when Rudd began his official involvement with the Labor Party. Dougherty remembers that 'it wasn't a very big branch, but Nambour was very active. Eventually, there were over 35 members,' he says. 'Some of them were teachers at the school—one of whom later became assistant state secretary of the party—and they formed a branch of Young Labor.'

'When we started it was just five men and a dog,' says Dougherty, 'but the branch built up. There was no factionalism; we'd just all get on together. We used to rent buses and run them down to Brisbane for the rallies and make a day of it,' he says. 'It was a lot of fun.'

Recognising Rudd's penchant for debating might have been enough to ignite discussions about politics. Interestingly,

Barber's son Ray was also to later become an ALP member, although of state parliament rather than federal.

Rudd's decision to support Labor was, however, significant. The teenager was clearly demonstrating that he would choose his own way of going through life, and would not just act in the way the family traditionally did.

Rudd's father had been a member—although apparently not an active one—of the Country Party. However, his uncle 'Eddie' De Vere was very prominent locally. Even today, years after his death, the large shire administration building bears his name emblazoned in metre-high letters. If you flick open a random page from a newspaper of the time, Eddie is often there, gazing back at you. Look up a school prize-giving ceremony and, as often as not, you'll see it's Eddie who's presenting the awards.

This was National Party heartland. Eddie was the top National Party official in Maroochy shire. His sprawling house sat up an incline at the top of the hill, with a bitumen road running directly to it. Ironically, one of the little houses that Eddie's property gazed over was the place where Wayne Swan was living at that time, down in the Bli Bli hamlet. Only a rough dirt track led down there.

Its possible to speculate that a number of factors encouraged Rudd to join Young Labor. He says a significant reason influencing him to join up was the extent of inequality of opportunity that he saw around him at this time; things must have seemed to be stacked against some people, through no fault of their own. Additionally, there was the anger at what he perceived to be poor-quality health care for his father. Compounding this might have been the fact that the Lows, who he thought had kicked him and his mother off the land, were a prominent and politically conservative family. The school, as well, had active, dynamic teachers who might have encouraged him towards Labor. And, finally, there might also have been some slight resentment at Eddie's wealth.

There was widespread suspicion of deal-making at every level in the Queensland government of the time, and Eddie certainly appeared to benefit from a number of decisions. In addition to the road up to his house, he also appeared to have prior knowledge of the assignment of sugarcane licences. As a result, although Eddie was really just a dairy farmer, he was able to obtain the licence and make a substantial profit.

The young Rudd also found that political contacts could come in handy. It was about this time that Rudd wrote to the army. He asked for 'my deceased father's service medals which he failed to collect following his participation in the war of 1939–45'. He baldly stated, 'Mr Barnard (who was then minister for defence) suggested that I supply the particulars of my father's war service,' Rudd wrote, perhaps to encourage the military to issue the medals quickly.

In fact, despite this name dropping, it appears the army still made a mistake. Although the Pacific Star, Defence Medal and War Medal were all issued to Rudd, his father also appears to have been entitled to the Africa Star. There's some further correspondence dating from 1991 on Bert Rudd's military file, which is embargoed until 2021. This may be a request to finally get Bert's full entitlement of medals issued.

In his final year, Rudd graduated dux of the school. Because he had dropped maths and science, his weaker subjects did not hold down his results in the matriculation exam. He scored 7—top marks—for Modern History, Ancient History, Geography, and Economics. In English, he received a 6 as his first mark, but this improved to 7 for each of the next three. French was optional, and this also proved to be his weakest subject. He received 6 marks for both the first two terms, but 5 for the two final terms.

Out of a possible total of 140, he received a remarkable aggregate of 139. It was an excellent result.

For a medium-sized school in the countryside, Rudd was a scholastic star. Having discovered the subjects he enjoyed, the boy threw himself into his studies. It wasn't hard for him to do this because he enjoyed learning. The study was not only interesting; he was also being rewarded for excelling. Other people had noticed him, and recognised his ability. This undoubtedly felt good. Now he was being admired for what he had achieved. This spurred him on.

It's difficult—probably impossible—to understand exactly how the young boy felt at this period of his life. In many ways he must have felt excluded from the wealth and prosperity that Australians still accepted as their birthright. His mother was poor and the family circumstances were straitened. As he set out each morning to walk past the hospital to school, Rudd must have been very aware that his house was not a sprawling Queenslander set on a hundred acres. On the other hand, he could see that his intellectual ability would provide him with the opportunity to establish himself in his chosen field. His decision to drop maths and focus on his good subjects had paid off well.

Although he was still young, a common portrait emerges from those people who knew him at this time. He was, firstly, polite. He always appeared courteous and respectful of authority. He didn't seek to challenge the established frameworks. Nevertheless, this attitude apparently hid a tension that resided within. The dux of the school still seemed to feel excluded from society.

His failure to complete maths meant that studying medicine was not an option. He never wanted to be a doctor; he just wasn't interested. At this time, the distinction between nurses and doctors was highly stratified, with nurses obviously the subordinate partner in the relationship. It's possible he may have harboured some hidden resentment about the way his mother was treated; or, equally, at a deeper, psychological level, he may not have desired to trespass on her territory.

Law, or a combined degree, was the other obvious alternative for Rudd. He says he flirted with the idea of moving into this field. Undoubtedly, by this stage the young boy felt that he could achieve a great deal. His knowledge of his own academic prowess, combined with his widely recognised ability to argue a case, must have inclined him towards the law.

Nevertheless, the child of a single mother from Nambour was aware of some of the subtle barriers that would have prevented him from walking straight into a set of chambers after graduating as a lawyer. There were few role models he could use to envisage himself working in the profession. Although he may have fancied himself as a barrister, arguing cases before the High Court, Rudd would have been well aware that before achieving this he would have had to spend years on plodding cases. He might have been terrified by the image of himself as a suburban solicitor conveyancing land title deeds, or by the idea of being buried in dusty books searching for arcane distinctions.

On the other hand, the image of being a diplomat must have inspired the young boy. In those days, diplomacy was seen as a worthwhile career — something to be proud of. The concept of the petty functionary had not replaced the image of the sophisticated negotiator. Even the idea of 'being sent abroad to lie for your country' held a sort of engaging allure.

Foreign Affairs trained and supported its people well. Everyone had images of them being whisked by chauffeured cars from cocktail parties back to their mansions populated by servants. Establishing himself on this career path appeared an exciting prospect.

When Rudd was asked, much later, why he chose to study Asian languages at the Australian National University, his reply was immediate and definite. 'To escape,' he said, appearing almost surprised at the question. At this time, a picture emerges of the young man that seems to contain inherent contradictions. He was a confident public speaker and brilliant student; and yet, despite these outward signs of success, he still seemed very determined to change his environment.

***

At this point, Rudd made an unusual choice. In the seventies most people chose to go straight from school to university. Taking a 'year off' was neither a usual nor even a popular choice for the year after school, particularly for a highly academic student who had managed to guarantee a place in the course of their choice.

After high school, Rudd hitchhiked down the east coast. He spent his time working at different jobs, including as a shop assistant, stacking books in a public library, working as a barman, a 'promotions assistant' and, finally, working back in the hospital as a wardsman.

In an attempt to find out more about this period of his life, I contacted a number of people to ask them to describe the young man. Rudd asked them not to speak to me, but there can be no secret about the person who headed down to university in Canberra to begin his first year in 1976. He had already proved to be highly capable academically. The foundation for this success was a solid application and disciplined approach to work. This drive obviously came from deep inside his psyche and was probably intimately connected with the death of his father. He had a confidence that was held in check by recognition that he still had a great deal to learn. His relationships with the others at school were friendly, although the difference in his personal circumstances had given him a maturity that not many others shared. Finally, and perhaps crucially, he was aware of his family's lack of means, and nurtured an ambition to change this.

Having already chosen his course—Chinese—at the ANU, Rudd had to find somewhere to live. He applied to stay at a residence in the university, Burgmann College. When he prepared his application, Rudd was staying in Sydney with the Freckelton family in Bayview Avenue, Earlwood. Although Frank Freckelton had only known Rudd for six weeks, he was an elder in the Church of Christ in the suburb who took his responsibilities seriously.

Perhaps because he didn't know Rudd particularly well, Frank's answers to the questions on the application form were positive, if somewhat terse. He said Rudd's general intellectual level was 'high'. His application to studies was 'good'. This word also was used to describe Rudd's willingness to take responsibility, and his interest in sporting activities. The question 'attitude to career, e.g. ambitious, easy-going' elicited the single word 'ambitious'. Later, after Rudd had become leader of the Labor Party, a Channel 9 reporter seized upon this as indicative of the fact that he had always been determined to rise to greatness. Mr Freckelton said that Rudd was 'courteous, willing to work, and with a happy disposition'.

Rudd also attached the two references he'd obtained before leaving Nambour. The first was his 'academic' reference from the deputy principal of the high school. This stated that the young man 'acquitted himself brilliantly at his studies and became Dux of the school'. But the college was searching for people who would make more than just a scholastic contribution, and so the principal was probably equally impressed that Rudd had been enthusiastic in participating in extra-curricular activities. The reference concluded that, 'without regard to Rudd's formidable academic and public speaking achievements, I find it more important to inform you that Rudd is a mature and responsible young man who has my highest regard and admiration. I cannot recommend him more highly.'

The second reference was on a Maroochy Shire Council letterhead, and signed by the chairman, Rudd's Uncle Eddie. He admitted to knowing Rudd all his life (although he did not mention their family relationship in the particularly glowing reference). As well as asserting that Rudd was held in 'high regard by the teaching staff' and 'popular amongst the students', his uncle finished with a flourish: 'I have every confidence in recommending him for any position of trust and responsibility to any person or institution whom he may apply.'

Rudd only put his religion as 'Christian'—he was already defining himself as something other than Roman Catholic, the religion of his mother. Interestingly, he chose to go to the Protestant college, Burgmann College, rather than the Roman Catholic one, John XXIII, which is next door. At that time, John XXIII was a male-only college, and had a considerably more sporty reputation than Burgmann.

Rudd was fixing up the final details of his attendance at university as the Whitlam government began its plunge into the final months of crisis. This would have been a crucial time for the development of Rudd's political views. It's easy to understand how the young man might have felt about the consistent opposition that the government faced every time it attempted to implement its policies.

As a Queenslander, he understood the shocking way in which Sir Joh had subverted the intent, if not the letter, of the Constitution by appointing Albert Field to the Senate. Field, ostensibly a member of the ALP, demonstrated no desire to assist the Labor government. Without control of the Senate, Whitlam could not guarantee the supply of money to fund basic services. The governor-general, Sir John Kerr, then made the unilateral decision to dismiss Whitlam rather than call a half-Senate election to resolve the issue. At the ensuing election the voters unhesitatingly turfed Labor out of office. The coalition gained a record majority of 55 seats out of 127 in the House of Representatives. The opposition had been reduced to a rump of just 36 members.

As Malcolm Fraser came to power in December 1975, Kevin Rudd was also preparing to live in Canberra. He had left Nambour for good.

CHAPTER TWO

China

1976–1988

'Render therefore to all their dues: tribute to whom tribute is due; custom to whom custom; fear to whom fear; honour to whom honour.'

–St Paul's letter to the Romans, chapter 13, verse 7

It was a very driven young man who left Nambour in early 1976 to study at the Australian National University. He was not just leaving the physical countryside in which he had grown up; he was departing the social restrictions and financial limitations that had surrounded him in Queensland.

The next decade would see a dramatic change in Rudd. Through sheer application he turned himself into a scholar and, later, a punctilious diplomat. He appears to have been totally dedicated to acquiring a new range of skills and abilities on which he could base his future success. Rudd used this time to establish an intellectual engagement with a new area.

The unifying theme in this period was China. Rudd threw himself into the study of the Orient with a determination exhibited by few young people at university. He applied himself with equal determination as a young diplomat to the requirements of the service. Most importantly, during this time he developed a personal relationship that would provide the crucial foundation for his later success. This was the period in which everything fell into place. But none of this would have happened without his determination to push himself hard and to keep achieving.

Rudd engaged with his university studies in exactly the same way that he had so successfully tackled school—with effort and hard work. He may have started off as a share-farmer's son, but he was well aware that he didn't have to remain shackled to his past all his life. The young man seems to have fiercely grabbed the opportunity to leave rural Queensland behind.

As we have seen, Rudd had already decided to stay in Burgmann College, one of the residential colleges affiliated with the university. He was quite definite in this choice. Although the application form advised students to indicate their order of preference for each of the nine different colleges and halls of residence; Rudd only placed a '1' in the box next to Burgmann, underlining the name. The reason he was so sure about where he wanted to stay reveals his methodical application to every issue.

He had already travelled down to Canberra and carried out a preliminary reconnaissance of the university. At that time, he had met Peter Maywald at the college. Later the administrator of Norfolk Island, Maywald had given Rudd the 1975 college handbook and application forms. Rudd quickly returned the completed form.

Burgmann had only been open for five years at this time, so it was relatively new and still developing its reputation. At that time the college consisted of two outwardly identical, long, three-storey buildings set amidst gum trees. The brown brick and raw concrete buildings were typical of the institutional/ functional architectural style that was embraced at this time. The straightforward materials used in the building technique appeared to mirror the way Rudd approached his studies.

Rudd had enrolled in the Faculty of Asian Studies. In his first year, as well as studying Linguistics, he took three, full-year units: Modern Chinese 1, Classical Chinese 1, and Introduction to East Asia. He intended to completely absorb himself in the one area of studies. This was not some sort of broad, general degree; instead, Rudd had chosen a difficult course with a narrow focus. His only language at school had been French, which had proved to be his weakest subject. Yet now he had chosen to embark on studying a language with which he was completely unfamiliar.

Understanding Chinese required Rudd to learn not merely a new alphabet but also a new way of writing. Chinese characters originated as pictures, each one representing a different word. Mastering the language from scratch required memorising many thousands of characters. Understanding speech was equally difficult. Chinese is a tonal language. Five inflections are used to invest a sound with meaning.

The Chinese language course focused on Mandarin—now called Putonghua, or 'common language'. It did not introduce the students to different dialects; however, separate courses focused on classical Chinese and modern literature (including the colloquial use of the language). The teaching used modern examples of all forms of social interaction. For a boy from a relatively sheltered background in Queensland, the differences in the way Chinese society worked must have come as a revelation. The further transformation of the country by the Cultural Revolution would undoubtedly have fascinated someone who had previously been trapped in a provincial Queensland backwater.

If Rudd ever felt that he was unable to cope there is no

evidence of this in his marks. He committed himself vigorously to his studies.

His main extracurricular activity seems to have been to lock into place a religious framework that he could use to interpret the world. His outside interest in this period at university was Christianity, and it was here that he found Thérèse.

Thérèse almost didn't met Kevin. When applying for residential accommodation at the ANU, Burgmann had been her second choice—after Bruce Hall which, it turned out, was already full. Thérèse came to university straight from school; she hadn't taken a year off to see the world like Kevin had. She had been to Firbank Church of England Girls' Grammar School in Melbourne, and she'd been brought up in Beaumaris, a bayside suburb.

Her father, John Rein, had suffered terrible injuries in a plane crash during the war. He became confined to a wheelchair, but retrained as an aeronautical engineer. He showed remarkable dedication, and continued working until his retirement at the age of sixty-five.

She had been an impressive student at school. Her principal, Patricia Turner, described her application as 'excellent—a keen student who has worked consistently well'. Turner also felt Thérèse would fit well into a residential community, as she was 'friendly and interested, with a wide range of interests'. In her last year at school, Thérèse had studied Music (including practical work on the piano) English, French, and Greek History and, unlike Rudd, had done Mathematics. But, as the headmistress suggested, Thérèsc shone through her participation in extra-curricular activities.

As well as drama, there was debating, the school magazine, hockey, sailing, and tennis. Interestingly, Thérèse also described one of her interests as being a 'religious instructor'. Her teacher drew a picture of a responsible girl whose attitude to her future career was also summed up in the same word used to describe Rudd: 'ambitious'. Thérèse intended to spend five years at university. She had enrolled in Arts/Law although, in addition to her legal subjects, she had also chosen to study Psychology and English. As she continued her studies, she seems to have realised that she was far more interested in people than technical legal issues. Thérèse eventually graduated in psychology.

Her other referee noted that the girl was 'inclined to underrate her own abilities and be needlessly reticent. As the eldest child of three in a family with a paraplegic father, she has borne considerable responsibility and attained a thoughtful maturity,' noted David Secomb, who was working as a senior research scientist in the Department of Defence.

In August of that first year at university, Thérèse caught glandular fever. She left college. The master, Trevor Wigney, was away in Melbourne at the time; however, realising how frustrated she'd be at not being able to continue studying, he immediately wrote her a letter. He said the illness could be 'absolutely exhausting', and advised her not to worry. 'The main thing is to get plenty of rest and not to fret about not being able to do things that you would like to do. If you push yourself too hard too soon there is real risk of liver damage and future occurrences, so *do* take it easy as long as you have to. And don't worry,' he wrote.

A number of people at the college had gone down with glandular fever that year. Assuming it had been passed by mouth, there was a sudden flurry in the master's office. The staff wondered if this had anything to do with the cups and cutlery in the college only being washed, rather than sterilised.

A resident of Burgmann at the time says, 'Oh yes, I remember Thérèse; she was lovely. Always a pleasure to be with.' When I ask her about Rudd, she draws a blank. 'No, he wasn't there at the same time as me,' insists the former student. 'I was there in 1976,' she adds. It takes a while to convince her that she shared a dining room, twice a day over a period of two years, with the person who may be the next prime minister. 'I really don't remember him,' she says.

Similar groups of people tend to sit together for meals at college, so it's not really surprising that Rudd could be missed—particularly as he seems to have been very involved with his studies at this time.

At an age when many young people were experimenting with different lifestyles, Rudd appears to have been happy simply working and studying. 'He already seemed to know what he wanted,' said another resident, 'unlike some of us'. Rudd was the opposite of bohemian. 'He didn't dress smartly, but he was neat.' Another sums him up in a single word. 'Poised.'

In the middle of that first year there was a meeting of the college residents' association. At this, Thérèse had asked some significant questions, because the master of Burgmann later wrote to her, offering to establish 'a series of solid Bible Studies on Christianity and Sexuality' as long as at least six people said they were prepared to come to all eight sessions. The college would run a series of study evenings on the topic, but 'the proviso would be that people would need to be prepared to do *serious* preparation ... as I have no time for "sharing of ignorance" in these things'.

'If you think that you can find people who are willing to accept this sort of disciplined approach to Bible Study I would be very happy to work very hard with you on this,' the master finished off. 'Hopefully, this would supply the sort of thing you were talking about when you came to see me the other night.'

Obviously, like young people everywhere, Thérèse felt the need to make some decisions about these issues. Unlike many people, however, she was also prepared to consider the issue from an intellectual basis, taking her faith into account.

At the end of that first year, Thérèse decided to work in the college during the holidays. Rudd was also working as a casual cleaner. One of the many people he was cleaning for included the political journalist Laurie Oakes. Rudd remembers being invited to watch the cricket on television with the political journalist one day after finishing his work around the house. They were to meet again in very different circumstances decades later.

Rudd only remained in the college for two years, deciding to move out while he completed his studies. In fact, there is no evidence that his life changed significantly as a result of leaving. According to another resident from the time, Rudd had played a continually diminishing part in institutional activities. He had obviously realised that there was a much wider world to participate in than offered by the insular nature of the college.

***

His lecturers were certainly impressed. Rudd was always well prepared. His application to studies was reflected by the care he took over his appearance. 'In those days, quite often students were barefoot,' says an early tutor from this time, 'but not Kevin. He was always appropriately dressed.'

'What he had to say in tutorials always had a bearing on the matter at hand,' he adds. 'His comments never digressed to irrelevancies or the personal.' In class, he was always keen and involved. He did the set homework and sometimes more. 'He gave off a sense of complete self-control, real self-discipline.' It seems Rudd was, basically, a swot.

'He was mature,' says the tutor. 'He was probably the same right the way through university. Very reliable, very self disciplined, always on time, no accidents. Everything planned and thought out.'

People at uni would often relate to others by finding common ground, talking about sport, music, or films. Rudd, however, appears to have been quite happy talking about more serious things such as study and philosophy.

'Even then, he had a vision of the difference between ideals and reality,' says a student who knew him at the time but prefers not to be further identified. 'He had a very keen awareness of just how far you could go, and he never wanted to push the envelope any further. He seemed fully focused on doing the right thing. He never challenged anything, unlike some of the rest of us.'

A later lecturer prefers to emphasise another aspect of this part of his character. 'Kevin understood the art of the possible. It's not enough just to have a vision, because you will smash up against a brick wall. It's not enough just to know the tricks of the trade, because you will never achieve anything lasting. You get nowhere unless you can combine both,' he insists.

A lecturer from this period describes the process by which students were swiftly whittled away from the faculty. 'It was natural selection,' he says. 'People who teach, say, English literature have to put up with all the people who say, "Look, I speak English, so I might as well enrol in the course because it will be easy." But with Asian Studies, it's not like that. A few join because of idle curiosity, but they drop out after a few weeks or months; because to keep up with the language course you need to do a lot of homework.'

Indeed, the courses demanded consistent application and hard work. It was demanding. Failure to keep up, particularly in learning vocabulary, was readily shown up in classes. Unless students kept on top of their homework they were quickly lost; catching up became increasingly difficult. 'People who stick with the course are obviously strongly motivated,' says the lecturer. 'If anyone is not intrinsically interested in the course, merely completing it would become punishment.'

'If you lose focus for a moment you can soon become lost. In no time at all you cannot read in class or translate the text,' he adds. Only strongly motivated people managed to keep the workload under control.

The course required a great interest in the subject, because otherwise just the simple attempt to keep up would have been torture. The lecturers felt this meant that the people who stuck with the course had much more to contribute. There was no need to motivate the students—that could be taken as a given. Instead, the course offered an opportunity for students to investigate a fascinating culture, although it demanded a great deal of them in return.

Anita Chang was another tutor who was keen to extend the students further than their official studies would normally take them. In Rudd's second year she wrote a musical play called *The Little Cowherd*. Fourteen students had roles in this amateur version of a Peking opera. Chang would often buy dinner for the performers during the two months of evening rehearsals. Rudd had the main role, playing an exploitative landlord with a wife and six concubines.

Chang says, 'I painted my Lancôme mascara moustache on his face, and he'd stuff a basketball under his gown to look fat. He was very eloquent. Just the right person to play the role of the powerful lord,' she adds. 'He was very good in the role, too; he performed exactly like someone from the gentry class.'

A crowd of 200 guests saw the students acting and singing in the play. Rudd organised a special lunch to thank Chang after the performance, where the players presented her with a special photograph. Rudd was thrilled by the reaction to the play. 'He said it was his ambition to organise a trip to perform it in Shanghai,' says Chang. 'He sang very well.'

In fact, Rudd was to sing in Shanghai many years later—although not as part of a performing troupe.

Although Rudd does not appear to have bothered too much with the Burgmann activities, he was very involved in the faculty organisations. None of his lecturers or tutors was aware of any political involvement while he was at university; nevertheless, he did become president of the faculty's student association.

'Once he was able to, Kevin would often speak to me in Chinese,' says Chang. 'It took a degree of courage to do this, but he practised hard and was very keen to learn. He was very determined and eloquent in the language.'

Pierre Ryckmans supervised Rudd in his honours year. He says today, 'Kevin Rudd was one of those few students who had ideas to exchange. Kevin had a totally adequate command of the language, but more importantly the ability to analyse, interpret, and present his ideas. I remember he did the type of work that we wished to see more often.'

A mutual courteous distance existed between Rudd and his supervisor. Already he had a very strong personality, although Ryckmans emphasises that this should not be confused with Rudd being headstrong. 'He was extremely articulate, clear, and courteous. Nevertheless, normally an understanding of life comes through experience.' Rudd appeared to be able to acquire his through study.

Very few people were taken on as honours students. Before anyone was accepted, they had to obtain at least a credit average for the proceeding years of study. Rudd had managed this, and his enrolment was approved.

The fourth—honours—year required the students to prepare a special long essay. 'The idea of this is to, first of all, see whether students can handle written material,' says Ryckmans. 'They have to find the sources, use and translate them into English, and make a coherent presentation of it. The basic idea of the exercise is to show and display their ability to make use of Chinese material. Interpret and analyse the documents.'

'I had many students ... with the passing of time and the weakening of memory, one forgets. But Rudd—I never forgot him,' says Ryckmans today. Rudd had joined a select company.

'They were interesting, the teaching experience was very pleasurable,' he says.

Undertaking the honours year demands real commitment from students. People in this small group always tended to be intelligent and hardworking.

'Often we have brilliant students. But sometimes they are erratic or inconsistent, or they have ups and downs. I had no idea what Rudd would go into, but there was one thing that always struck me. He knew what he wanted. He had an air of quiet certainty about him.'

'Sometimes when you meet people again, 25 years after you've taught them, people change,' says Ryckmans. 'But Rudd didn't change. When you saw him as a student, he looked older than the others. But now as you see him as a politician, and he still looks young. Yet he's obviously very much the same man.' Ryckmans sees this as an impressive consistency.

'I was absolutely sure that he came from a rather privileged background,' says Ryckmans. 'I thought he'd been educated in a good private school, and had enjoyed a very protected life. It was just the reverse, and I think he harboured a deep insecurity. As it turned out, he applied himself with a great deal of that industry to his studies,' Ryckmans emphasises. 'He didn't just have self-control, self-discipline. He was cool and seemed to display great reserve.' This struck his lecturers as unusual for someone of this age.

'Kevin analysed his thesis topic on dissidents completely in modern terms,' says his supervisor. He was in fact using modern Chinese, which was translating these concepts with no reference to traditional culture. This meant that, in addition to proving a mastery of modern Chinese language, Rudd also developed a detailed understanding of current political movements within the country.

'For a brief period (in the late '60s), young people in China were told that the fate of the country was in their hands. That it was up to them to expose the corrupt officials,' says Ryckmans. 'Of course, it turned out that this was simply for the benefit of Mao Zedong.'

Just before Rudd had begun his studies, China was filled with chanting cadres waving their copy of *The Little Red Book* (containing quotations from the works of Mao) in the air. 'At this time, any sophisticated understanding of China required direct engagement with the dissident movement that emerged in the wake of the revolution,' says Ryckmans. 'Understanding the way the Cultural Revolution had first been developed and then manipulated offered a glimpse into the way power worked inside China,' he adds. After disillusionment set in, the dissident movement became the interface between the individual and society. This was the intellectual space that Rudd wanted to explore.

Honours students choose their own topic and supervisor. Rudd decided to ask Ryckmans if he'd be prepared to supervise him. It is unknown what first attracted the student to this particular lecturer, but in retrospect a striking fact stands out. While he was at school, Rudd had been interested in Thomas More, the great English humanist who opposed King Henry VIII on a matter of conscience, and was gaoled and executed.

Ryckmans takes up the story. 'At that time I had on my table a small postcard which I always kept displayed. It was the portrait of Thomas More by Hans Holbein, which I had inscribed with the Chinese phrase, "A minister doesn't follow the ruler; he follows the truth." I don't know if Rudd ever noticed it, but it struck me that it "clicked".'

'He came to see me to ask if he could work on political dissent,' says Ryckmans. The professor had often used this kind of material in his classes—more as an interesting basis for translating modern Chinese than political study. 'There were some very pungent writings,' he says. 'Aside from that, it's far more interesting than boring textbooks.'

This was not a fashionable topic. 'It was not something that, at that time, would help you get a scholarship to China because, quite obviously, it was dealing with the heterodox.' The idea of resistance apparently fascinated Rudd. 'I encouraged him,' says Ryckmans, 'because he was obviously someone capable of a high distinction.'

'I felt very deeply for the democracy movement,' says Ryckmans. 'We investigated the potential conflict between the individual and the state and whether a person should follow their conscience or the imperatives of the despot. He was very attuned to this type of problem.' Issues were not always discussed in these moral terms; however, his supervisor felt there was a more significant reason that Rudd was interested in the topic.

'It was the type of problematic that Rudd was attuned to,' Ryckmans emphasises. 'We were investigating the conflict between the individual and the state. Should I follow my conscience, or the imperatives of the despot?'

Ryckmans, using the pseudonym Simon Leys, is also an award-winning writer. Rudd was lucky to be offered the opportunity to engage with such a distinguished scholar, and appears to have taken full advantage of this.

Of course, for an ambitious student keen to become a diplomat, tackling a subject like this didn't only show a superior command of modern Chinese language. By demonstrating that he understood the dissident network, his thesis would also form a fantastic complement to any application form. It would display the fact that he had an undoubted capacity not simply to analyse the overt politics of the country but also to understand the hidden forces that explained the political dynamics of China.

'I had no idea — we never discussed — what he wanted to do,' says Ryckmans. 'The only thing I was sure of was that he would go far. He seemed very certain of who he was and what he wanted,' he adds. 'His was the certainty of the man who knows himself. But he was also a very reserved person. We never talked about it. He never exposed his own aspirations.'

'Certainly there was deep interest and sympathy from Kevin for a movement of people motivated by high idealism,' says Ryckmans. 'These people can have had no illusions about what their fate would be.' Rudd understood this, and must have been interested in a political movement that would have a long-term future but was doomed in the present. 'As he researched it, it was already being suppressed,' his supervisor notes.

'A purely pragmatic person would have looked at, say, who is in charge of the economy, what are the implications for foreign affairs,' Ryckmans points out. 'But if you get interested in the democracy movement, you get interested in people who are landing in jail. So, in the short term, it's not a very pragmatic move for future employment.' To Ryckmans, this is all suggested a deeper commitment to something higher and more meaningful. 'It also gives you a much better understanding of the duality of China,' he points out.

Rudd's study of China suggested he was interested in much more than simply mixing with the diplomatic cocktail set. It appeared as if the young student was attempting to gain an understanding of the undercurrents swirling within Chinese society.

There was an impressive mass of documents and texts to study. Although the democracy movement only flourished for a brief period, it was a very active time. Thoughts were being articulated and powerfully expressed. There was an enormous mass of information, varying from photographs of the democracy wall in Peking to pamphlets circulated around the underground. The big source of information came from the listening post of Hong Kong. 'This had everything from escaping Red Guards who were swimming at night across to the island, through to bundles of roneoed notes being smuggled from the mainland,' says Ryckmans. 'These provided news of what happened, or information about what was going to happen.' Rudd had a rich and reliable source of documents, which allowed him to interpret exactly what was happening, down to the testimonies of individual dissidents who had escaped from China.

It was easy enough to get a picture of the orthodox China, the official view, or how China wanted to be seen. For that, there was an abundance of material. But if you wanted to know if there was more to it, another side to that duality, you needed to unlock the opposition perspective.

'The dissenters transformed the one-dimensional propaganda of China into something with relief,' says Ryckmans. 'Without that,' he adds, 'you really get a false idea of the country.' There is always another face of China, which remains shrouded in mystery. Rudd's studies gave him access to the hidden face of China, with its victims and martyrs.

'At certain times, there is no access to anything beyond the façade, the curtain that covers the real China,' Ryckmans insists. 'But sometimes the façade suddenly cracks open, and you can see what is behind the veil.'

This appealed to Rudd, who always wanted to see the full picture. By the time he was posted to the country years later, political developments meant that the environment had changed considerably. Nevertheless, all the hard work at university opened up two doors for him. He gained not just the possibility of joining External Affairs, but also a real understanding of China that could later be put to work.

By the time he'd finished his studies, Rudd had acquired a remarkable speciality that was later to put him at the forefront of engagement with a vital neighbour. The young student had also developed a finely honed ability to analyse political and economic events. Now he needed to begin putting this to work.

***

The official title pretended it was just a *Statement of Service Appointments and Biographies*. Those in the know called it the 'stud book'. It was a vital means of allowing everyone employed by the Department of External Affairs to measure themselves against their colleagues, work out promotion prospects, and figure out who was winning the race to the top. When 'RUDD, Kevin Michael', began work as a diplomat, his entry was brief.

Those reading the book could find out that Rudd was appointed to the Australian Public Service on 28 January 1981 as a Foreign Affairs trainee. One of those on his selection panel later privately asserted that Rudd did not shine out as an outstanding applicant during the interview process. 'Nothing special at all,' he confidentially asserted with the unique benefit of someone able to use hindsight to make a point about how good the overall calibre of the department had been. Nevertheless, Rudd was obviously good enough to be offered one of the highly regarded cadetships. So was Alexander Downer, although not in the same year.

Rudd was meant to spend that first year in Canberra, gaining experience with different sections of the department. It also offered the senior diplomats a chance to evaluate their new recruits before sending them on an overseas posting. At this stage, the department was still small. It had a reputation as the elite, particularly amongst its own members. All its recruits were required to be graduates. Many had honours degrees. They had to be capable of the detailed analysis required by the service—weighing up many different factors in tightly argued appreciations, before coming to definite conclusions and then recommending a sound course of action to be followed.

Nevertheless, Rudd quickly realised that more was required of diplomats than the simple production of reports and papers. His integration into the department depended on being much more than just an assiduous bureaucrat. He needed to be able to demonstrate complete mastery of his work and, perhaps even more importantly, the vital ability to negotiate the subtle shoals and waters of interpersonal relationships in a complex political environment.

In those days, much more so than today, Foreign Affairs was thought of as doing 'intellectual' work. There was an air of quiet superiority about the place, although this was really grounded in the quality of its work rather than the background of individual recruits.

Later, Stuart Harris took over as secretary. He was an outsider, because he hadn't come up through the ranks of the diplomatic service, and he decided to commission a survey of the make-up of the department to see if any of the rumours about social elitism were true. Much to the surprise of some, this showed that, as a group, the diplomats themselves reflected ordinary society. Those who'd come from public schools outnumbered those who could wear an 'old-school tie'.

If there was any similarity amongst the recruits, it probably came from self-selection. Many of his new colleagues spoke English using just the same accent as Rudd. This was the way they wanted to be, the way they saw themselves. Not only was their pronunciation like his, they also articulated their ideas in the same logical, precise way that he loved, using similar words to the ones that sprang so naturally to his lips.

Rudd was keen to make a good impression, and so he did. A senior officer at the time says, 'Careful attention was paid to the way the new recruits were fitting in. Sometimes those who had achieved good results at university didn't manage to produce similar outcomes once they began working as diplomats.' There was a good deal of difference between the ability to shine in an academic environment and the need to maintain positive relationships with colleagues while working under pressure.

'Instead of finding it difficult to mix with others, social skills came naturally to Kevin,' he adds. 'As well as that, his work was up to the standard the department expected.' This should not have been a surprise really, because Rudd already appears to have been quite sure of his abilities and the direction he wanted to take by this time.

Negotiating his own way through life must have become natural for a young man who, in many ways, didn't appear typical. It would have been easy for him to be picked on at school because of his academic interests. At Burgmann he'd been surrounded by wealthier students who must have appeared less interested in their studies. But Rudd mediated in his own way through this maze while keeping his cool and concentrating on achieving success. He was already a natural diplomat. All that was required was the official imprimatur.

Rudd's expertise was, of course, China, so the department made a conscious decision to give him a job that would require him to demonstrate that he had the ability to expand his focus. After a brief induction period, in which the workings of the department were explained, he started in the ASEAN section, which looked at Australia's relationship with the Association of South-East Asian Nations. Richard Woolcott, a later departmental secretary, insists that the focus of the department had never changed. 'There has always been that special focus on Asia,' he says. 'It's only an issue of degree. But at this time North Asia was perceived as being a little bit secondary. A lot of emphasis was placed on the countries that are closer to us.'

It was part of a subtle test for Rudd to check if he was the 'right sort'. Not all the 'bright young things' could survive being taken out of their comfort zone. Occasionally, even the best wouldn't be able to cope with problems that they hadn't been exposed to before. There was a need to make sure that intellectual rigour and discipline was innate within an individual. This would mean that analytical skills could be applied to any problem, not just issues that the diplomat was already familiar with.

'Rudd was very across the detail; most capable,' says Woolcott today. 'There is the occasional feeling within the department that people who do well academically don't do quite as well in the field. Well, that wasn't the case with Kevin at all.'

This period also gave the department an opportunity to weigh up how well Rudd could work with other people. Before he went overseas it was necessary to make sure that Rudd had the right sort of personality to get on with a small group of other Australians, sometimes in considerable isolation, working together in a foreign country. 'Someone's first posting is very much just "on the job" training,' says Woolcott.

Rudd fitted in well. His superiors noted the way he dealt positively and respectfully with his colleagues. If the term 'team player' had been made up by this stage, it would have suited Rudd perfectly. His written skills were above average; however, it was the dedication he displayed that caught the attention of everyone.

In May, Rudd took leave. He had a number of little things to sort out, but most importantly he wanted to make sure that, if the chance came up, he'd be able to head overseas at a moment's notice. When he returned in July he was posted to the Economic Relations section. By now there were no real questions about Rudd's suitability for the department. Everyone was happy with his work, and this posting was seen in an opportunity to develop his skills in a new area. Rudd had eschewed economics, along with anything mathematical, while he was at school. This posting probably challenged him far more intensely than had the earlier one in the ASEAN section. Colleagues from the time say that Rudd appeared to throw himself into everything at this stage, and this was certainly a new area for him. One feature that marked him out from other people in that intake was his enthusiasm to take on any task, along with his dedication in getting to grapple with the subject.

But he didn't have to wait long for his first-ever chance to leave Australia. Because air travel was not as common then as it is today, Rudd had never left the country. He must have felt the incongruity of being a diplomat who had only ever seen Australia. If he was going to reach the top, he needed to understand what the business end of the operation looked like. And the only way to do that was by obtaining a posting. His chance came before the end of the year.

The Stockholm embassy urgently required a third secretary. This is the lowest rank on the department's hierarchy, but it is the point at which everyone has to begin.

There was just one other thing the excited diplomat needed to do before departing. The weekend before leaving, Kevin and Thérèse were married in a ceremony in Canberra.

***

A capable young diplomat posted to Sweden as a junior officer leaves few traces in the official record—which is probably very much as it should be. Although a posting to Europe is normally for three years, the couple returned in October 1983. Thérèse was back in Australia for the birth of their daughter, Jessica Claire Rudd, on 7 December that year. The proud father then spent two months working on a desk job in the department before he was sent to Point Cook in January 1984 for a further eight months of intensive language training in Mandarin.

This was standard for officers about to be appointed to Beijing. It was a way of ensuring that the command of the language he had achieved at university was up-to-date with modern colloquial expressions. There were certainly no gaps in Rudd's linguistic ability by the end of this time. Although later he would pretend he was not an expert, this was simply Rudd being self-effacing. There was no doubt about his mastery of both the intricacies of the language (formal or colloquial) together with Chinese culture. This was about to become very useful for his career.

'Australia has always had an intimate engagement with Asia,' says Woolcott today. 'Remember, Harold Holt's first visit overseas was to Indonesia. Until recently, Australia's main diplomatic effort has always been directed primarily towards our neighbours and the region. After all, this is where we live.'

The situation in China at this time was even more exciting than when he had studied the country at university. The opening up of the economy had begun in 1978, but back then it had moved very slowly. By the late '80s the momentum for reform was reaching a high-tide mark. After Tiananmen Square in 1989, it would again be repressed. But, all through Rudd's period in China, change was happening. It was an exciting time to be in Beijing.

At the time, Westerners thought the Chinese premier Zhao Ziyang was an intelligent leader who might lead the country in a different direction. He developed an analytical approach to both international relations and internal politics. He'd made a significant trip to Australia in 1983, originally organised by the Fraser government. Hawke followed this up with a return trip the next year. After this, relations between the two countries had flourished.

Mutual suspicion prevented America developing too tight a relationship with Beijing. The Europeans' knowledge of the Asian country had also languished in the preceding decades. Similarly, many Asian countries that were not members of the communist bloc had failed to even establish diplomatic relations with the People's Republic. After Whitlam established links in 1972 Australia was at the vanguard of international engagement with China. This continued during the Fraser years.

A surprising feature of Australian society is the depth of the relationship with such a vastly different country. Opinion polls show that, just after the Second World War, attitudes to Chinese migration were far more favourable than, for example, Jewish migration, despite knowledge of the atrocities perpetrated by Hitler. The attitude towards Asians generally has become far more mixed since that time. Now, instead of being primarily engaging in small business, Asian immigrants have tended to work in more professional occupations. It seems that this may have increased feelings of insecurity amongst others in the population.

But, at that time, Beijing thought that Australia was a good country to experiment with. As a small Western nation in the Asia-Pacific region, there was considerable advantage for Canberra in developing a productive relationship with the superpower. Australia was the first signatory to a foreign-aid agreement with China and, after the *open policy* began to take hold in the early 1980s, there was considerable interest in further developing the relationship.

Rudd was appointed as a second secretary to the embassy in September 1984, although he was quickly promoted to the more senior rank of first secretary. Working in the political section, Rudd's main job was to keep an eye on what was happening on the political scene. Another staff member says, 'He never took anything for granted.' By the next July, because of staff shortages, he found himself acting in the even more senior rank of councillor for five months, until the end of that year.

Former *Asiaweek* correspondent Linda Jaivin subsequently told the *Australian Financial Review*, 'I quickly found that he was one of the best-informed diplomats in Beijing ... and his analysis of the labyrinth of Chinese politics was astute.' When I spoke to her on the phone she similarly emphasised this to me. Unfortunately, after texting Rudd to get permission to speak, Jaivin never found the time to get back to me. When I later contacted her, she would only say, 'He was brilliant, with an exceptional knowledge of the country.' She then claimed she was unwell, and rang off.

It's probably important to note at this point that any desire to veil his activities hasn't been erected as some sort of 'cover' for spying. Although diplomats in China at this period were on the lookout for information they could report back to their home country, it appears that Rudd did not hold any position as a spy-master. Instead, his tasks at this time were simply those of a capable, mid-level embassy staffer.

One of Rudd's important duties in the embassy was to watch China's relationship with North Korea. Others from the embassy at the time say that he found this particularly interesting. The contrast was quite dramatic. On one side of the Yalu River, separating the two countries, was China: still very much a communist regime, but nevertheless one that was opening to the world. North Korea was called 'the hermit kingdom'. It was remained locked in its own interpretation of 'communism with Asian characteristics'. *Juche* or 'self-reliance' was the peculiar state ideology that was destroying the country.

If Rudd had needed any experience to remind him of the disastrous role that central planning could play in economic development, this should have been enough. The contrast with South Korea was dramatic. Some two decades after the end of the war, Seoul was thriving, even if the country was not yet a fully functioning democracy. At least people could eat and live with a degree of security. The regime in Pyongyang, however, had yet to find out that ideology couldn't replace food.

Everyone in the embassy also watched the see-sawing relationship between mainland China and Taiwan. The situation across the straits presented a particularly delicate diplomatic problem for Australia. Canberra was committed to a relationship with Beijing. Nevertheless, the linkage between

Washington and Taipei was so close that it was important that Australia not be forced to pick sides if a dispute suddenly escalated. In the mid-1980s the China station really was the front line of Australian diplomacy.

There were many visits from politicians, and that's how Rudd's name was mentioned for the first time in federal parliament. In July 1985 an Australian delegation had visited the country. In a report on the trip, the parliamentarians noted that the ambassador, his wife, and a 'Mr Kevin Rudd accompanied the Delegation throughout the visit. Their understanding of China and the Chinese people contributed greatly to the success of the visit.'

Providing helpful advice and assistance for parliamentarians visiting China later placed a big strain on the small embassy staff. 'Introducing cabinet ministers, premiers, and other visitors to China became a big job,' says another diplomat, recalling that time.

While Rudd was in Beijing, the ambassador, Dennis Argall, became ill and had to leave early. There was an urgent need to fill the ambassador's position quickly. Prime minister Bob Hawke was certain whom to appoint. His economic adviser was Ross Garnaut, who'd previously been an academic at the ANU. The relationship with China was going to be vital for Australia, so Hawke asked Garnaut to take on the job.

Because he'd come from outside the department, the new ambassador had to make some quick assessments of his staff. Rudd had received a good rap from the outgoing ambassador, but Garnaut says, 'I was making up my own mind. He was earnest, serious about his job, conscientious, and keen to learn about my approach.'

'I was asking him to report about some economic issues,' notes Garnaut, who came to the job with a particularly strong understanding in this field. 'What I found impressive was how earnestly he set about briefing himself,' says Rudd's former ambassador. 'He would shamelessly come to ask me what a whole lot of economic terms meant—he didn't know, but he wanted to learn. We spent some time talking about economic concepts.'

Rudd was a political analyst, but by this time the idea of political change in China really meant economic change. These reforms were at the front of the political agenda. Rather than try to avoid it, Rudd threw himself into attempting to understand the implications of it.

Interestingly, Garnaut notes the overall quality of the embassy at this time. He says a number of 'particularly sharp minds' were working in Beijing then, and it was difficult for Rudd to stand out. 'Kevin was one of a small group of very, very good people,' says Garnaut. 'Nevertheless, he was obviously destined for higher things in the diplomatic service.'

Kevin and Thérèse also fitted in well with the relatively closed embassy scene. There were a number of young families in the diplomatic community in Beijing, and they made good friendships.

For more casual meetings, Rudd would sometimes translate for the ambassador, and he tells a story against himself about one of these occasions. 'Garnaut began with an official greeting,' Rudd later told a meeting of the Kokoda Foundation. It was a suggestion that 'China and Australia are currently experiencing a relationship of unprecedented closeness'.

Rudd says he translated this, only to be greeted with gales of laughter from the young audience while blood drained from the faces of the older listeners. 'Apparently, what I said in Chinese was that China and Australia are currently experiencing fantastic simultaneous orgasms,' Rudd claimed.

Garnaut does not challenge this story, although he will not endorse it either. More probably, Rudd has chosen to tell this story as a means of making light of his exceptionally good command of the language.

Rudd also spent his time interacting with Chinese government officials, as well as with the other diplomats. A good deal of information was swapped between observers of the domestic political scene. He also made many contacts within what were described as the 'think tanks' of China—the various research academies located within the universities.

'We had the visits of the various government delegations and politicians,' notes Garnaut, 'but at no stage did Kevin nail his personal political colours to the mast. This was even though he knew I'd worked with Hawke,' Garnaut adds. 'Rudd was diligent regardless of the political affiliations of the people he was serving.'

'If you'd asked me then where I think Kevin would have gone,' says Garnaut, 'I would have said rapidly up through the ranks into a very senior position. China would have been an important part of his career right through, and one day he would have been ambassador. He was 100 per cent a career diplomat. That's how I would have expected things to progress ... of course, it didn't turn out that way at all.'

'Even then, though, his motivations were all about implementing good public policy.' Garnaut says he is not surprised that Rudd's career veered-off in the particular direction it took.

In the mid-1990s, a considerable argument developed about whether Australia was a part of Asia or not. The debate became highly politicised. Eventually, it seemed to become focused on lines on the map or the number of 'Asian' faces that could be seen when you walked down the street.

Richard Woolcott, himself something of an 'old Asia hand' in the department, had helped Alexander Downer draft the Liberal Party's foreign policy in 1996. Called 'A Confident Australia', this made engagement with Asia first priority. Woolcott regrets, 'That all changed on September 11th 2001, when John Howard developed this highly compliant relationship with the Bush administration.' He holds Rudd in very high regard.

***

The couple's second child, Nicholas, was born just at the end of the family's posting to China on 20 August 1986. They did not return to Asia, and Thérèse later took a part-time job as a rehabilitation counsellor.

Ironically, Rudd departed Beijing just as crucial political developments were taking place inside China. The end of 1986 saw severe new constraints suddenly placed on the possibility of political and economic change. The period of open-ended discussion came to an abrupt halt. Huge demonstrations in eastern China were suppressed. There is a sense in which the later destruction of the pro-democracy demonstrations in Tiananmen Square in 1989 was an end-point of repression that had begun in Shanghai, three years earlier.

A rumour still goes round the department that, when he returned from China, Rudd felt he should have been promoted to deputy secretary—a promotion that would have jumped a number of pay grades. 'People were astonished that anyone should expect such a meteoric rise,' says another diplomat today. Thinking back on that period he shrugs, before adding, 'That's just Kevin though, isn't it?'

When Rudd did come back to Australia in September 1986, he was posted twice within the department. First he went to the policy-planning division for just over a year, and then to staffing policy until June 1988. To an outsider at this time, 'He looked like, for all the world, the complete diplomat—shiny bum and all. I thought he was obsessed with the department.'

Diplomats need to work overseas, and Rudd had begun to search around for his next posting. He had already notched up considerable expertise in Asia. To continue to rise, he needed another appointment in the West if he wasn't to be typecast as just a Sinophile. The careerist in him would also have considered the advantages of an analytic appointment, where his reasoning would mark him out from the pack. A position such as the Office of National Assessments job in London, reporting on intelligence and strategic matters directly to the prime minister, was an obvious fit. It was so obvious that Rudd applied for, and was soon appointed to, the job.

But, while waiting to take up the position, Rudd claims the department sent him briefly back up to Queensland. He says he was in Brisbane reading the paper when he saw an advertisement for quite a different job.

CHAPTER THREE

Goss

1989–1998

> 'The trip had been flawless and successful. It was a pity that … the Prime Minister made unflattering remarks about Wayne Goss and called his adviser, Kevin Rudd, a "menace".'
>
> –Don Watson, *Recollections of a Bleeding Heart*

The relationship that Rudd developed with Wayne Goss was to provide the third seminal experience that would define the way Rudd would approach the world. From the time Rudd returned to Queensland, his story would become bound up inescapably with that of Goss himself, who was premier from 1989 to 1996.

For the previous three decades, Queensland had been held firmly in the grip of premier Joh Bjelke-Petersen's National Party government. The state had become an intellectual backwater, where the dulling heat and tropical rains defined the mental environment as well as the physical. There was enough prosperity to keep people happy without the need to change too many things, and the myth had grown up that this was the way Queenslanders liked it. The idiosyncratic premier had orchestrated the system; it only played the music that he wanted to hear.

Labor had become accustomed to fighting over the crumbs of defeat. In opposition, ideological purity had taken on a sanctity all of its own. Some people, particularly those on the party's left, occasionally seemed to value this virtue for itself far more than melding it into policy that might appeal to the dazed electorate.

Into this mess strode Wayne Goss. It wasn't the case that nobody else could see what needed to be done to bring the party to power. However, for more than a generation, no one had been able to achieve it. Goss soon proved that he was much more than just the 'right bloke in the right place at the right time'. Through longevity, a series of particular mistakes, and other instances of general incompetence, the Bjelke-Petersen government certainly appeared as if it ought to collapse. But it never had. Even with the findings of the Fitzgerald Inquiry into corruption casting their long shadows across the landscape, it was obvious the opposition could not simply expect power to fall into its lap. Real authority is never just left lying around; it has to be seized.

This was the situation when Goss took over as the state's Labor leader. The party was accustomed to opposition and was far from united. Divisions wreaked the party, both within its parliamentary wing and also organisationally, where bitter feuds occasionally surfaced into the media, reinforcing a more generalised feeling of chaos.

Goss' task was to reform the party organisationally, create a policy agenda to carry into government, and then to campaign until Labor won office at the next election. Methodically, he set about his assignment.

His first key ally in achieving this mission would be Wayne Swan. The former Nambour High School student had studied economics and then law at Queensland University, before realising that politics was his great love. After graduation he was lucky to become a lecturer in his chosen field at what was to become the new Queensland Institute of Technology. But the Vietnam War, Sir Joh, and the general malaise in Queensland had politicised the young man. He had become involved in Labor, so when Goss appealed to him to take over (from, ironically enough, the current premier, Peter Beattie) as the party's state secretary, he agreed.

Swan would provide Goss with the firm support-base he needed from which to launch his offensive. However, the opposition leader still needed to craft policies and develop a political agenda. This was his own responsibility, but in order to achieve it he urgently needed an office that could support him effectively. When the chief of staff announced his intention to leave, Goss realised that he'd have to find the right person for this vital job. Rather than just appoint someone from inside the party, he decided to advertise for the best applicant.

Goss takes up the story. 'When I became leader in March 1988, I wanted to make sure I took the time to get the right chief of staff. There were 80 applications, and I shortlisted five people,' he says today. 'Three of those were eminently appointable. But Kevin stood head and shoulders above the others.'

In May 1988, Goss was scheduled to travel down to Canberra for the opening of the new Parliament House. Rudd met him at his hotel. Goss says he quickly realised he had the right person for the job. Indeed, at that time it would have been nearly impossible to imagine a better candidate. Rudd ticked all the right boxes: he had demonstrated his commitment to Labor by having joined the party at an early age; his intellectual ability was on clear display with a first-class honours degree; and, perhaps most importantly, Rudd had acquired a strong policy background, together with the ability to negotiate his way through a bureaucracy, thanks to his experience with Foreign Affairs.

As soon as he was offered the job, Rudd seized the opportunity. Fortunately, at that time the department had adopted a new policy that was supportive of diplomats gaining experience in other areas of the public service. Rudd was allowed to retain his position while on leave without pay when he left the diplomatic service on 11 July 1988.

When Rudd arrived back in Queensland he found he needed to improve the efficiency of the leader's office after so many years in opposition. For example, there were no business contacts. 'I thought to myself, hmmm, this isn't good,' Rudd later told *Australian Financial Review* correspondent Lenore Taylor. 'I identified the top 40 companies in Queensland and I obtained their annual reports. I identified their CEOs and directors and I tracked them down. I organised meetings between myself and Wayne and all of those people, as well as with all the peak industry bodies in the state.

Rudd called in consultants from the accounting firm KPMG to work on a detailed transition-to-government plan. Many might have floundered in a new environment without firm signposts indicating the correct direction to take, but Rudd didn't. He undoubtedly received firm support and guidance from Goss, but another politician says he also demonstrated his own initiative in running the small office.

Together, Goss, Swan, and Rudd rapidly became known as the troika. Goss drove the policy reform, Swan ran the political campaign and Rudd's key role was to co-ordinate the agenda. The youthful team worked together remarkably well. There were clearly delineated areas of responsibility and, although extensive input was called for and valued by Goss, there was no doubt about who led the trio.

Goss' deputy was Tom Burns. A significant and widely respected Labor figure himself, he was happy to throw his weight behind the younger leader. He provided advice and maturity—together with a link to the older 'working-man's' roots of the party. Burns describes himself as an old-fashioned Labor man, but he grew to like the young former diplomat who was determined to achieve things. He says, 'We wanted to win. That's what it's all about. But after you've been in opposition for a long time, some people think it's just about being in parliament.'

The election was held 17 years (to the day) after Gough Whitlam had won power federally in 1972. Whitlam's victory had seen the party return to office after a gap of 24 years. In Queensland, the party had been in the wilderness for a desperately long 32 years.

The night he won office, Goss told people not to get too excited. To be precise, he suggested they all needed to 'take a cold shower'. It was a vivid image, so effective that one of his listeners that night would later enthusiastically take it up as his own.

On the Sunday night after the election, three excited people sat down to begin mapping out plans for the new government. Goss knew it was vital to avoid chaos. First, a clear agenda was established. This ensured that, right from the first Monday morning, a methodical approach would be used to tackle the reforms that the government had in mind. Australia had seen nothing like it since Whitlam came to power in 1972.

On that first morning, the police Special Branch—which had been used to harass opponents of the former regime—was closed down. Thousands of extra teachers were appointed to the schools, and the government boosted the number of university places available. A sudden gust of wind began to blow through the creaking ranks of the Queensland public service.

'There was a real need to clean out the stables,' says Goss. This is a reference to one of the labours of Hercules in the old

Greek myth. In it, the hero had to clean out the stables housing King Augeus's massive herd of cattle. They had never been cleaned before, and as a result an enormous mass of filth had accumulated. It could only be cleared by diverting a whole river to clean out the mess. Goss felt the situation in Queensland was the same. Everything needed to be tackled.

***

'We inherited 27 public service departments,' says Goss, 'and in only two were the departmental heads chosen after their positions had been properly advertised. As it happened, one of those people was the head of my own Premier's Department. He stayed. What we were doing wasn't just some sort of ruthless political blood-bath.'

Nevertheless, within a month of the election, eighteen departmental heads had been removed, and nine of their departments had been abolished.

In order to understand both Goss and the reason the voters dismissed his government two-and-a-bit terms later, it's necessary to understand the key role of the Fitzgerald Royal Commission into corruption in the state. Goss was voted into power with an agenda to institute reform. The problem was that serious changes inevitably caused resentment while, on the other hand, nothing Goss did seemed to be enough for those on Labor's left. Or, to look at things another way, perhaps everyone in the party did not share Goss's concerns.

Working so closely with Goss meant that Rudd was intimately involved with this process.

There are different conceptions of the role that a chief of staff should fulfil. Obviously, the key task is to keep the leader's office working smoothly. But the second element is an ability to influence policy outcomes, and it appears that Rudd enthusiastically sought the opportunity to do this.

A close observer looks back at this period. 'The problem with the story at the moment is that it suggests everything that happened in Queensland happened because of Kevin. Well, that's not right. Goss was nobody's patsy,' he says. 'I've been there when there was a difference of opinion between them, and Goss always made the decision.' This commentator pauses for a second. 'Don't you worry about that,' he laughs, echoing a familiar saying of Sir Joh's. 'The premier is always right.'

Very clear commitments had been laid out as part of the election platform, and Goss wanted to ensure that they were achieved as quickly as possible. As an example, one promise was to double the amount of land under National Parks in Queensland. But simply working this through posed an immense task for the bureaucracy. It was not just settling the negotiations to acquire large swathes of countryside. One of the most radical features of the changes—in some areas—was the emphasis placed on the need to find long-term ways of resolving problems.

The government said it would end sand-mining on Fraser Island. But after Tony Fitzgerald had reported on the broader implications of this policy, a structural-adjustment plan was implemented that specifically considered the development of alternative industries and workforce transition procedures, as well as simple compensation arrangements.

The cabinet process was reformed from day one. A big problem with the previous government had been that there was not enough co-ordination between departments. Goss himself wrote a two-page document outlining the way ministers should set out their submissions to cabinet. One particular heading was marked 'consultation', which was intended to be a way of ensuring that the different government departments spoke to each other to ensure that a co-ordinated approach was developed.

Shortly afterwards, Goss had to amend the document

to include another heading: 'results of consultation'. This was because ministers (or their departments) simply ignored the 'contributions' of other departments with which they disagreed. It was not always a case of Goss attempting to thrust reform on Queensland; sometimes the premier was forced to rein in others who endorsed their own pet projects without any concern for the wider ramifications.

Before the government came to office, academic Patrick Weller had been commissioned to prepare a paper called *Making Government Work*. 'The state of Queensland was quite ossified at this time.' Weller smiles dryly as he recollects the situation. 'There was actually nothing radical in the changes that were introduced,' he emphasises. 'It was just portrayed that way by some people who were losing out as a result of the reforms. A lot of this was people who didn't want the state to move into the 20th century.'

After 32 years in office, the former government had established itself firmly. There seemed to be a strong case for restructuring and broad-based reform of the public service. Goss found he could trust Rudd. As a result, the two worked closely on reform of the public service and policy issues. Today, Goss says, 'Kevin knew my ideas, and he'd run through things with me. At times this would create tension and friction. But the relationship was vital.'

'Kevin and Wayne had particular interests and, basically, the public service was not one of them. The present vice-chancellor of Griffith University, Peter Coledrake, and the current vice-chancellor of Melbourne University, Glyn Davis, were in the Public Sector Management Commission. They managed the reform and, let me tell you, they are not shrinking violets,' Weller insists.

Some people believed that the commission was just being used as a way of centralising power in the hands of the premier. That was not the intention. However, a lot of noses were put out of joint. Another ex-minister says, 'Some of our own politicians very quickly got cold feet about reforming the public service. But it was something we had to do. Well, Kevin took a lot of the kicks ... a lot of the kicks.'

Professor Ken Wiltshire later noted that people quickly 'made a connection between the restructuring of the public service and the political allegiances of those overseeing it'.

Queensland academic Scott Prasser insists that 'Rudd was the de facto power behind the throne. He was Wayne Goss's closest adviser and the premier's Mr Fixit. He was the key man.' But he does not admire what was achieved. 'Executive government control, secrecy, and manipulation of appointment processes remained embedded during this time,' he says.

There were a couple of different issues. The first was the speed with which change was implemented. After so long out of government, Labor pushed the transformation—hard and fast. At that time the public service was meant to be apolitical. But Labor had been out of power for so long that many felt that the institution had become captured by conservative ideas. Rightly or wrongly, the incoming government felt the service was too responsive to and friendly with the previous regime.

'I've seen allegations that the Goss government "politicised" the public service,' says a senior public servant from that period. 'Well, hang on ... it would be wrong to characterise the pre-existing structure of public servants as being purely non-partisan and highly professional. That would be a myth. It's not as if they could just keep in place all of these people who the National Party had installed and had great confidence in.'

Rudd challenged established structures with his attempts to shake up a deeply entrenched bureaucracy that had long operated without accountability. But this soon fuelled resentment with what appeared to be a lack of respect that resulted from his managerial style. Many people felt that he disregarded their expertise if their proposals didn't fit in with his preconceptions. These people added that there was a tendency to disregard anyone outside his own close-knit circle. Such people, who declined to speak on the record, felt that alternative opinions were simply disregarded.

'I watched him at close range for six years,' says another person from the Queensland public service at the time. 'He would intimidate people. It was quite deliberate and very calculated. If you did what he wanted, things were fine; but if you chose to suggest there might be some other solution, you were berated and ignored.'

Former colleagues have suggested that Rudd 'had a hand in everything'. When he was director-general of the cabinet office he still occupied an office right next to the premier. A door, called by workers the cat-flap, linked the two rooms. Some thought he 'controlled everything'. Others emphatically disagree.

Nevertheless, Rudd did play a vital role in the Goss government. A former Labor politician says, 'Discipline is one word to describe his approach. But he didn't suffer anyone he thought was a fool lightly, either. And not everyone happened to agree about who the stupid person in the relationship was. Arrogance is another word.'

***

'Listen, mate, you're not going to get very much because everyone's been lent on pretty heavily,' says a person who knew Rudd at this time and who refuses to speak to me further. 'You know, for the good of the party. Just shut up. Don't say anything. That sort of thing. The Rudd machine has gone to work.'

'He had a one-track mind focused on whatever he thought the issue of the moment happened to be,' says another politician. 'And *his* solution. That was always the right one. He didn't have a lot of time for people who weren't up to his standard. It must have been a great pity to him that so few of us measured up,' he adds sarcastically.

'He had a reputation for intolerance,' says another person who observed him from the outside. 'This may or may not be fair—I'm not going to argue. But he wanted to get things done.'

There were clear distinctions between the political arena, the policy process, and the administrative work that needed to be done. 'Rudd worked extraordinarily hard and was impatient with substandard offerings. But he remains just one light in a bright team,' says a third observer.

At first, a special policy division was established within the Premier's Department in an attempt to develop ideas and ensure the agenda was implemented. This department should have been the engine room of government, but within a couple of years it became obvious that something more was needed.

'Wayne Goss saw Nick Greiner's cabinet office in New South Wales,' says Weller, 'and he said, basically, "I want one of those." ' Goss disputes this, saying rather that he adopted the model that was initially developed by Neville Wran a decade before the Liberals took over. But this may be a 'political truth' rather than the real one. Goss realised he needed someone who understood him to run the new department effectively. Perhaps not surprisingly, Rudd got the job.

His role was no longer to act as a barrier between Goss and the parliamentarians. Instead, he had a much more critical role in formulating policy, and with this came a style that didn't always go down well in the intimate surroundings of the small capital of Brisbane.

'I think where Kevin *was* important was in pushing policy agendas through,' speculates Weller, 'and at times *pushing* was exactly what was needed. His model was Foreign Affairs. He came from a department with highly qualified staff that was used to producing well-argued policy advice, and he comes to Queensland and finds this isn't happening.'

'The problem with that job is you're doing so many things at once,' Weller asserts. 'Getting across everything the ministers are doing, following up desires of your premier, and then, if you've got the chance, slipping your own policy interests into the mix. There's a lot to do.'

Rudd explained his style. 'I am by nature methodical,' he told the *Australian Financial Review*. 'You identify the problem, you identify a range of solutions, toss them, you decide, only then do you look at it through the political prism. That's the way in which I believe advice should be structured.'

'You know,' says another academic observer, 'we are in danger of reading every event in Rudd's life as if they were simply stepping stones to where he is today. Well, they weren't, and there was no inexorable path he pursued that was destined to arrive in Canberra. He may choose to believe that, but it's not the way things were.'

This observer points out that, although 'Kevin was interested in getting things to happen, there were some other pretty clever people sitting around him who were concerned about process. Things didn't just happen because Kevin had a bright idea. The routines of government are vital.'

When it's put to Goss today that Rudd sat like a spider outside his office, with his web entangling unwelcome visitors and preventing them from seeing the premier, he just laughs. It's a rich, honest laugh, which comes from a concept he seems to find genuinely amusing. Certainly, Goss himself is in no doubt that it was *his* government. Others, including particularly Rudd, may have assisted him, but they did not run the government.

The two men were very close, but they did have their differences. 'Saying "no" can create tension and friction. Some of that rubbed off on Kevin.' The point is that Goss needed someone to separate out the submissions that were not up to scratch.

If politicians really had a problem, they could always approach the premier directly. 'All my ministers always knew how to get hold of me,' says Goss. 'They could phone me at any time. Every Monday, before and after cabinet, I was always available. And, of course, there was always parliament. No, this idea that he was somehow vetting who I saw, it's really quite silly.'

***

The Rudd family was settled in Brisbane, and the children were eventually enrolled at private high schools. Thérèse began part-time work as a rehabilitation counsellor. She realised they were going to build their future there, and decided to start a business, which she called Work Directions. Money was needed to start, and the couple borrowed, securing it with a mortgage over their house. Rudd says things became a bit tight for a while and there wasn't a lot of spare money. Nevertheless, he backed Thérèse, saying, 'If that's what you want to do, that's what we'll do.'

But it proved to be a wise investment. The company grew with Queensland. A physiotherapist, Frances Edwards, said, 'We had a lot of people like bricklayers or nurses who had back injuries and couldn't work at that job any more, so what we did was work with them to see where they could get a job.' The company expanded quickly.

Later, an office in northern New South Wales at Lismore was opened, and then one in Sydney in the early 1990s. The company was effective and growing well. Then, in 1993, the Keating government decided to outsource job placement for people who had been unemployed for a long time. Thérèse's company won a contract.

Far more significantly for the family, though, in 1993 Thérèse gave birth to the couple's third child: another boy, Marcus.

***

Rudd was attempting to negotiate his own way in the narrow space between politics and government, but his confidence seemed to grow daily. He was a relatively young man with the majority of his work experience in one, somewhat unrepresentative, Commonwealth department. He was on a quick learning curve while having to establish his own role in the government. This led to particular conflicts with a number of the elected politicians.

It was not just Rudd by any means who was pushing for personnel changes. Indeed, a senior public servant at the time—one of the new people wanted by Rudd—says that, sometimes, 'It was all he could do to prevent shocking appointments and decisions. Nepotism and favouritism was the only way of explaining what some ministers were trying to do,' he says. 'If Kevin hadn't centralised things, the disaster would have come much earlier.'

'When I saw some of the criticism that was being levelled against Kevin', says another very senior Goss government bureaucrat, 'I nearly puked.' This person has no doubt whatsoever about what was motivating the attacks on Rudd. 'People had been passed over for promotion. That was it, purely and simply. They thought the new government would suddenly recognise their sparkling genius and elevate them. They became bitter when their talents were not recognised. Perhaps they didn't have any to begin with.'

Tom Burns had not been sure about Rudd when he first met him. 'I've never been a fan of bringing people straight from the universities into politics. Those sorts of people have never had a real job and are consumed by what they've been taught. But at least Kevin was lucky enough to be both,' he says.

'Other ministers would come along to budget review with their dreams,' says Burns, 'but they weren't properly worked out. They got knocked back, so who are they going to blame? Kevin. They called him Doctor Death, the Mandarin, a whole range of things like that; well, that's because he was tough.'

It might have been one of those ministers who first gave Rudd the nickname 'Doctor Death' because he 'put dreams to sleep'. Others say it began as a joke. At first Rudd seems to have believed the nickname suggested a grudging respect. As internal fights continued, it appears the name developed another, less pleasant, edge.

'The thing is,' says a political player from the time, 'some people would have been unhappy if they didn't get their own way on everything. They'd say "that fucking Rudd". That's because they had to blame some bastard. It was never their fault.'

'The ministers would get very annoyed,' adds Burns. 'They'd leave messages for him to call them back. I'd go past his phone and there'd be all these post-it notes stuck on it, you know, just saying so-and-so called, please call them back. Well, I'd just say to Rudd's secretary, "You might as well throw all them notes in the bin." Kevin just didn't ever bother phoning anyone back.'

Burns says the Labor team in Queensland still 'vividly remembered the dramatic failure of the Whitlam government, where ministers were running off in all directions, with no one in control'. Since that time, every state and federal Labor government has had to ensure it didn't fall into this trap. 'I had to remind them of what had happened federally,' he pointed out. 'Well, we lost in 1949 and then we didn't win again until 1972. There'd been a lot of people who'd been waiting forever to change things. The lesson of that period was that we needed discipline whenever we came into government,' says Burns.

Although Goss was to develop a fierce reputation as the power in Queensland, this wasn't always the case in the beginning. At an early cabinet meeting, Burns recalls a decision of the premier's being rolled. Burns was furious. He later spoke to Goss and insisted that such a thing should never happen again. The premier had to be in charge. Burns says today that, 'We needed a system, because we had no experience of government,' says Burns. 'Kevin put that together.'

Burns describes himself as being enthusiastic about further contacts with China, having been involved in the original decision to switch recognition from Taipei to Beijing back in 1972. Initially, Rudd and Burns appeared to be unlikely friends, but they shared a passion for China. At this time they travelled there on government business.

'One night we were staying at the Hilton or somewhere in Shanghai,' says Burns. 'Well, the prices at the bar there were ridiculous—an arm and leg—so we went across the road. And there were some kids down there singing. So Kevin starts to sing, too. He sang beautifully. Very soon, the kids stopped and they wanted him to sing more. Then they all joined in together.' Burns smiles and nods his head as he remembers.

'Whenever he knew I was a bit down,' says Burns, 'because the government couldn't borrow money to get a project I believed in through, or something like that, he used to come and have a talk about the issue. He'd say, "G'day, Burnsie" and have a chat and cheer me up.'

Burns remembers that he particularly respected Rudd's political judgement. 'One day,' he recalls, 'there were these firemen protesting down at parliament. Well, I'd spoken to their leaders the day before, and we'd got it all sorted out. But their protest was already scheduled, so it still had to go on. As I went into parliament I called them—the leaders—"wankers". Unfortunately, the media thought I was using the word to describe the firemen.'

Burns wanted to sort it out, but this risked making the whole thing an even bigger media disaster. 'Kevin phoned me and said, "Don't take it any further." Well, I still wish I'd gone out and explained it, but I accepted his judgement—at a personal cost to me. But I admired and trusted him, so I didn't.'

Craig Emerson also provides an insight into Rudd's style. Emerson had spent four years with Bob Hawke by this time, working as his environmental adviser. When the Goss government took office, he was keen to move on. The two had already spoken of the phone a number of times to discuss policy issues when, one day, Rudd found himself in Canberra. The two met to have a chat over a drink at the Hyatt Hotel towards the end of 1990.

Impressed, Emerson decided to apply for the position of Queensland director-general of the Department of Environment and Heritage. He went through what he still remembers was a 'particularly tough' interview process. Though he had worked as a senior level as a policy adviser and as an assistant secretary in the Department of Prime Minister and Cabinet, there was no 'inside track'.

The questions at the interview were to do with what structure he felt was appropriate for the department. Emerson felt this demonstrated the willingness the new team had to consider different ways of doing things to achieve a better result. Nevertheless, he'd had to scrub up on the detail of the criteria, and referees' reports were sought. Although he found it gruelling, Emerson respected the professionalism of the process. 'People might have said, look, he comes out of the political office, but I don't think anyone would have said he's without ability.'

Another person backs this up. 'Rudd is very professional in the way he approaches these things. He'd only insert someone in there if they were genuinely the best person for the job. That's not the same as fixing it up for your mates. He's not "matey." '

It was during this period that Rudd first met Bob Carr. Goss had been asked down to New South Wales when Carr was still opposition leader. Very keen to depict himself as part of a new wave of change, Carr attempted to get some of the 'Goss gloss' to transfer itself across the border. Rudd flew down with the premier to meet the Labor team. For the media's benefit, this was dressed up as a 'transition to government' seminar.

Carr saw an opportunity like this as a means of displaying a confident and united team to the public. He decided to milk the association with the victorious Labor premier for all it was worth. At that time, some members of his shadow ministry were not of a particularly high calibre, and the idea of using all of them to nut out hard policy was likely to have brought a gust of laughter from Carr. Nevertheless, the opportunity of getting the leadership team together had a more significant effect than simply creating some sort of media façade.

At this stage, a Labor victory in New South Wales was looking possible, but events rapidly conspired against the opposition. First, the state government had won the Olympics, and premier John Fahey's leap of delight was plastered across the daily papers. Then a bushfire crisis around Sydney early in the New Year helped the government look like the saviour of people's homes. Finally, Fahey bravely threw himself into a scuffle on Australia Day to disarm a man who looked as if he was going to shoot Prince Charles.

But the first time that Rudd really came into focus for Bob Carr was when the opposition leader was travelling to Parramatta to campaign for a by-election. Suddenly, the car phone rang. Although the state election was still months away, Rudd had formed a personal link with the head of Fahey's cabinet office, and wanted to make sure that Carr kept him on if he did win victory. At that particular time, the conversation was something of a bizarre distraction.

Nevertheless, Carr heard Rudd out while he praised Roger Wilkins as being 'co-operative, with a first-class brain. A great public sector talent'. Then Rudd said something that surprised Carr, who prided himself on his cultural fluency. 'You know,' said Rudd, 'Wilkins's family used to gather around the piano singing Wagner when he was a child. He grew up in a very cultured house.' Rudd had seized on the exact argument that was likely to appeal to Carr. This conversation struck the opposition leader, because he felt that by this stage Rudd was obviously confident enough in his role to consider himself a 'player'.

Rudd was determined that there was no point being in government unless policies were changed for the better. He took the opportunity to press for things that he believed in whenever possible.

For him, education was vital. It offered the opportunity for children to improve their lot in life: empowering them with knowledge. He also saw education as playing a key role in the economic development of Australia. He decided to tackle this on two levels—first, by providing assistance to kids who were behind with their reading in school and, second, by pushing a particular subject area that he believed would assist in the future development of the country.

The Reading Recovery program was initially developed in New Zealand. People working in government say that Rudd enthusiastically pushed it in Queensland as the government's first educational reform. The second, far more significant initiative was the introduction of Asian languages into schools.

Surprisingly, this simple idea aroused hackles of resentment across the country, particularly amongst some in the ALP. Despite the broad genuflections in the direction of Asia by the Keating government, within the different states there was a refusal to embrace the study of Asian languages. Eventually, a combination of state government inaction and a lack of federal government support demolished most of Rudd's initiatives in this field.

At the time, Goss (and therefore Rudd) had an up-and-down relationship with Keating. The worst flare-up arose on a joint trip to Asia in mid-1993. Just before the trip there'd been a Melbourne meeting of COAG (the Council of Australian Governments). In this meeting, the Mabo decision of the High Court to recognise Native Title had been the central issue. Keating's dismissive reaction to the premiers' land-management proposals had provoked another of their customary walkouts.

Shortly afterwards, Keating and Goss (and Rudd) travelled to China. Somewhere between Seoul and Beijing, Keating walked down the aisle of the plane to speak to Goss. The Queenslanders suggested a compromise on Native Title, with Rudd going into detail about how this might be achieved.

Goss says, 'We were actually trying to help. Keating wanted to *do* things, to take giant strides. Our point was that we couldn't go far, but at least we could actually take half a step forward to help resolve one issue.' Goss goes further. 'The states had some expertise in land title—the Commonwealth didn't.'

'Keating said he'd think about it and went back up the front of the plane,' Goss continues. 'He came back a little while later and rejected Rudd's compromise, saying, "Those are weasel words, weasel words." This was not politically very smart. There was the occasional explosion—well, Keating had a mercurial temperament.'

'Today,' says a person who knows Keating well, 'he's just consumed by loathing for Howard and where that man has taken the country. He may have thought Rudd was a little upstart back then, but that's a long time ago. He'll be there supporting Kevin when the time comes. With bells on.'

By this stage, Woolcott had taken over as secretary in Foreign Affairs back in Canberra. 'We'd lent about four diplomats to various state governments, but none of them had ever come back. It was obvious that Goss had come to depend on Kevin by this stage. I told him his secondment couldn't continue indefinitely. Later, Wayne Goss phoned me and asked if he could stay even longer.'

But by this stage the time had well and truly come for Rudd to make a decision about his future. Although he'd been keen to hang onto his position, he eventually relinquished it. He now had other ambitions.

Woolcott had earlier been instrumental in making sure Rudd joined the Australian American Leadership Dialogue. 'Phil Scanlan was starting it, and he asked me, "Who do you think will be in your position in 20 years' time?" I gave it a bit of thought and said, "Well, why don't you invite Kevin Rudd?" He joined up and, of course, that has served him very well in blunting allegations that he is anti-American,' says the former diplomat today.

***

'If Kevin and Wayne were both such bloody geniuses, you have to wonder why the Goss government got turfed out after just two-and-a-bit terms,' says one of Goss's former advisers.

The reasons Labor lost are complex. Three months before the election, Goss had widely been regarded as unbeatable. There was also a huge reservoir of resentment, both federally against Keating and at the state level, because of the way things were done. The Nationals tapped into this to win back government.

The Labor victory in 1989 had changed Queensland—too fast for some, too slowly for others. Goss himself did not seek controversy. In fact, the government became the butt of jokes from some on the left of the party who became frustrated at the slow pace of change. 'How long' they would ask, 'does it take Wayne Goss to change a light bulb?' The answer was, 'No time at all, because Wayne doesn't change anything.'

Many nitty-gritty domestic factors were to cost Labor government—individual issues in different seats. But the image of the Keating government, which loomed large over the state issues, also cast a darkening gloom over Labor's flickering light.

To be defeated so comprehensively after just two terms in office points to something else—a much more profound alienation from and hostility towards the government. Some insiders suggest Goss's high personal-approval ratings simply hid real problems that voters had with the party. The result was a government insulated from reality by a sense of complacency. Unfortunately for Labor, the premier's personal rapport with the electorate did not easily translate into votes.

'If Wayne wanted something, then he got it,' says a former Labor parliamentarian. 'We weren't being politically smart. Goss and, I think, Rudd, believed in things and so they pushed ahead with them. All that was just stupid.' He says the government didn't use basic political judgement.

The refrain was similar—whether the government was building a road, reforming the public service, or changing the education system. The parliamentarian adds, 'We were fixing problems, but at the same time the way we went about it created another political problem that was far worse. It was bullshit,' says the same politician.

'We were seen as arrogant, there's no doubt about it,' admits Burns when this is put to him. 'We forgot where we came from. By the end, we'd started to think we knew better. Well, when they got to the ballot box, some people thought *they* knew better. That's why we lost Queensland in '96.'

***

In 1994 Rudd had become both president and secretary of the party's Bulimba branch in the southern Brisbane electorate of

Griffith, a quick drive across the river from the CBD. Now Rudd decided he wanted to stand at the 1996 federal election. It was obvious the local federal member would soon be retiring. The seat was solidly Labor, although the demographic was changing to the party's detriment. Nevertheless, there were some lovely places within the electorate in which to live.

In the summer of 1995, the political journalist Glenn Milne spoke to Rudd at a Council of Australian Governments meeting. As they ate at the Pier Nine restaurant, Milne suspected his dining companion had a more political agenda that hadn't yet come up. In a bar afterwards, Rudd finally broached the issue that was on his mind. 'I'm thinking about running for federal Labor pre-selection,' said Rudd, as casually as he could manage. 'I was wondering if you had any views?'

Milne insisted he should stand. 'Run,' he said, 'because you will be an adornment to federal Labor's caucus. Secondly, you will probably one day make a fine foreign minister in a Labor government.' Then Milne added his third bullet-point. 'But if you're thinking about leading the ALP, forget it,' he said. 'The punters will not take to a bookish, Mandarin-speaking former diplomat as a Labor leader. The voters will think you are from Mars,' he insisted.

An electoral prize like this isn't available just by putting up your hand. At this time there were bitter feuds within the rival factions of the ALP; in fact, a person on the left of the party was keenly eyeing off the same electorate. For a while, it looked as if there would be a real fight for pre-selection. At this time the ABC's *Four Corners* program reported on the sudden establishment of a new branch in the electorate by a small group of people who all, coincidentally, worked in the Queensland government. Almost immediately, a large number of Vietnamese people were rapidly signed up at this particular branch.

The television program did not allege anything suspicious

about this; it simply reported on the facts and noted that branch-stacking had been prevalent in the ALP. As it happened, the electoral boundaries were eventually changed, and Rudd easily won the pre-selection.

Rudd also informed his old friends in Foreign Affairs. 'Kevin told me that he was standing for pre-selection,' says Woolcott. 'Perhaps surprisingly, I'd never really understood his political leanings.'

But by this time the Liberal Party also realised it had a chance of winning Griffith. It started to ramp up campaigning. In late-August 1995, Rudd received his second mention in federal parliament, although this time it was not friendly. In an attempt to cause trouble for the Labor candidates in Queensland, Liberal senator Ian Macdonald drew attention to an edition of the newspaper *Keep Left*.

He noted that this paper described the state president and secretary as 'liars and abject failures who should be dumped'. The paper then went on to describe Rudd as 'an extreme right-wing fundamentalist Christian with no understanding of fundamental Labor principles'.

Senator David MacGibbon followed up this assault a month later. He claimed that Rudd and Wayne Swan were known as the 'boys in suits' around Queensland ALP circles, and emphasised their links with the Australian Workers' Union faction. He said, 'They're called Ludwig's office boys by the community in general', adding, 'the boys came up with the idea that they would frighten the electorate (into voting Labor)'. But it appears that the senator hadn't done his homework, because Rudd was one of the few politicians not associated with the AWU in the state.

As it happened, these attacks were not needed. Goss's assessment was correct; it was the Keating government that the electorate wanted to dismiss. Voters had no hesitation in meting out retribution to Labor candidates across the state. Federally, the party was reduced to a parliamentary rump, which didn't include Rudd. He failed to hold Griffith for Labor.

'The true measure of the man is that he stuck his head down and kept trying to win the seat,' says a federal party insider. 'Well, a lot of people wouldn't have bothered. It was very hard going, and there were no guarantees. Particularly in that particular electorate, because it was changing so fast.'

He recollects the mood of despair that encompassed Labor at the time. 'The Keating government wasn't just defeated; it was booted out. With gusto! The punters had finished with us.' He pounds a fist into the palm of his hand. He seems to feel an almost cathartic release as he describes the mood. It's a reminder that many in the Queensland ALP were, at best, ambivalent about Keating by this stage. But then he remembers the party, and Rudd's predicament. 'There were no guarantees Rudd would win the next time; none whatsoever.'

A political contact from Queensland state parliament says, 'He was busy earning his living at that time, so we didn't really see too much of him.' Rudd kept quietly plugging away in Griffith.

Bob Carr also occasionally travelled up to Brisbane during this period. He noticed that Rudd continued his political involvement, even if he was out of office. At least one casual meeting was hosted on the Rudd veranda, where the NSW premier and Wayne Goss came to discuss political events.

'There's quite a lot of federal bloody politicians who don't bother to get around their electorates. Well, Kevin does,' says a former state party official. 'It would be very hard to criticise him on his grass-roots campaigning. He really worked that place between the elections in '96 and '98.'

'I think he handled Bill Ludwig very well at this time,' says someone who's not a member of the AWU faction, 'because it was a very delicate relationship. Bill can deliver money, which helps, but he doesn't deliver the votes that will get you into parliament. You've got to campaign for them yourself. Well, Ludwig and his people never supported Kevin in that first election, and it was disappointing to see some of the double-dealing that went on at the time. A great disappointment.'

He continues, 'The AWU has got to learn it doesn't own the party. Kevin definitely wasn't one of the boys, and so he didn't get a lot of support. He had to do it all himself.'

'If Howard hadn't introduced the GST, if he'd just kept things ticking over smoothly, then Kevin might just be remembered as a footnote in a very dull and boring electoral history textbook,' he comments. 'You can even imagine how it might read. Something like: "two-time loser Kevin Rudd narrowly missed out again in the 1998 election and returned to consulting full-time". Not a particularly vivid commemoration of your life, really, is it?'

But, of course, that wasn't to be Rudd's political epitaph at all.

He did work hard. In all the research for this book, no one has ever suggested there is anything fake about Rudd's prodigious work ethic. When the next election came around, Rudd was ready. And it was in part thanks to the campaigning talents of the leader that he'd later supplant—Kim Beazley—that Rudd entered parliament.

CHAPTER FOUR

Backbencher

1998–2001

> 'We are all the product of our own experiences and ideas with which we have been confronted. These are the simple experiences and unremarkable beliefs which cause me to sit proudly here, rather than on the benches of those opposite.'
>
> –Kevin Rudd, 11 November 1998

In the last months of 1998, Rudd travelled to Canberra not just as a bureaucrat, but for the first time as an elected representative of the people. This thrilling moment granted the narrative of his life a coherence that few are lucky to achieve.

He was married to a successful, dynamic woman; he had three children (already successful at school, and giving every appearance of being well integrated into society); he had a secure religious belief; he was an intellectual with a scholarly understanding of Chinese language and society; he had solid experience at the highest level of bureaucracy; and now, finally, to crown his achievements, he had a seat in Australia's parliament.

Rudd had come a long way from Eumundi. Although others had provided assistance along the way, he'd secured his achievements through determination and energy. Perhaps it was true that not everyone liked him, but he doesn't appear to have made a large number of enemies either. And the ledger was well balanced with many quite genuine friends on the other side.

Today, Beazley calls the 1998 election 'the one that got away'. Despite this, the accomplishment was significant. In 1998, Labor came very close to winning government. It secured more than 50 per cent of the vote, but this was concentrated in too few electorates to give it a majority in the house. The opposition won 67 seats, the government took 80, and there was one independent member.

'In the last week of the election campaign there was a lack of focus,' says Beazley today. 'Debate over things like the application of the Capital Gains Tax didn't cost us votes, but they cost us airplay. When you think about it, we probably didn't have some of the mongrel sharpness of a truly successful opposition,' he notes regretfully.

'We had in our mind the process of government,' Beazley continues. 'There is a multiplicity of influences on an election result. But probably in the end there just weren't enough people who thought the government had been given a fair-enough go.'

'We didn't have the full "Mandate of Heaven", but we did have a few sparklers left,' says Beazley. He explores the idea further. 'The "mandate" is the electorate's view that you have a capacity to govern and this has settled on you. At least there were some residual effect that we were capable of forming government.'

'We certainly did do very well in Queensland, and that did bring Kevin into parliament. I always thought it likely we'd pick up seats there, because we were badly hammered there in '96.'

Rudd's old friend Craig Emerson was also elected to represent the southern Brisbane seat of Rankin. 'It was pretty exciting. I remember, for some reason, there were a number of us in the same car on that first morning,' he says. 'There we were at last, going to parliament again, but this time as members. It was very exciting. We were laughing and joking on the way.'

Emerson knew the house well. As one of Hawke's advisers, he was often seated in the little enclosure that they were allocated near the dispatch box. But he'd never been allowed to walk on the hallowed floor of the house as a member. 'We all had separate entrances to use, and all the staff knew exactly where we couldn't go. So this time it was all pretty amazing ... to actually walk on that green carpet without expecting an attendant to shoo you off it.'

In his first term, Rudd knew he would have to establish himself as someone who was going places. He didn't want to be categorised as 'just a good local member'; he was ambitious to achieve much more than that. It was almost as if he set himself two concrete tasks to achieve by the end of his first term: he wanted to ensure that he was the obvious person in line to be foreign minister when Labor next won office; and, just as importantly, he had to ensure that his own electorate was secure.

In this regard, Rudd was determined to take nothing for granted. He had been the beneficiary of many of the preferences from Pauline Hanson's One Nation Party. The candidate for this party had received 7 per cent of the primary vote in the electorate. Griffith could by no means be classed as a 'safe' seat: with the ALP receiving just 52.4 per cent of the vote, it was still very much a marginal electorate. As well as that, out of the 27 electorates in Queensland, all but three had produced bigger swings to Labor. There was, quite plainly, a lot of work to be done.

However, Rudd could see there was light at the end of the tunnel. His own personal campaigning style was obviously having an effect. He had attracted more than 44 per cent of the first-preference vote, and this was nearly 6 per cent higher than the number of people who had voted for the ALP in the Senate. Although a similar effect could be seen in some other electorates, it usually meant that the candidates concerned had managing to attract their own degree of considerable support.

The changing demography of the area was working against Labor. The electorate was gentrifying relatively quickly; the days when it was part of the semi-rural fringe of Brisbane were just about over. Today, the lovely old Queenslanders still grace the water fringes, but they are much more likely to be the homes of millionaires. Although parts of the electorate—particularly the southern edge—still retain the old feel, the rest of the area has changed considerably. Another parliamentarian says, 'Twenty years ago, or so, parts of Rudd's electorate might have been regarded as being "outlying", but I don't think you could make that case any more. It's pretty much jumped straight into being more-or-less an inner-city electorate.'

In 1996 many of the electors deserted Labor, and there was no guarantee they'd go back to their old ways. On the other hand, because of the type of politician Rudd was, he believed that the new crowd would probably take to him if they got to know him. As a result, he set out on what appeared to be a one-man crusade, attempting to speak to electors and impress upon them the need to vote for him. Rudd's work in the electorate, combined with his local profile and position in the party, have all added together to make it a much safer seat as the years have gone on.

In 1988, it looked as if Labor had lost its hard, disciplined edge at the last moment. Bob McMullan was one of those bitterly disappointed that Labor had not managed to keep the campaign running tightly in those last few days. 'I think, after

1996, that a lot of people were too slow to realise that the next election was winnable,' he says.

This seemed to be the problem for Labor. 'I never heard Kim say it was a "two election strategy", but some other people did and that was a very foolish thing to do,' says McMullan. 'Because we've got fair electoral boundaries, it's rare in Australia for anyone to get a majority of the vote but still fail to win government. I think the result shocked all close political observers. I have no doubt that, on the night, the Liberals had been briefed to expect to lose. Particularly those on the television panels.'

McMullan had appeared somewhat testy on the night as he watched victory slip away from Labor's grasp. There's little point now, of course, in attempting to allocate blame for the failure of the national campaign. It may have been a couple of slip-ups towards the end of the campaign, but might in turn have originated because some of the older party members had lost their edge.

Nevertheless, that election saw an influx of bright new people entering parliament. 'The landscape was crowded with good people. We were very lucky,' McMullan continues. 'In some cases, the selection processes themselves were not particularly good, but the outcomes were, often surprisingly so. Nicola Roxon is a person like that who obviously comes to mind.'

'People say that Kevin, and people like him, are ambitious,' he adds. 'That's true, but it's a pretty inadequate description. People like this—not all of them become leaders, of course—are, perhaps most importantly, people who have a vision of what might be.' McMullan insists that what sets these politicians apart is their sense of what can be achieved. 'Good people are driven to *do* something. Perhaps partly for themselves, but most importantly it's also for society. There's nothing wrong with ambition as long as its ambition to do something, rather than just to be someone,' he says.

After many years in politics, people quickly become swift judges of character. They have to be. 'It's all subjective,' says McMullan, 'but you can tell the difference between people who just want to advance themselves and those who have an enthusiasm to get a position because they can do something with it. Of course, no one falls simply into either of these two categories, because it's a continuum.'

'Obviously,' admits McMullan, 'people who come here have an element of personal motivation, as well as a desire for good policy and outcomes.' No one could really yet be sure exactly where the balance lay for Rudd.

***

The new member for Griffith was also beginning to work on accommodating his own personal philosophy within that of the Labor Party. 'Look at his maiden speech,' says a person who has worked closely with Rudd. 'It's all there.' He pauses. 'And it's all about power,' he adds. 'This is not the man who came to Canberra in any doubt about the nature of the beast. He knew exactly what he was searching for—and he found it.'

Rudd stood for the first time to speak on the floor of parliament at six minutes past six on 11 November 1998. The numbers were auspicious, and so he began his speech provocatively. 'Politics is about power,' he asserted. In those four words Rudd demonstrated with clarity that he was not going to obfuscate why he had come to Canberra. Yet after this admission he laid out the principles that he would use to guide him in the exercise of this power.

Some people would seek to do this with examples. Rudd chose instead to base his principles on a foundation of ideas. 'I believe that ideas are important. Ideas shape behaviour,' he insisted. Quoting Keynes, he continued, ' "The ideas of economists and political philosophers ... are more powerful than is commonly understood. Indeed the world is ruled by little else. Practical men, who believe themselves to be quite exempt from any intellectual influence, are usually the slaves of some defunct economist." '

But this was just rhetoric. What Rudd sought to do was deal Labor back into a debate that had supposedly ended with the collapse of communism and the death of the Soviet Union. 'Put crudely, (this) is the view that, because parties of the traditional right and traditional left have now moved to some mythical place called the "centre", all that is left is an essentially technocratic decision between one team of managers against another.'

This was something that many people felt Labor had forgotten, and Rudd was determined to overturn this orthodoxy. He said his father's death had caused him, as a young person, to think. 'It made me think that a decent social security system designed to protect the weak was no bad thing.' He listed two requirements of a healthy society: public housing and a decent universal health system. Education was also vital, and he devoted a significant proportion of his speech to this issue. 'If equality of opportunity does not begin in the school system, it begins nowhere at all.'

The frontispiece was, however, the economy. Rudd insisted that market regulation was necessary because 'markets sometimes fail'. He did not say he was advocating Tony Blair's 'third way'—his was instead a much more fundamental and simple 'repudiation of Thatcherism'. He used the speech to accuse Foreign Minister Alexander Downer of failure to engage with the region and multilaterally.

Finally (and significantly, considering the electoral impact Rudd was beginning to have in Griffith), he insisted, 'I am in this place, first and foremost, as a representative of my local community.' This was the continuing theme that Rudd would return to, time and time again over his period in parliament. Even when he became Foreign Affairs spokesperson, he'd find time to note that he'd attended local schools or perhaps acknowledge the contribution of volunteer groups within the electorate.

Then came the thanks to his family and colleagues in the Labor Party. The formalities are important to Rudd, so those close to him all got a mention.

***

Rudd had already developed his own rhetorical style. From now on, he would polish rather than change the way he naturally expressed himself. As a style it is revealing—because it demonstrates clearly the way he thinks. Listening to his speeches in parliament, it becomes apparent that Rudd has arrived at his decisions through a careful, rational analysis of the options that are available.

Particularly in parliament, his arguments have always been powered by reliance on reason, rather than emotion; politeness instead of vindictiveness; and by a quiet determination.

The reputation of the dynamic new member for Griffith was spreading in Queensland. Carl Ungerer was on leave from the Department of Foreign Affairs while he was at Queensland University completing a PhD thesis on Australia's arms-control policies. He approached Rudd to see if he could work for him in his spare time—about one day a week.

Justifiably proud of his academic credentials, Ungerer's first task was to prepare a speech on the situation in North Korea. He worked hard to impress his boss, making sure that he was across all the issues—and there were a plethora—in the relationship with Pyongyang. Rudd came back after he'd read it.

'Oh, it's okay, I reckon about a seven out of ten,' he said.

Ungerer stood there stunned for a moment, thinking, is that good? Surely it must be good? 'I learned later that this mark was actually a really high mark from Kevin. It turned out to be the equivalent of a high distinction. I didn't always score that well,' he laughs.

'Rudd is interested in the ideas of others,' says Ungerer, 'but he is also confident that he is able to grasp issues better than others—except on points of very fine detail. So, for example, I'd get a call at seven in the morning and we'd go through the nuclear fuel-cycle before Kevin had to do media at 7:30 a.m. Perhaps Kevin wasn't too sure about the difference between gas centrifuge and enrichment. It was that sort of level of detail,' Ungerer insists. 'But the fact is, for every media interview, he prepares so meticulously that he knows he really can't get caught off-guard by a question on either the policy side or the minutiae.'

'He has a steel-trap mind and really does try to get across it all,' says Ungerer. 'He can be advised—there is a role for advice in Rudd's world view,' he adds, somewhat less emphatically.

Nevertheless, his advisers found that Rudd didn't need to be taught. He was more worried about points of detail to ensure that he didn't trip up over them. In speaking about Foreign Affairs, he was dealing with something that he knew about intimately, so it's not surprising that Rudd was across the issues.

Journalists are driven by the requirements of the news, which doesn't permit anything more detailed than a glib and superficial response to whatever the issue of the day happens to be. This form of writing has its own discipline, even though reports often appear superficial to those who possess greater knowledge of the subject. The demands of news reports are often compared to 'pap' (poor quality porridge). Even so, at this time Rudd always ensured he was available to reporters, many of whom enjoyed talking to him. It seemed he was always happy to speak to them as well.

Perhaps more significantly, some other parliamentarians later noticed that once he'd made up his mind he wouldn't change it needlessly or without concrete proof that he was wrong.

At the early stages, Rudd seemed to go through a number of staff members in his office. Colleagues began to refer to Mr September and Mr October until Alistair Jordan joined the office and remained. He is still there today.

'When he arrived in Canberra, there was no one to beat Kevin's knowledge of international affairs apart from Kim,' says ANU professor Hugh White, who had worked for Beazley when he was defence minister. 'His intellectual engagement was unparalleled,' adds White.

Rudd was always keen to get more advice and to talk through ideas. White remembers having lunch with Rudd's family in Brisbane. 'The relationship they had was very impressive,' he says. 'You really learn something about a person when you see them with their family. He related to his children, always dragging them into the discussion as active participants,' White adds. 'Considering that our discussion was probably about strategic affairs—not one of the most interesting subject-areas for many people—it was fantastic to watch him challenging and encouraging them in the conversation. He wasn't condescending at all.'

'I came away thinking of that as a real model for family relationships,' says White. 'It was a charming lunch.'

White is a fan. Some others are more critical, although no one will go on the record. These unattributed judgements are fiercely contradicted when they are put to others. 'No, I don't think he's got a problem with his sensitivity to others,' says another person who has seen Rudd at work. 'He just thinks, right, this is the way the world is, so it's up to you to get on with it.'

One former staff member from this time found him 'hard, abrupt, and exploitative'. Others, observing the way his relationships in the office sometimes worked, suggest that the only way of accounting for the differences is to divide his personality into two different personas—the public Rudd and the private Kevin.

'I was with him once when he had to phone his office to get a message through,' says another person who works in Parliament House. 'No one answered the phone for ages. When they finally did, he dripped with sarcasm as he apologised for disturbing them. He can be very different depending on just who is listening and who he is speaking to.'

Far more credible are indications of his explosive temper or—and this is apparently much worse—the dismissive politeness he responds with that seems to suggest a staff member has failed to measure up to Rudd's high standards. This apparently indicates someone has been cut off. There's nothing more to be said. Certainly, there are numerous accounts of shouting coming from his office, and assertions that if advice doesn't fit in with his own preconceptions it will be ignored.

But most people insist Rudd is a delight. He is adept at casual contact. This is a key political skill, and vital for a leader.

Years later, in May 2006, Whitlam opened Rudd's new electorate office in Morningside, retelling a story he'd originally been told by Rudd. Whitlam insisted the younger Labor politician had learned a priceless lesson from the former Liberal minister Jim Killen. 'Jim had shown Kevin how to nurse a marginal seat into a healthy majority,' Whitlam said. 'He visited a shopping centre in his electorate every Saturday morning. What Jim Killen had done in Moreton, Kevin Rudd decided to do in Griffith,' said Whitlam, pausing dramatically for emphasis at the end of his sentence.

As a good friend of Killen, Whitlam would have particularly appreciated this story.

There was also criticism that Rudd was, somehow or another, not really a Labor person. This came mainly from people who didn't know him well.

Just before Rudd entered parliament, a former senior bureaucrat was speaking to a senior coalition minister. The minister is supposed to have said of Rudd, 'What a pity he joined Labor. He really should be one of ours.' When this was put to the minister, he flatly denies it, insisting that he wouldn't have even known who Rudd was at that time. 'But,' he says, rubbing his hands together ever so slightly, 'why don't you focus on his use of Christianity for political advantage?' By the end of our conversation it's become difficult to work out exactly who has been the most ruthless in co-opting religion to support his argument.

Bob Carr insists that any suggestion that Rudd isn't really 'working class' or, in some unspecified way, not a true Labor representative places him in a long tradition. Carr remembers a branch 'blowhard' back in the '70s complaining that 'Gough Whitlam's not a real Labor man', calling the prime minister 'coat-and-tails Gough'.

'These sort of claims are always rubbish; just rubbish,' says Carr.

The dynamics within Parliament House itself are unusual. Casual contact is necessarily minimised by the long sterile corridors. Instead of allowing chance encounters, the geography of the building focuses on barriers. An arid blankness frames the rooms in pristine white. Small black numbers etched onto square brass plates are the only markers identifying the individual rooms.

Backbenchers sometimes try desperately to have a bit of fun. 'Some politicians around this place are far from normal,' says one. 'They're not the sort of person you'd have a beer with.

Although I'd happily pull up a stool with Kevin.'

'He'd participate in a few of the games we'd play, you know, like making sure you used a particular word in a speech, or something like that. He was great fun once he knocked off.'

Every politician is allocated a small suite of offices. Once inside, insulation from the outside world is complete. The white walls are, by edict, decoration free. The only exception is for appropriately framed artwork on loan from the parliamentary collection. Paintings, which should be full of life, become 'artworks', and the process of official approval drains away their soul as they are confined and hung.

The stories of staffers leaving trails of breadcrumbs so they can find their way back to their offices are not true, but that's just because nothing is allowed to deface the cleanliness of the official spaces, even for a minute. Members are also subordinated to these fierce regulations, seemingly drawn up simply to expunge any sign of humanity. Sticking a poster on a wall represents a highly insubordinate act, which will be quickly corrected. Monotony is ensured, by edict.

Rudd tried hard to impress his own personality on the place. Behind his desk he hung some scrolls he said he'd picked up late one night in Taipei. His bookcases were full of books that he'd read and was interested in, rather than just copies of Hansard that would look impressive. Right from his arrival at the end of 1998 as a little-known backbencher, Rudd made sure he cut his own swathe through the parliamentary jungle.

***

During his first term, Rudd prepared a caucus paper dealing with the relationship between Australia and Indonesia. The point of this was to place party policy on East Timor into context—and this lay at the heart of what was to become a long-simmering dispute with Labor's spokesperson, Laurie

Brereton, who was responsible for overturning Labor's earlier decision to recognise Indonesian sovereignty over the whole island, calling instead for the people of the island to vote on their future.

'I'm sure Laurie thought that taking a pro-independence position for Timor would benefit him politically,' says a person who does not wish to be identified. But this analysis ignores the fact that it was also absolutely necessary for the party. If Brereton had not changed the policy, the progressive left would have abandoned the party later when the pro-Indonesian militia wreaked their revenge after the independence ballot. 'It was a very politically farsighted move to take,' says another politician, 'regardless of his personal motivations.'

The big speech Brereton gave to re-position Labor on the Timor issue was followed immediately by fireworks—but not of the celebratory kind. In achieving what he did, Brereton had pulled apart not only Whitlam's policy, but also questioned the close relationship that Paul Keating and Gareth Evans had forged with the Indonesian government. Brereton was accused of just seeking to enhance his popularity with *Sydney Morning Herald* readers and ABC listeners.

Gough Whitlam quickly jumped in, claiming that 'this is the least qualified shadow foreign minister Labor has ever had'—a stinging rebuke that substituted vitriol for argument. Others amongst the old guard had the wisdom to simply remain silent. But picking at this running scab didn't endear Brereton to those in the party who had ignored the continuing human-rights abuses on the island for years.

Brereton's stance simply recognised what had long been obvious—that, more than twenty years after the original invasion, the east of the island had still not become integrated with Indonesia. But his decision to place human rights ahead of *realpolitik* traumatised those who had previously privileged the relationship with Jakarta.

Despite this, there was an almost audible gasp of relief once the policy change was forced through. Former Labor president Carmen Lawrence is still very enthusiastic about the role Laurie Brereton performed at this time. 'I think Laurie did a marvellous service for the party when he re-positioned us on East Timor. He also performed an important role in emphasising a new, broad, human-rights agenda,' she says. 'Up until then, the party had nearly a 30-year history of getting it wrong on East Timor, so it was a big achievement for him to step around a few of the very big egos in the party. Somebody in the foreign affairs club probably wouldn't have been able to do this.'

'The success or failure of this policy over the long term will be answered by the success or failure of East Timor,' says one of the party's former luminaries. 'Recent events suggest the state is corrupt and barely viable. But what is its future to be? It's a big leap to say they'd be better off as part of the Indonesian republic.'

Brereton's speech allowed Rudd an opening to present his own paper on the Indonesian relationship. This emphasised that, while East Timor and the human-rights issues were important, the bilateral relationship with Jakarta was absolutely vital for Australia's long-term security.

It was a coherently argued case—but Labor people wondered why Rudd had picked a fight with Brereton. Many suspected that, behind the ostensible desire to engage in a policy debate, there was a hidden agenda at work to boost his credentials in the party.

By this stage Rudd had begun to intensively network inside the party. He took every opportunity when he was visiting a city around the country to do so—dropping in on premiers, seeing factional allies—and, gradually, carefully, he let his ambitions be known. One of the people he was lobbying at the time derisorily commented, 'It all looked a bit impertinent, but he kept doing it anyway.'

A close acquaintance of Brereton says of this period, 'He hated Kevin. It's easy to see how it happened. Laurie was a professional politician—a politician's politician—coming into contact with a professional diplomat who was busy activating all his old contacts.'

Brereton became very critical of Rudd to other colleagues in the party. Unsurprisingly, he saw Rudd's development of a foreign affairs agenda as undermining him. He also pointed out that Rudd was on two (domestically focused) parliamentary committees at this time. 'If he's so keen to develop policy, why doesn't he do something with these?' Brereton demanded, pointing out that although Rudd had sought the positions, he appeared to have made few contributions to either. Rudd already believed he had credibility on macro-economic issues as a result of his time in China and through working as a consultant for KPMG.

One Labor caucus member now says, with just the hint of a smile on his face, 'I can't remember any conflict between Laurie and Kevin.' When pressed, however, a recollection seems to return of one caucus meeting in particular. 'Each meeting of caucus has its own dynamics,' he adds. 'Sometimes people get very passionate about an issue.' This was one of those occasions. 'Rudd was told, in front of everyone, to stop undermining the spokesman. Laurie's not a fool; he knew what was going on. But there's no point in dredging up the bitter disagreements of old times,' he adds.

Brereton has always possessed a politician's eye for possibilities and realities. He positioned the party where he felt it had to be. At that time, Rudd had less experience and a very different point of view, but there have been changes in their relationship over the subsequent years. Brereton was close to Latham, and enthusiastically underwrote his leadership credentials. More recently, other MPs quote Brereton endorsing Rudd—and, more particularly, his ideas.

'Rudd had to do something about Beazley,' Brereton said recently. 'We have moved well past any disagreement we may once have had. And we desperately need someone who can get rid of Howard.'

As a new member, Rudd also began to cross Mark Latham. He defended the Labor Party against criticism from Latham, who had accused the ALP of being intellectually bereft and lacking policy. Latham claimed he wanted to reposition the party, whereas it seems Rudd held more traditional views during this period.

The relationship between Rudd and Foreign Minister Alexander Downer also seems to have been quite varied. At times, Downer appeared to assist Rudd. Other parliamentarians suspect that this had more to do with an attempt to cause friction within the opposition between Brereton and Rudd rather than anything else.

Later on, a Foreign Affairs diplomat notes that 'Rudd was taken off the invitation list.' He added cryptically, 'It all depended on Downer.'

'I think one of the reasons Downer and Rudd so dislike each other is because they were both together in the department,' says another diplomat. 'Well, Downer was FAQ—fair average quality,' this person says dismissively. 'The sort who got very modest assessment reports. I think there may have been a little jealousy there.'

A senior policy analyst attacks the Howard government by suggesting that 'good domestic politics can make very bad foreign policy,' although he later pointed out that Rudd has been guilty of the same thing. 'An example of this is calling for Indonesia to ban the Muslim organisation JI. Well, this sort of thing is just *not* going to happen. It's a stupid demand. I pointed this out to him. For a start, in their language it just means little brotherhood. But neither of them listened. Good domestic politics outweighed good foreign policy.'

Then there's a pause. 'Kevin is also a Christian. I think he's genuinely worried about what radical Islam might do.' I ask if more should be read into this, but the analyst clams up.

***

Early in the parliamentary term, Janette Howard held a lunch at the Lodge for the wives of the new parliamentarians. Thérèse went to Canberra for the function, where she was placed next to Judith, the wife of Liberal MP Bruce Baird. After a brief—and possibly inadequate—introduction, the two women began to talk, and soon realised they had a great deal in common.

Later that evening, Judith told Baird she'd met Thérèse and they'd had a lovely chat. She asked where Rudd stood on the political spectrum. 'Oh, on the right I should think,' replied Baird, and then noticed the surprise on his wife's face. She had obviously not picked the husband of the lovely woman she'd been speaking to as a right-winger. Suddenly, the cause of her mistake dawned on Baird. 'You do realise he's Labor?' he asked.

'Oh, I had no idea. Absolutely none,' she laughed. Because she had a similar outlook to Thérèse, she had assumed Rudd was, most probably, a Liberal wet.

Over time, Rudd and Baird were to find that they had something else in common: a strong Christian faith.

Ten years before, Baird had been a popular and effective minister in the Greiner government, which had surged to power in New South Wales after the voters dismissed the Unsworth government. Today, Baird is a highly experienced and capable federal politician, but Howard has never promoted him to cabinet despite his obvious qualifications for a senior ministry. Analysts have assumed that is because of his small-l liberal views, combined with his concern about implementing a progressive social agenda.

'Kevin has an absolutely genuine belief in Christ, I have no doubt about that,' says Baird. 'It's not just something he's adopted because it's politically convenient.' Later in our conversation he repeats this. 'His belief is deeply held; it's not superficial,' says Baird, 'but it's also a very contemporary Christianity—not of the overtly proselytising sort. He appears to be keenly aware of the church's failings.'

As referred to earlier, Rudd has identified himself as belonging to the Church of England, deciding to abandon his mother's Catholicism. 'He could sit comfortably anywhere,' emphasises another friend. 'He doesn't accept that a person is defined by their religious denomination. You interpret your faith through your life,' this person insists. 'It's not your particular "brand" that necessarily assumes an overarching significance.'

Indeed, even in this early part of his parliamentary career, Rudd's faith would sometimes pose quandaries for someone needing to reconcile his personal belief with the discipline required of a party member.

'He has no problem praying for guidance,' says Harry Quick, one of the few Labor parliamentarians who has also publicly identified himself as a Christian. Quick's father was a Gallipoli veteran and was 20 years older than his mother. He'd been a butcher, and the family had often relied on the generosity of the church to survive. Quick, who repays this with a strong Christian faith, had worked as a primary-school teacher and principal before becoming a politician. He says, 'There are two or three other guys, some on the other side of the fence, who I can relate to in a religious sense. We are of a similar ilk in the way we minister to our electorate, and it seems to help us to keep getting re-elected.'

Baird notes that, 'As politicians, we sometimes find the biblical injunctions to retain our humility particularly difficult to obey,' says Baird. 'These canons can seem to contradict the natural requirements of the job to push yourself forward. Kevin is very aware of this tension.'

'Kevin is also particularly interested in the journeys of St Paul,' says Baird. 'He'd buy old maps and attempt to trace the routes the saint had taken as he travelled across the eastern Mediterranean.'

Rudd's choice of St Paul is interesting. This particular saint's title is 'the evangelist', and he is remembered for spreading the gospel through his trips and letters. Today, proselytising religions are viewed with suspicion; however, there is another way of looking at what Paul was attempting to achieve. His religion was inclusive—in fact, he had a big argument about the need to take the gospel to the Gentiles (those who weren't born Jewish).

It's difficult for many people to know what to make of Rudd's interest in the evangelist. Some may choose to focus on the fact that Paul devoted himself to his mission, working indefatigably and being extraordinarily self-reliant. He supposedly survived three shipwrecks, and was stoned and imprisoned. He was also very aware of his own weaknesses, but found hope in the unconditional love of God. Those who are suspicious will worry about elements of anti-feminism and control residing within this interpretation of Christianity.

Easy familiarity with the Bible and church history led to Rudd acquiring some other unusual qualities. Much later, a parliamentary staffer recalled being in a large meeting with him and others. 'Everyone was droning on, talking about the usual issues, which weren't particularly interesting,' she says. 'Suddenly, although I wasn't really paying attention, I heard the words "in extremis". It was quite unusual to hear people in our party talking this way, so I suddenly sat up and paid attention. I started noticing the religious phraseology he was using. It wasn't just for effect; it was obviously the way he normally spoke. After that, I began listening for him using these sort of words, and it was surprising how often he speaks in this way. Or makes use of those unusual word constructions that are often used in the Bible.'

A significant danger with Rudd's declaration of Christianity is that other religious communities might feel excluded. Aware of this, in late 2004 Rudd engaged in an argument through the pages of the *Australian Jewish News* with the former Labor parliamentarian Barry Cohen. Cohen claimed that his old party had become 'rampantly anti-Semitic'. Rudd quickly leapt in to fight this slur.

'It is dangerous for people to start throwing the term anti-Semitic around indiscriminately,' he said. 'I find it profoundly personally offensive,' he continued. Rudd was also aware of the political dimension of religion, asserting that, 'I also fear that (the government) is actively seeking to create a political wedge between Labor and the Jewish community as part of a long-term electoral strategy.'

Perhaps the key point is that Rudd believes in the necessity for some sort of spiritual engagement. After the Second World War, the poet T. S. Eliot had come to believe that the basic idea of culture was under threat. He insisted that civilisation required religion for it to flourish. Without the shared set of beliefs that come with religion, he felt there was nothing to bind people together into a society.

But not every politician who thinks about these issues necessarily turns to religion. Carmen Lawrence, for example, would occasionally rib Rudd about his Christianity. Nevertheless, she says that beneath the light-hearted banter lay a recognition that something different was motivating both of them. 'We are concerned about more than simply the success of the economy,' she says. Lawrence had been brought up a Catholic, and spent a couple of years away from home at boarding school at a young age. 'I would occasionally remind him that I knew exactly where he was coming from, particularly on those so-called "moral" issues,' she says. 'We can respect each other's views — while knowing how far apart we are.'

Because she was on the left of the party, the two were not factional allies. Nevertheless, when they met there would be the occasional discussions about books and writing, as well as the more political ones. The main issues that they ended up talking about were, in fact, their differences, 'but this was an interesting engagement in an intellectual sense,' she says. She felt that the positions he took were often somewhat conservative; however, there was never any personal antagonism in the relationship.

'I regard him as a friend,' says Lawrence, 'but in that quite light way that we use the term in politics.'

***

Rudd was not the only person in the family who was succeeding in their chosen endeavours. Thérèse's company was expanding rapidly. The biggest boost came in 1998 with the Howard government's decision to abolish the Commonwealth Employment Service, establishing the Job Network. This outsourced the placement of all unemployed people.

Thérèse now had links of her own. The company boasted some big names on the board. As well as Goss, Mike Codd (the former head of the federal public service) was on the board; he is also a member of the Qantas board. Barrie Adams, a former Queensland regional commissioner of the Australian Securities and Investments Commission, was another member.

By the year 2000, Thérèse's company had been renamed Ingeus, and had opened an office in Britain. This was followed by more expansion, first into France and then Germany. Eventually, more than half the company's revenue would come from offshore operations.

***

In early 2001 the defence minister, John Moore, resigned. The relationship between the prime minister and Moore had been long and sometimes icy—Moore had been one of the key plotters who had assisted Andrew Peacock in overthrowing Howard during his first stint as opposition leader in 1989. Moore had first taken the Brisbane suburban seat of Ryan in 1975, and over time had cemented his position in it. Even in the 1998 election, which had seen Labor roll back the significant gains made by the Liberal Party in 1996, Moore had still won more than 59 per cent of the two-party-preferred vote. This was a seat that should have been unwinnable for Labor.

But support for the Liberal government was collapsing across the country. At the time, the pollster Gary Morgan said that if a federal election had been held in late February, the ALP would have won in a landslide. Since the previous year, the Liberal government's fortunes had become locked in a downward spiral from which it seemed unable to pull out. Just before the by-election was held, Morgan's polling showed that primary support for the coalition had fallen to an all-time low of just 30 per cent. This was even lower than when the GST was introduced. Even after the distribution of the notional preferences in the polling, Labor still received a massive 63 per cent of the vote. Quite suddenly, the unwinnable was looking possible.

Labor's candidate in Ryan was Leoni Short. A medical researcher, she had been preselected to contest the seat well before Moore had decided to depart politics. At that time, victory appeared a distant prospect, but now everything had changed. Labor's team in Queensland threw everything into winning the campaign. Rudd and his factional friend Arch Bevis accompanied her around the electorate as she tirelessly sold herself. The stifling heat sucked the enthusiasm out of all but the most determined party workers, but Short kept on: walking from door-to-door, smiling her greetings at the shoppers frequenting the markets in The Gap, handing out pamphlets and walking through the shopping centres.

Labor had another difficulty, which would compound the problem of gaining the seat. Because of the difference between state and federal elections, it was necessary for voters to mark every box on the federal ballot paper. At the recent state election, premier Beattie had campaigned on the slogan 'Just Vote One'. This meant that the opposition expected it would suffer a greater percentage of informal votes.

As the counting began, however, it became obvious that none of this would matter. The electorate was furious with the government, and that anger outweighed anything else. Labor won Ryan easily. The message seemed obvious: if it could win in the Liberal heartland, it seemed as if it was just a matter of time before the opposition coasted to victory in the federal election, due later that year.

Complacency quickly spread through the Labor ranks. It was hard not to be sanguine. Equally, a looming realisation that the Howard government faced not merely a narrow defeat but a complete and utter rout fiercely concentrated the minds of the leadership. The fight to return from the brink of electoral disaster began on the Sunday morning after the poll.

The budget that year represented such carefully targeted generosity that each announcement would have sent alarm bells ringing for the opposition. Fine calibration was used to ensure that the swinging voters — the people who were flirting with voting Labor — were wooed back to the Liberal fold.

The budget give-aways were not simply across the board. Making the calculation that the wealthy were going to vote Liberal anyway, the government focused on the so-called Howard aspirational voters. New measures were introduced that would directly appeal to these people.

The first indication that Labor was beginning to lose ground came from Victoria. A by-election was held after the sitting member in the seat of Aston, Peter Nugent, died. Labor warned journalists that it would be a 'hard ask' to grab this seat from the government because of demographic changes. Indeed, since that ballot was held, the seat has become progressively more and more safe for the government, and it now sits on a buffer of 13.2 per cent, making it almost impossible for Labor to win.

Nevertheless, in 2001 that was not the case. Despite Labor's warnings, most pundits confidently expected it to fall. Although there was a significant swing against the government, the seat held, and returned a Liberal candidate to Canberra.

'Idiots, and there are many,' says Beazley pointedly, 'assume that we did badly in the Aston by-election. We actually did better in that seat than we've ever done before. Basically, one of the things that depresses me about the media in Australia is they don't read anything. It's info-tainment. There's not much you can do about that.'

Beazley was disappointed, according to his staff, but he was not perturbed by the result. He used a simple argument. Translating the swing nationally, he confidently asserted that the party would romp it in.

Was this hopeful buoyancy, or smug self-satisfaction? The government increased its efforts to turn back the tide. It redoubled its intensity at the same moment that Labor nationally appeared to loosen its grip on the reins.

Significantly, Rudd did not let up on his personal campaign to turn Griffith into a jewel in the Labor crown. As a backbencher, his time was largely his own to allocate. This was his biggest resource, and although he devoted a lot of energy to positioning himself within the party nationally, his real focus was directed towards making his seat secure.

A campaign worker insists that the result in 1996 had a

significant effect on Rudd. 'He would never accept that the electorate wouldn't turf him out,' this person says. 'Every weekend he would get out there. He wanted to meet people and explain to them why they had to vote for him. And then, there was also the big issue ...' he says, his voice trailing off towards the end of the sentence.

'No politician actually wants an issue like the airport,' he says, 'because you never know when it will turn around and bite you on the bum. But Rudd ran with it hard and positioned himself as the defender of the local community. He threw himself into it. It worked a treat for him.'

Another political colleague says, 'The airport became a genuine issue in his electorate, and he felt he had a need to address that. He received a lot of media coverage—television, the *Courier Mail*—and I think it all helped to lift his profile.'

Brisbane airport was expanding. This meant that more aircraft would fly over his electorate. It was nothing like being under the Sydney flight-path, but it was significant for Brisbane. Rudd's seat wasn't necessarily the worst affected, but he led the fight against development of the airport site. The changing demographics had made the runway issue particularly significant. 'People were out there watching their property values,' says a resident who was involved in the protest. 'We needed to see that someone was out there fighting for us.'

'I think Kevin managed the issue quite well. As a consequence, his profile was lifted to very high levels within his electorate,' says a person who used to work for Rudd. 'He talked to every pilot he could get hold of,' says the resident. 'He'd ring the airports around the world to find out what noise patterns are like with particular wind velocity. The detail was incredible.'

It was this command of the facts that allowed Rudd to have the confidence to stand before people and tell them what should be done. He took the issue to court in a bid to prevent the airport going ahead, but the judges were less impressed. Rudd lost the court case against the airport amid suggestions it had been a 'frivolous litigation'. But this had more to do with the fact that there was no law against the development of a parallel runway, rather than the fact that Rudd was doing everything he could to keep faith with his electorate.

***

Beazley confidently asserts that 'An election campaign—for a opposition leader—is pure joy.' He smiles. 'Courtesy of television and radio, you get your unexpurgated message through. You can get up on television for 30 seconds every night.' This is the key. 'Newspapers are just part of the background noise—white noise,' he insists.

'We were trying to get up the alternative agenda,' adds Beazley. 'I took on board the view that perhaps there were not enough sharp edges—points of distinction between us and the government. But there's not much point in having a disagreement when the electorate won't agree with you.'

There are two, diametrically opposed, explanations for the 2001 election result. Beazley still has absolutely no doubt about what it was that caused Labor's destruction. For him it will always be the Tampa and September 11.

'Polling showed a week before Tampa we had 58 per cent of the two-party-preferred vote in Mal Brough's seat. It looked as if we'd romp it in,' says Beazley. 'He ended up with a swing of nearly 2 per cent *towards* him. He should have lost.'

'The fact of the matter is, I've always believed in an election campaign anyone can win,' says Beazley. 'By the end of the 2001 campaign, we'd had some bad setbacks, but I still thought it was possible we could win. We lifted about 7 per cent during the campaign.'

'We were winning on the domestic issues. I suspect it was when *The Australian* tumbled to the fact that the kids had not been tossed overboard that we lost. The agenda swung back to the government's strong suit—national security,' Beazley still insists. 'It played a sharp role. All of a sudden, our message was jumbled.'

But there was a rival explanation advanced immediately after the poll by Liberal strategists: the government had learned from its mistakes and changed. This argument asserts that the government was looking better to the voters long before the Tampa's Norwegian skipper decided to pluck people from their sinking boat and sail into Australian waters.

It seems best to go to as neutral a source as possible to arbitrate between these competing claims to truth. Right through this period, the polling organisation Newspoll was regularly surveying the political scene. Rather than asking a small group of people *why* they were feeling a particular way, Newspoll asked large numbers of people *what* they were going to do as a result of these feelings. In particular, how they were going to vote.

'The Liberals were competitive well before the Tampa,' says the company's head pollster from the time, Sol Lebovic. 'September 11 just had the government looking more comfortable. The problem Labor had was that it couldn't lock the electorate into supporting it. I'm convinced that it wasn't the case that those two events destroyed Labor's chances.'

'First, the electorate will look at the government,' he says, 'and if they don't like it then they'll evaluate the opposition. But they weren't convinced, and they felt that Labor still had a lot of work to do. It hadn't converted the potential into votes.'

Some analysts claim that because the majority of voters say they don't make up their minds until the election itself, much of the work beforehand is wasted. Lebovic disagrees. 'By the time a campaign starts, it's too late. Messages won't sink in;

people need time to absorb them.' He quotes an old marketing saying: "Until you're bored with it, people haven't even noticed it." 'If you leave everything to the last moment and rely on the campaign itself, it doesn't give you very long to win a policy debate.'

'I seriously damaged Labor's chances of winning the election when Howard brought me the first border-protection legislation,' says Beazley now. 'Without consulting caucus, I brought together the strategy group and said, "Under no circumstances will I accept this." We collapsed nine points in the polls in the next 48 hours.'

'That was my stand on principle, but it was the right thing to do,' insists Beazley. 'Weeks later, Philip Ruddock turned up in my office with the amended legislation. It became obvious that my speech opposing the first Bill had provided the drafting instructions.'

'Out there, amongst the sea-green incorruptibles,' adds Beazley with a hint of bitterness, 'there is no understanding of that. But I was prepared to lay Labor on the line.'

After the election, Beazley decided to go to the backbench, and so did Brereton. This left the way open for a new team to contest the next election. In 1998, a few people had been desperately disappointed that Labor hadn't won. Nevertheless, most in the party thought that they would soon be sitting on the government benches. 'Everyone thought that Howard would unravel after 1998,' says one Labor MP, summing up the mood of optimism in the party after the election. 'But he didn't unravel at all, because we didn't manage to keep the pressure on him.'

In 2001 that sense of optimism was lacking. The party became introspective as it tried to work out why it had failed so badly. Rudd saw his opportunity, and urgently wanted to contribute to renewing the party. This was his chance to make a mark.

CHAPTER FIVE

Shadow

2001–2003

> 'There is no debate or dispute as to whether Saddam Hussein possesses weapons of mass destruction. He does.'
>
> –Kevin Rudd on *Lateline*, 24 September 2002

Around the country, election night 2001 turned into a disaster for Labor. But in Griffith the results were very different. Nationally, there had been a devastating 2.26 per cent swing against the opposition. Yet Rudd managed a 4.4 per cent swing *towards* him on first preferences. His margin of safety had increased to 5.7 per cent. All the work at the shopping centres, all the constant effort courting the media, was finally paying off.

Significantly, Rudd had widened his appeal. Pauline Hanson's vote had collapsed, and Rudd seemed to attract most of her supporters. But it was more than this. Once again, a comparison of the vote between the two houses of parliament revealed that now his personal following in the House of Representatives was more than 12 per cent higher than Labor's

Senate assault—the biggest differential in the state. In other words, people who weren't voting for Labor in the Senate were voting for him. This is often the case, but not to this extent. Rudd's personal vote was just slightly greater than the one Swan was managing to achieve in Lilley.

This campaign, the AWU—Ludwig's boys—had decided to back Rudd more fully. He'd received a far greater degree of support than at the two previous elections. But this alone did not explain his personal triumph. There was undoubtedly a 'Rudd effect' at work.

'That's just Kevin,' says a campaign worker. 'In some ways, it's a contradictory part of his personality. He is an intellectual man obsessed by policies and ideas, and yet I've seen him, every week, out there in the mobile office that he sets up somewhere around the electorate just talking to people. He talks to a whole range of very different people.' This worker insists that Rudd's interest in people's problems is not feigned. 'You know Kevin. It's as if he's got us under the magnifying glass and he's thinking, "I wonder how this works." He is fascinated by people.'

'He's done very clever things. The bicycle thing has been a huge hit,' adds the worker. This is a reference to the fact that Rudd personally gives a bicycle to every primary school in the electorate once a year. The school then raffles it off, using the money to pay for improvements it otherwise couldn't afford. 'It's very, very clever,' the volunteer points out. 'It's about kids, about fit kids, and its about delivering money back into the school community. But, wait for it, because this is the real kick: all these mums and dads think it's fantastic, but the people this stunt really appeals to are the gentrifying mums in their four-wheel-drive vehicles. These are exactly the people who might otherwise be voting Liberal.'

'When they see their children developing independence,' he smiles, 'and being helped to do so by a *Labor* politician, who speaks very nicely, they think, "Yes, I'll vote for him." Rudd's got all his bases covered. But it's through hard work.'

Rudd was appalled by the electoral devastation that encompassed the party. Nevertheless, he would also have been well aware that the disaster also provided him with an unparalleled opportunity to showcase his credentials in a senior role. Beazley had decided to step down. So did others on the frontbench team—including, as Rudd noticed with particular interest for his own personal future, Brereton. No one else had made such a determined pitch to be appointed to the Foreign Affairs job in the previous term of parliament. He was the most obvious candidate to take the portfolio.

Rudd's fellow Queenslander Craig Emerson was also elevated to the shadow ministry after the election. 'When you're promoted to the front bench, lots of groups and organisations want to meet with you. You really need to be meeting people and doing a lot of travelling. That takes up a lot of time,' he says. 'As well as the requirements of the portfolio, there's also the need to get out and about in the marginal electorates to reinforce the vote. Between that and policy work there's not a lot of time left over for things like life.'

Rudd couldn't have achieved this without the complete support of Thérèse and the children. She managed the family, and kept it ticking along in the background. She also successfully managed a dynamically growing business. She contributed financial resources to support him in his efforts.

Inevitably, when dealing with politicians, you hear gossip, because there is usually a lot of it around. There's talk about relationships, people on the make, or affairs, off and on the road. One of Rudd's prominent Christian colleagues was Ross Cameron. His infidelity later became common knowledge, and Australians don't like unfaithful politicians. The swing against Cameron was just 1.9 percent, but that was more than enough to see him off. Perhaps the voters suspected he might shortly break his promises to them as well. He didn't return to Canberra.

The point is that there is none of this sort of talk about Rudd.

***

When Beazley stepped down from the leadership in the wake of the defeat, Crean was the obvious candidate to take over. No ballot was necessary. Later on, some parliamentarians tried to argue that Crean had forced his way into the position by shoving others out. It didn't appear like that at the time.

Some people in the ALP might have been apprehensive about Simon Crean taking over. Others might just want to have had a go at leading the party themselves. But as it was always clear that Crean had majority support, there was no point in anyone making a fuss. In hindsight, some assert there was a campaign of destabilisation against him right from the beginning, but the work the whisperers were doing wasn't obvious until much later.

Labor had turned to a former unionist to lead the party at a time when the electorate was consumed with international issues. Crean relied on Rudd to help guide him through the foreign policy and strategic issues that were to bedevil his period of leadership. His assistant was well experienced diplomatically, and intellectually equipped for the task. But the party failed to score any hits politically.

This was not Rudd's fault alone. The caucus was being pulled apart over the Iraq War. On one side was the old, working-class, socially conservative base of the party. They had no time for a dictator like Saddam Hussein, and were worried by Islamic fundamentalism. Then there was the intellectual class, virulently anti-Bush, who perceived that the invasion of Iraq would become a military disaster like Vietnam.

Finally, there was the government, using all its resources to continually poke and prod the opposition, goading it mercilessly. The real mission was simply to avoid defeat. Victory looked impossible.

Rudd's first major test in the portfolio came in the lead-up to the Iraq War. Labor found it extremely difficult to establish a policy. There were no easy or obvious solutions; the old shibboleths all seemed to have been thrown out at the time of the attack on the World Trade Centre. In the turmoil that followed the terrorist assault on New York and Washington, everyone had supported the decision to invade Afghanistan. After all, that was a renegade state (not even a member of the United Nations), and it had definitely been nurturing Al Qaeda. Iraq was quite different.

Many of those on the left of the party were in no doubt that the plan to invade Iraq should be opposed. For a start, it was being drawn up in the Bush White House. A suspicion of US motives came naturally to some, while others doubted the ability of America to successfully mount an invasion, let alone create a flourishing democracy, in the Middle East.

Tony Blair then significantly complicated matters as the party groped its way about in the dark. Suddenly, a Labor government was giving credibility on the international stage to the assertions about Saddam possessing weapons of mass destruction. There was just enough doubt to make these well-publicised fears seem reasonable. Rudd was certainly a believer.

There were two issues that needed to be resolved. The first was what was the correct thing to do. But this had to be based on a realistic understanding of what was possible.

'Kevin began by being very sceptical about Iraq, for the best strategic reasons,' says a military analyst. 'But he was always more of the diplomat than the strategist,' he continues. 'You could always see him thinking, "How can we work our way through this?" Military men have a more fundamentalist approach.' The problem was that, while Rudd was genuinely trying to find solutions to a problem, Washington remained implacable. The White House had already decided on war, and had no interest in other ways of resolving the conflict. 'Rudd's attempt to find a way to talk the problems through was very soon completely irrelevant,' insists the analyst.

'When Howard visited Bush in Crawford, Texas, in the middle of 2002,' another person who was working in the military intelligence community at this time says, 'it was pretty clear that Australia was informed of the impending war with Iraq. But, of course,' this specialist says, smiling slightly at the thought, 'the Australian people didn't know that.' Neither did Labor. One of the party's strategists is bitter. 'Howard always said there was never an undertaking; we weren't committed to war. Like hell we weren't! The fact was he *did* commit. Early and often.'

Ungerer was Crean's foreign-policy adviser by this time. He says that, together, Howard and Downer attempted to ruthlessly demolish the opposition, using all the resources of government. 'They were saying things like, Simon is an appeaser; he talks like Saddam Hussein. They directly prosecuted the case for war for the next six months. They knew it was coming. We didn't. It's not difficult to out-manoeuvre your opponent in that sort of situation.'

'They were there all the time,' says Ungerer, 'and the refrain was always the same. "You're weak, you're weak, you're weak. You don't know what you're talking about." '

Rudd did, in fact, personally write a major shadow cabinet paper on the war in April 2002. Never previously released publicly, this document set out Labor's approach to the issue of war. It contained two vital policy recommendations. The first element was the preservation of 'reasonable flexibility within a diplomatic stance'. This was important because it allowed

Australia to join with America if solid evidence of a WMD program or Al Quaeda links suddenly turned up. The second element was 'to establish a clear set of principles and process before Labor would support any military action in Iraq'. It concluded that, 'We do not believe the case has yet been made that would warrant a direct attack on Iraq'.

The difficulty was that, although the solution that the paper proposed was an intelligent compromise, it did not prove to be a workable policy—the divide between opponents of the war and those wanting to invade was too wide to be bridged. The ambiguity within this policy soon bedevilled the opposition, which was unable to send a clear message in the media. Those on the left of the party increasingly turned away from Labor. They were implacably opposed to any military action.

'Many also felt that Kim Beazley (in particular) was quite ready to jump in with the Americans,' says an observer. This is a very simplistic characterisation of a delicate and nuanced position. Others disagree, saying that it was actually Rudd who pushed the most pro-US line. Regardless of the specifics, there was no unified approach on the issue. At the time, many blamed Rudd for the failure to create a workable position. Some felt that their foreign-policy spokesman was not working for Labor at all.

The resultant policy left Crean crucified. He was attempting to find a workable path in the centre, but his left and right hands were pinned so that he could not move. He was hammered in, and the government was driving in each nail.

***

A member of the shadow cabinet at the time insists that many of Crean's later problems came from Rudd's failure to articulate firm political positions over security issues early on. 'It took a long time for us to get to our final policy, and it wasn't just on issues like the Iraq War. This was a very big problem and part of the reason he (Crean) lost his leadership. For too long there was a lack of clarity about what we were saying.' This senior politician has no doubt it was the inexperienced Foreign Affairs spokesperson who was to blame. 'I don't know that he knew which way he was going some of the time, and I think that was part of the problem.'

By the time of the debate over the Iraq War, it had become obvious that the old factional positions were becoming less and less relevant. It was extraordinary that even in a policy environment such as this, the old left and right divisions had begun to disintegrate. According to Carmen Lawrence, 'Personality had now become the dominant issue in determining support within the party, rather than ideological posturing.'

When it's under pressure, the Labor Party can sometimes look as if it's formed from an unusual coalition of disparate groups. Simply keeping the party together can prove a full-time job. Insiders say that this problem confounded policy-making in the lead-up to the war. The difficulty is that many on the left of the party harbour intense anti-American feelings. Those on the right, however, genuinely believe the alliance with Washington is a vital, necessary, and valued centrepiece of the party's foreign-policy platform. Reconciling these two diametrically opposed positions is fraught with difficulty.

Those who had less patience with the relationship with the United States wanted to see greater scrutiny applied to articulating Australia's interests, rather than slavishly following Washington. Labor's right insisted that this ignored the dominant role of the US alliance as the bedrock of policy-making. Since the Second World War, maintaining the ANZUS alliance has always been the starting point for any discussion of Australia's foreign-policy options. New Zealand was prepared to risk the rupturing of the alliance over the nuclear ship issue, whereas Australia never would. However, the key political factor that underlay all the policy formulation was the need to keep faith with those people who were slowly returning to the party after the Keating years.

Leaving aside his natural strategic inclinations, Rudd was well aware that these voters required reassurance that Labor would defend Australia's interests. When such people saw Saddam Hussein on television, they saw a petty despot. Ordinary people didn't like him. They liked him even less when they found out what he'd done to the Kurds and the Marsh Arabs in the south. They heard John Howard suggesting he was developing nuclear weapons and that he was dangerous. People knew President Bush was likely to invade Iraq, anyway. For people like these, the idea that Labor would not be prepared to go along with the US was anathema. If Saddam was bad, possibly even evil, many people couldn't see why he shouldn't be deposed, particularly if America was going to do all the 'heavy lifting'.

Labor votes were being lost over the war and terrorism. A political strategist says, 'If people are talking national security, Labor loses. And there is nothing, absolutely nothing, the party can do about it.'

The roots of this problem grew from the original foundation of the party. Since the time of Federation, conservative politicians have emphasised the important security-role of foreign alliances, first with Britain and later with America. Labor, instead, has stressed the defence of the continent of Australia. Beazley openly articulated this policy in the 1980s, when he was defence minister. Howard managed to successfully portray this policy as simply waiting passively while dangerous threats developed. Rudd realised the importance of being part of the debate, but had a great deal of difficulty in reaching a position that had firm intellectual foundations and would also meet with the approval of different elements of the party.

A member of shadow cabinet recently suggested that Rudd's problem in formulating a workable policy on Iraq stemmed from a desire not to alienate anyone. This appears unlikely. Those on the ideological left were concerned because they did not think clear policy was articulated right from the beginning. But Rudd was spelling out policy, *his* policy, although he was working hard with Crean at hammering out a position that would be acceptable to both sides of the party.

What emerged was strong in a policy sense. But the equanimity shown by the party attracted the ire of the intellectual left, while at the same time failing to make its case to the general public.

Initially, it seemed to be a politically smart move to insist that the war should be contingent on what the United Nations decided. But, as the debate dragged on, Labor was left to swing in the breeze. Crean began by insisting that Iraq should not be invaded. This was firm, clear, and popular with many in the party. But then, in an effort to reach out to traditional Labor voters and not be outmanoeuvred, Rudd insisted that, if the UN supported an attack, the opposition should also endorse the war. Then, as the debate wore on, it became clear that the US had already decided that it would go to war, regardless. Together with Rudd, Crean's policy then became to support a war if the majority of the Security Council voted for it, but not if it was vetoed by a country acting 'unreasonably'. Speculation quickly developed. Did this mean that a French veto alone would be unreasonable, but a combined French and Chinese veto would be, somehow, 'reasonable'? The position was untenable.

Mark Latham wrote in his *Diaries* that you could draw a basic lesson: 'never listen to Rudd on foreign policy. If that guy's an expert, then I'm Henry Kissinger.' He asserted that Rudd had earlier briefed shadow cabinet that none of the

Security Council members would veto the war against Iraq. 'You could almost feel Crean urging Rudd on, praying that he's right about the Security Council. Simon doesn't want to get between the Americans and their dirty little war,' Latham confided.

In September 2002, Rudd certainly felt confident enough to emphatically state on the ABC's *Lateline* program that 'there is no debate or dispute as to whether Saddam Hussein possesses weapons of mass destruction. He does.' Others in the opposition lacked this absolute certainty. They felt that the case for war had not been proved and that there were serious doubts about this central issue.

Rudd was apparently sure that he knew about Saddam's weapons of mass destruction. He'd travelled to America and received extensive briefings on the issue. This suggests he believed the information he'd been given, despite a series of warnings at the time flagging the possibility that the US government may have concocted the intelligence. In other words, he'd been sold a pup and had bought it completely.

'He was always given a lot of respect by the left, although we often disagreed with him,' says a parliamentarian. 'Later, we realised he'd just bought Bush's argument hook, line, and sinker. This was the problem that lay beneath the eventual disaster that our policy formulations became. Well, things might be better if there was a bit of room for self-doubt in Rudd's world.'

'He never understood the far more finely nuanced argument that was anti-Bush, rather than anti-American,' he continues. 'Some things are not certain. Kevin needs to recognise that, and listen to other people.'

By the time the troops were sent off, there was still confusion in the public mind about Labor's position—for example, when Crean wished good luck to the departing troops while at the same time also insisting that he disagreed with the need to send them. Yet that message was one of the more simple ones that Labor was trying to send about the war. Rudd had played a role in drafting this response, but after the wording was attacked at a right-wing factional party meeting, Latham asserted that Rudd stood up and proclaimed it 'hopeless'.

Oppositions often suffer the difficulty of not being able to articulate a position quickly because they don't want to alienate public opinion. This is not simply because they are poll-driven; it's also because there can often be a significant deal of quite healthy policy disagreement about an issue within the party. Without the power to effect events, a usual default position is to choose a popular policy. This time, that opportunity wasn't available because Labor's base remained fundamentally divided. The left was against the war; but many other people, including those who had abandoned the party after Tampa, swiftly became strongly in favour of overthrowing Saddam before he threatened Australia (however unlikely this might have appeared).

But what was worse, the voters just switched off. They'd stopped listening to Labor's message. Instead of developing a flexible position, senior Labor insiders felt they were suddenly talking in a vacuum. All the equivocations had the effect of making the party irrelevant. Another parliamentarian said, 'No one was listening to us any more. Instead of being at the cutting edge, we'd become so irrelevant that we weren't even taking part in the debate.' At the time it was formulated, the policy had looked sensible. A majority of Australians agreed that Saddam should be deprived of his weapons of mass destruction. The popularity of the war swelled with the speed of the invasion and the sight of jubilant Iraqis pulling down the statues of Saddam Hussein. However, as it became obvious that there were no WMDs, and also that America did not have a workable plan to install a new government in Baghdad, public enthusiasm for the war turned. Because Labor had never firmly articulated its anti-war policy, the party wasn't given any credit for its position.

Later, Rudd lambasted the government for never having strategies, and instead for using slogans to make their arguments. 'Every element of national security policy (is) driven through the prism of one man. That one man is Mark Textor,' he insisted, naming the key person who provided market research for the Liberal Party. Rudd was angry because he felt, 'Government is a serious business; it is about what really works'. This was true, but equally it was not the point. The electorate had become conditioned to simple messages. So when Rudd asserted, 'The market researchers say, "Don't argue a strategy, you might be held accountable to it. Give them a slogan and that's all they'll remember",' he was speaking from bitter experience. Nevertheless, Rudd was unable to win over the undecideds without a simple policy. He needed to find something that could be summed up in one sentence, but which would also incorporate the complexities that he saw in the argument over what should happen. This remained elusive.

When the resolution on the war came to a vote in parliament, Labor united to vote it down. Given that the party eventually came down to oppose the conflict, many in the ranks had wondered why a firmer anti-war stance could not have been taken earlier on. Some, particularly those on the ideological left of the party, were angry about the equivocations that had lost them the chance of pushing a simple anti-war message to the electorate.

At this time, it was difficult for many analysts to properly envisage the quagmire that would soon engulf Iraq. The regime collapsed as predicted, but the Bush administration had failed to prepare for the next phase of the conflict. Some in Labor felt that, at this time, Rudd was relying increasingly on his own contacts with American analysts for information. As a result, he appears to have been blind to the dangers that were already emerging. The ground war had ended in victory, but this didn't mean that peace had been achieved.

A criticism others make against Rudd is that he didn't seem willing to concentrate on this question. 'Why was Rudd so ready to accept the way the government had framed the debate?' says a parliamentarian, adding, 'He accepted it was just about Saddam's WMDs.' She felt there was room for the opposition to quiz the government much harder about what would happen after the war was over. Critics such as this felt that if firm commitments had been successfully obtained from the government, it would have been much easier to have held it to account for the later failure.

Gauging the public mood would remain a complicated problem, particularly as many of the reputable left-wing commentators overseas began to barrack for the Allied forces. But the problem remained that, in Australia, the Greens had now effectively usurped the role of opposition to the government. Rudd was still being heard, but most of those on the left of the party had stopped listening. His personal disappointment was that the so-called 'Howard battlers' did not seem to understand Labor's policy either. Although the party had been willing to jettison the 'progressives' in an attempt to rebuild its working-class support-base, it looked as if it had not even succeeded in this attempt to regain its foundations.

***

By early 2003, Crean's supporters were frustrated. 'The *real* Simon wasn't coming across on television,' they still insist. 'If the voters could see him the way we do, or if they saw him barracking for North Melbourne, you couldn't help but love him.' But Crean remained unable to reveal himself to the public.

A number of Labor parliamentarians became very worried about Crean's leadership. Many of those hanging on to the outer-suburban seats in the capitals were watching their vote collapse. 'In 1996, under Keating, I'd seen my majority of 10 per cent cut down to just one-and-a-half per cent in a single election,' one says. 'I went from a majority of 15,500 down to two thousand. Then, in 1998, it went back up again, from 2,000 to ten thousand.' But now things were looking dire. Very dire.

Secret party polling, which hasn't previously been released, showed that Labor stood to be reduced to a rump of barely forty seats in the 150-seat parliament. The party was going backwards, and there appeared to be no way that Crean would be able to turn this around. This information provided the spark that ignited the second move to install Beazley. But there was another factor that made the challenge particularly urgent. Another senior Labor figure had received information that John Howard was preparing to call an early poll. Shifting to a campaign footing requires a considerable amount of prior preparation, and this person had become certain the Liberals had begun to prepare for an early election. This would have enabled the government to capitalise on Labor's disarray.

For his part, Rudd had even less support in caucus. By this time, his nicknames included 'Pixie', 'Harry Potter', the 'God Botherer' (because of his Christianity), 'the Professor' (because he always seemed to know everything with absolute certainty), and 'Heavy Kevvie' (from Latham in particular, who thought Rudd's policy positions were quite lightweight).

It was only a matter of time before Crean's enemies in the party began moving to depose the leader. At first, this didn't include Beazley.

'I'd anticipated this would be my last term in parliament,' says Beazley today, 'so I did what I enjoyed. I joined lots of committees, like Foreign Affairs and Defence. There was no plotting. I was right out of the loop.' He travelled to the Middle

East and studied in Israel, where he became aware of serious opposition to the American project to invade Iraq.

Then he came back to Australia and gave an interview to Maxine McKew of the *Bulletin*. 'Maxine over-wrote it,' says Beazley, but it launched the possibility of a challenge and he doesn't deny it was true. 'I knew—and I won't say how I knew, but it was Liberal sources—that Howard was preparing for an election at the end of the year. We would have been devastated. Polling suggested we could lose 20 or 30 seats.'

'I went early, but we're talking weeks,' says Beazley. 'The first challenge would never have been successful.'

'I thought the first challenge was mistimed,' says Bob McMullan. He pauses before adding, devastatingly, 'and the *Bulletin* interview was bungled'. Beazley's interview with Maxine McKew reopened the possibility that he could take on the leadership again, and this was immediately seized upon as the announcement of an actual challenge. Beazley was forced into declaring his hand prematurely, well before he had corralled enough support to guarantee a victory in a leadership ballot.

After the Keating assault on Hawke in 1991, the assumption had grown that anyone who wanted to challenge the party leader needed to adopt a 'two-challenge strategy'. In other words, the first assault would weaken the incumbent, and then the assailant would come back a second time to finish him off. It looked as if Beazley had decided on this sort of approach.

But it didn't necessarily work the way he had hoped. 'The way Kim was talked up in the *Bulletin* interview meant that Kim's hand was forced before he was really ready,' says McMullan, 'and launching the challenge in the media was a tactical bungle. It was portrayed as if Kim had just accidentally allowed himself to get carried away over lunch with Maxine McKew. I couldn't believe it.' The incident reminded some politicians of Beazley's lack of discipline in the past. 'It was unnecessary and it damaged the party. That first challenge didn't serve Kim's interests,' said McMullan 'and it didn't serve the party's interests either. I decided not to vote for Kim.'

Rudd was frustrated when Beazley launched the first challenge to Crean. He appeared to feel that he would soon be ready for the job. 'He may have thought that,' a parliamentarian derisorily snorts, 'but at that time you certainly didn't need more than one hand to count the number of votes he would have received.' The weakness of Rudd's base in the caucus had been exposed.

'There was also an element of sibling rivalry with Wayne Swan,' says a Labor political player. 'Kevin believed he was the superior political talent.'

It was at this time that the two Queenslanders fell out and stopped sharing a house. Swan will not say what caused the serious breach. Some suggest it was 'because of some AWU thing in Queensland'. A more likely suggestion seems to be that in some way these two people, both highly capable, recognised that they both aspired for the same position. Swan, older and in parliament first, may have felt that he had seniority. If so, Rudd obviously didn't agree. Although they continued to see each other regularly, the firm bonds that had existed in the past had been broken.

Together with their wives they would, inevitably, frequently be guests at social events. On these occasions they continued to find a way of engaging socially. It was much the same at work. Some observers suggested they hadn't really noticed a change. Nevertheless, the warmth had evaporated from the relationship, and mistrust had taken its place.

When President Hu Jintao visited the Australian parliament in 2003, Rudd spoke to him in fluent Mandarin, and Rudd gained considerable respect by showing that he at least understood the issues in the relationship with China. Many on the left of the party remained concerned that the economy and trade were placed above other issues in the relationship, such as human rights. But Rudd also knew that when Keating had brought up this matter at a banquet in Beijing, Hu had abruptly stood up and left the table. At least Rudd was able to engage in a conversation, albeit a short one.

With a booming business, Thérèse could provide extra assistance with polling, secretarial support, and travel. This included speechwriting. Rudd made remarkable use of the extra opportunities provided to him.

Rudd was now obviously an ambitious man, one who didn't stop. He would travel the country urgently, meeting as many people as he could. At one moment he'd be working the electorate in Queensland; the next moment he'd be attending a middle-level function in an art gallery in Sydney's Woollahra devoted to Australia-Israel relations. He'd attend second-rank Labor Party functions in different state capitals, just to be there and meet people who might, one day, help him move forwards. There would be barely an acknowledgement—typically just the brief mention, 'And among our guests tonight, blah, blah, blah, and the shadow minister for foreign affairs, Kevin Rudd'—before the speaker moved on to the next minor dignitary. Rudd went to everything, so much so that some friends warned him he was spending too much time travelling around. But no one could be more assiduous. So as not to miss anyone, he paid court to everyone, making sure he was noticed.

'Swan was also there, doing this sort of thing, but Kevin seemed to do it more,' says Carr. 'Around the middle of the year he'd attend the Australian American Leadership Dialogue in Sydney or Melbourne, or, every alternate year, in Washington,' says the former premier. 'Next you'd see him at the Australian Davos Connection on Hayman Island with business people, and then at the Centre for Independent Studies Concilium at Coolum, with the think-tanks. He just went to everything.' It was an indefatigable work ethic, particularly as he never stopped doing constituency work, or speaking at other meetings that backbenchers had arranged for him.

Brereton pronounced at the time, 'Mate, he says whatever the Americans want him to say. They own him—lock, stock, and barrel.'

Those of a more pro-American bent disagreed. 'There was something quite gutsy about the way he participated in these events,' comments another person at the Australian American Leadership Dialogue. By this stage, the general flavour of the forum was very pro-Bush. 'It was very hard to advocate a line that differed from the White House view of the world,' he says. 'But Rudd didn't back down. He handled the heavy hitters very adroitly. Kevin always found a way to make his points without getting marginalised.'

But Rudd wasn't the only person travelling widely at this time. It had become increasingly obvious to everyone that Crean was on the skids. Even his supporters began to realise that the leader would probably have to step aside.

Laurie Brereton was promoting Mark Latham, and would encourage him to go to fundraisers for backbench politicians. Because Latham was a well-known and controversial figure, a good turnout could always be guaranteed. Brereton had also become aware that Rudd didn't hold back when it came to sharing his opinion of Brereton with the world.

A politician, one of those who played a moderately significant role in the backroom number-crunching at the time says, 'There are politicians who spend a lot of time in the press gallery talking up their viewpoint. They sometimes generate jealousy. But those of us who don't do it can't complain. There is no door up there that says we can't do it; it's just we choose not to. We want to work in different ways.' He pauses for a second. 'Kevin, Wayne, and Stephen were diligent in doing this, and it generated some hostility amongst their colleagues.'

No Labor leader had ever been deposed before he'd had the

chance of taking the party to an election. That tradition was about to be dispensed with.

***

On a cold November night in 2003, the ABC's Jim Middleton broke the news that significant figures in the party were meeting to tap Crean on the shoulder and tell him to resign. In the urgency of the moment, he may have gotten some of the details wrong—but the report itself was absolutely correct. Devastatingly so.

The next morning, after the normal tactics meeting, Crean asked McMullan if the stories in the media were true. Although McMullan had not been a member of the group who had come the night before to ask Crean to resign, those people had allegedly telephoned to check that he agreed with what they were doing.

McMullan admitted that he had withdrawn his support from the leader, saying, 'Yes, Simon, I think you should go. For the good of yourself, and for the good of the party.' McMullan said Crean should go quickly because, 'We can't afford to have a long, drawn-out debate.' As far as he was concerned, the polling conclusively demonstrated that a change was needed. Driven by the need to make the party competitive again, McMullan was determined that Crean had to go.

'When it comes to voting for the leader,' says one of the people on the backbench at the time, 'people feel an obligation to make a choice that is in the best interests of the party. Whether they get that right or wrong is a completely different matter,' he laughs, before continuing, 'The need to choose the right leader definitely overrides factional considerations.'

Beazley was the obvious candidate for people to turn to. He telephoned around in an attempt to build support, and asked McMullan who he'd be voting for. Frustrated and angry about the political situation, McMullan said he was ready to vote for 'anybody'. But he was quite angry, because he felt Beazley's challenge hadn't been managed properly.

Later, he explained his concerns. 'At that stage in the electoral cycle, as we neared the election, my view was that the only sensible person to change to was Kim. I seriously believed it was too late to change to a new face. I didn't think that there was any chance of anyone else getting majority support, other than Kim. It was just too late in the electoral cycle.' Although he'd voted for Crean during the first challenge, this time he decided to change to Beazley.

'In retrospect, I still think that Kim was the only person who could have taken us to victory in 2004,' says McMullan. 'I'm not saying that he would have—there are still too many imponderables. Nevertheless, I thought he was the only person who would give us a chance to win then, just as I thought he was the wrong person after 2004.'

Many Labor politicians were very angry at the destabilisation that Beazley's supporters were perceived to have participated in. This was a big factor, particularly after the earlier, failed challenge. Others asserted that the party had to turn to a new generation to lead it forward.

As Rudd considered putting his hat in the ring, he spoke to Tasmanian MP Harry Quick, who was factionally independent. Quick provided some very honest advice. 'Kevin,' he said, 'I've got to tell you something man-to-man. In my eyes, what you really need is a good dose of humility.' Rudd was taken aback, perhaps because his one weakness had been fingered, perhaps because he felt the Tasmanian should support a fellow Christian. Quick continued, 'Your aura is of a diplomat, with diplomat-speak. People don't know what you're like. We all try to project invincibility, and humanity is never shown—because it's a sign of weakness. We need to know what you're on about, where you come from, who you are.'

'He was very shocked when I said he needed a good dose of humility,' says Quick now, 'but he took it on board. Saying something like this was obviously very hurtful to him.' The comments had indeed touched a raw nerve, particularly as they came from someone who had supported Mark Latham.

As the two politicians continued speaking, Rudd began talking. Slowly, the story of his father's death and his past tumbled out. Until then, Quick had no idea of this personal history. 'Look,' he said, 'people should be aware of that. There's no need to go on and on about it, or wear it on your sleeve the way an American evangelical might, but you need to tell people about yourself.'

Quick's view of leadership was quite straightforward. The reason he didn't vote for Beazley at the time was that he believed a real leader would always involve everyone in the process. Otherwise they wouldn't be committed, really committed, to the goal. He didn't feel that had been happening in the party up until then, and that's why he hoped the change to Latham might work. Nevertheless, he was impressed that Rudd was 'straight up', and said he'd be prepared to consider him 'next time'.

For Rudd, the blow was more significant. Quick was a committed Christian and an independent. Rudd realised that, if he couldn't convert someone like this to his cause, there was much more work that needed to be done.

Rudd's problem was that out of the people who might possibly vote for him, almost all decided they wanted Beazley more. If it had been a simple choice of Rudd versus Latham, some people consider he might have had an outside chance of victory. But Beazley's supporters also included a couple of Rudd's own rivals. It's just as likely that if Beazley hadn't stood, one of these people would have received this bloc of votes.

This was obvious to Rudd's potential rivals. They'd counted the numbers, and then gone back and counted them again. They were as certain as they could be of where the votes would flow. As a result, they decided to back Beazley, who was determined to try to regain the leadership in an effort to staunch the constant flow of support away from the party.

Latham later admitted that Rudd's candidacy had, perhaps inadvertently, kicked along the argument for the party to make a change to a new generation, to a new group of people who hadn't been part of the Hawke and Keating governments. He believed that as this idea began resonating in the media, it had the effect of weakening Beazley by moving support over to Latham.

Rudd nominally remained in the ballot until late Sunday afternoon. 'He was only fooling himself,' a former parliamentarian said of this time.

***

At different times, up to ten people had supposedly ended up promising Rudd their vote. There may have been a hard core of five votes that would stick with him, regardless. But there was nothing like the necessary surge of support towards his candidacy, and Rudd had needed at least 30 secure votes if he were not to look like a self-promoting spoiler.

After Rudd had decided to withdraw from the contest, a group of independents went to him. Their message was simple: they spelt out for him what he needed to do to become a serious contender for the leadership.

Two of them were former teachers, and one said, 'Look, the best school principal is one who knows the name of every kid in the school. They get the teachers to work as a cohesive team, helping one another.' They pointed out that, in the party, policy often seemed to be determined by the leader and one or two acolytes. However, the members emphasised the way that even 'ordinary' backbenchers were desperate to contribute—particularly those members who'd won a seat from the Liberal Party. 'People like that must be doing something right,' insisted one frustrated backbencher.

Rudd took the lesson to heart. He knew he had to offer something very different from the other potential candidates. He also realised that the game was about much more than simply being focused on victory. The way victory was achieved was also important—not just for its own sake, but because the team could not be united unless it was involved in the game.

Rudd set up a quasi-religious discussion group as a first step towards getting to know backbenchers better and, incidentally, as a means of combating the obvious religious affiliations of some parliamentarians on the other side. These had been given a good run in the media, leading many voters to think that Labor was a party of atheists.

He also spent much more time just 'popping in', sitting down, and chatting with other parliamentarians. Rudd began to ask people, 'How are things? What are the vibes? What's happening here, and what's the message?' He also learned to ask the most important question of all, 'Where do you think we want to go?' He made an effort to become much more accessible, asking people in for coffee. The other parliamentarians felt that they were more welcome than in the past, and the conversations with Rudd started to range over far wider areas than before.

CHAPTER SIX

Frustration

2003–2004

> 'We've had many, many meetings on this subject and I'm very careful about not misleading you about what was said when.'
>
> –Kevin Rudd on *Lateline*, 29 March 2004

Latham won the ballot. Rudd didn't vote for him, supporting Beazley instead. As he walked out of the caucus meeting, he rolled his eyes to the waiting journalists, muttering quietly, 'This will be interesting.'

Latham records in his *Diaries* that Rudd wanted to be shadow treasurer. Given that Rudd was very keen to expand his portfolio responsibilities, such a move would have been quite understandable. One of the reasons some people were not prepared to support him for the leadership was that he didn't have any experience in a domestic shadow portfolio. He'd been told he'd never become leader if he was 'just dealing with stuff that's happening half a world away'.

After Latham was installed, he asked to see Rudd. Latham understood that he needed to straighten out US alliance issues and to find out if the two of them would be able to work together. They particularly needed to decide what they were going to do and say about America.

It was the morning after the vote when the two met in the leader's office. As it happened, Latham was very upset and distracted with what he described as a 'black cloud'. Late the night before he'd become worried that his former wife, Gabrielle Gwyther, was going to lash out at him. He wanted to check if she had given any interviews, or if she was about to. At ten that night, Latham had telephoned her. A 'weird, weird' conversation ensued. He later said that she reassured him with the words, 'Oh darling, don't you worry about things; you have achieved what you wanted.' But Latham was troubled. The reasons that caused the relationship breakdown had not formerly received the intense scrutiny to which it would soon be exposed.

Someone who knew Latham very well during the marriage break-up confirmed that he had been distraught when the relationship failed. This person insists that, 'For all the "hard man" image that Latham conveyed, he didn't want to lose her. The bond between them had changed, but a connection like that doesn't just disappear.'

Latham was in a very emotional state when he saw Rudd the next morning. He'd just achieved his constant goal, to be elected leader of the party, but now saw that the bitter disintegration of his first marriage was threatening to imperil his new honeymoon before it had even started.

That morning, he'd heard that Gwyther had supposedly taken a shot at his mother on the radio. In fact, it had been a thinly disguised attack on him. Latham's composure failed. He began breathing heavily. Tears formed. When Rudd asked what was the matter, Latham broke down. Rudd did the only thing he could: he embraced Latham to give him some physical and emotional support.

When Rudd later told the story to someone who knew both him and Latham well, he insisted that he felt a genuine sadness for the leader at that moment. He was also surprised at just how upset the new leader was. Rudd's friend suggests that, in retrospect, this moment offers an insight into why Latham was later to fail in his ambition. His emotional range wasn't masked and disguised. Here he was, admitting extreme vulnerability in front of Rudd.

Nevertheless, the brief rapprochement did not last long. Over the weekend, Latham put together his shadow ministry team. He'd already asked Rudd to remain in his job. Rudd asked for his title to be expanded to 'Foreign Affairs and International Security' and Latham had agreed. But then, according to Latham, Rudd found out that Robert McClelland would be shadow minister for Defence and Homeland Security.

Worried about the potential for overlap, Rudd objected, and threatened to quit and go to the backbench. Latham thought the objection was absurd and decided to bluff Rudd. The new leader said he'd accept the resignation, because he was certain Rudd would 'fold'. Latham asserts that Rudd phoned him back at eleven that night to say he'd take the job.

This was not, as Latham apparently felt, just a silly or pointless dispute. Politically, titles mean a lot. By defining responsibilities, titles can be used by the various shadows to capture as much public attention as possible within their own personal bailiwick. The larger the title, the more broadly the spokesperson is able to roam. Gradually, this allows people to stand out from the crowd—something an ambitious MP is always keen to do.

The illuminating aspect of this incident is not so much that there was a small fight over language. The point is that Rudd absolutely understood the power of words. Titles were, basically, irrelevant as far as Latham was concerned, but they are important as part of the internal political game and in defining who can take the fight to the government.

Later, Mark Latham was to reveal in his *Diaries* that Rudd had cried in front of him after the death of his mother. A senior Labor figure (not one of Rudd's supporters) was utterly furious. 'It's outrageous. If a son doesn't cry when his mother's died, there has to be something wrong,' she says. 'Of all the things in that *book* of his'—and at this point she shudders, again, in anger and horror—'of all the things, that has got to be the most outrageous statement. And that is really saying something.'

There was another incident that some of the people who had worked in Crean's old office felt counted against Latham. As a matter of course, immediate briefings were arranged with the heads of all the intelligence agencies—ASIO, ASIS, and others. When his international security adviser Ungerer asked Latham about when he'd like a briefing, he didn't even look up from his desk. Waving his hand, he said, 'No, mate, not now. I've got important things to do.' Ungerer left in despair. He departed the office a few days later.

***

When it's put to Senator John Faulkner that Rudd and Latham were always at odds, he raises his eyebrows archly. 'I have read Latham's *Diaries*, and he lists his five favourite journalists, writers, and God knows what,' he says, dismissively, 'and there it is—Rudd's in his list of five favourite politicians. It's in the *Diaries*.'

I suggest that, at other times, Latham displayed an almost visceral hatred of Rudd.

'Look,' says Faulkner, 'again you're asking me to comment on other people's personal relationships. I don't like speculating about these things.'

Speaking for himself, Faulkner admits, 'Of course, I've not always agreed with Kevin—but we're not in a mutual-admiration society here. It would be more surprising if we agreed every single time. He'd never shirk entering a debate; well, that's what you'd want him to do.'

'He is active, hardworking, and ambitious,' continues the senator. 'Well, we need people who are driven and motivated. I want him to succeed in his current ambition to become prime minister. It's a prerequisite. Don't read it as a negative; it's critically important.'

'Kevin wasn't consumed by self-doubt,' he adds before again becoming pleasantly taciturn. 'But whatever disagreements there may have been in the party at the time, I won't tell you about them.'

Latham's relationship with Rudd wasn't constant. In 2002, for example, he thought Rudd was 'thoughtful and considerate' by comparison with Smith and Swan. Latham dismissed the latter pair as 'mostly useless', asserting that ' their only answer is to follow the polls'.

***

Yet later that same year, Latham fingered Rudd as the source for anonymous criticism that appeared in a newspaper article: 'his pompous language is a give-away'. Latham also vented his spleen at the sort of publicity that Rudd could achieve. 'Rudd reported on his recent trip to Washington and New York, but he need not have bothered, it's all in Glenn Milne's column this morning. As ever, Rudd is insatiable for publicity.' At other points, Latham called Rudd a 'crazy bastard' and 'a terrible piece of work: addicted to the media and leaking'.

At first, Latham's emphasis on issues such as children's literacy appeared to be a cheap stunt. But soon the voters were interested. People began to notice someone who was talking about problems that affected them. 'Voters initially liked what they saw,' said one of the new leader's supporters, 'but they didn't decide to buy. His weakest point was a propensity to act without due regard for later consequences. He was successfully provoked, and he slipped up. It was a risk we took.'

At the beginning of 2004, Latham's elevation to the leadership looked like a masterstroke. Bob McMullan was in no doubt that, until then, Howard was ready to call an early election. He'd hoped to capitalise on previous leader Crean's unpopularity. But after Latham took over, that option was off the table.

Latham began playing his own tune, and it wasn't long before people began dancing to it. Television viewers were treated to the bizarre spectacle of Prime Minister John Howard—a besuited man in his sixties, who was normally pictured standing alongside foreign dignitaries—uncomfortably trying to find a space on the floor so he could read a picture-book to a four-year-old.

It took a long time to demolish the new opposition leader, but Howard was relentless. The constant pressure began to take its toll, and negative headlines helped to create a spiral of scepticism. In the centre of the whirl, Latham would occasionally 'ad lib' as he was talking to the media. This just made the situation worse—fine detail is the lifeblood of political argument. A few slips provided the government with the only chance it needed to turn around popular perceptions.

As speedily as a meteor passing across the sky, the phenomenon burned out. By playing his own game, Latham had successfully discomfited Howard as he rocketed skywards in the polls. But then came the reckoning. The Liberals moved in.

His past was dredged up, including his fight with a taxi-driver and his period as mayor of Liverpool. Eventually, his first wife weighed in and told her expansive story to the media. The detritus of a marriage break-up is never pretty, particularly when it's spread all over the front page. Even his use of colourful language—such as his description of the Liberal Party as a 'conga line of suckholes' because of their subservience to the US—became a liability. Every detail was hammered home, like nails being driven into a coffin.

Canberra has no end of people willing to offer a plentiful supply of gratuitous character analysis. There is always somebody who will tell you they know the real reason why Latham slowly self-destructed over that long year, as the country waited for Howard to pull the trigger and call the election. The truth is, of course, that there was no single reason for it all falling apart and for Labor's hopes to drain away.

One of those who had voted for Beazley later admitted that Latham had managed, for a while, to convince voters that things could be better under Labor. 'The problem was,' he says, 'Latham had been unable to manage the other part of the equation for victory. He had to not only inspire people, but also reassure voters that change wouldn't be a risk.' Because Latham failed to convince the public of both of these elements, his appeal for votes was destroyed in the mortgage belts of the capital cities and the rutted timber roads of Tasmania.

At the end of March 2004, Rudd was on *Lateline*, attempting to defend Latham's 'troops home by Christmas' policy. When compere Tony Jones asked him to confirm that the policy had been endorsed a year before, Rudd evaded the question by saying, 'We've had many, many meetings on this subject and I'm very careful about not misleading you about what was said when.' In Question Time the next day, Howard enthusiastically quoted Rudd, making the obvious point that his every utterance had been totally at odds with Latham's assertion. Nevertheless, Rudd remained silent.

The next day he got the chance to respond properly. He did not directly counter the assertion that the policy had been made on the run. Rudd obviously knew that Latham had simply chosen to suddenly announce his decision; but he wasn't going to go public, and limited himself to raising an eyebrow whenever the 'troops out' policy was mentioned in private forums, such as tactics meetings.

Rudd decided that if he had to be accountable for what he said, the government should be questioned about its statements as well. Labor was particularly infuriated that 'the foreign minister goes on and on' about Latham who, Downer alleged, was not even asking for briefings on Iraq from his department. Rudd pointed out that this claim was incorrect, because Latham had already been in contact with the Australian Secret Intelligence Service, or ASIS. Carefully, using his considerable ability with language, Rudd went through the government's claims one by one. He identified how careful use of language, coupled with 'bald statements', seemed to place the government in an alternative 'George Orwell universe'. This was a reference to his book *1984*, where facts are rewritten at the Ministry of Truth until they accord with the current political reality.

Although Rudd's own ambitions had been thwarted—perhaps even destroyed—he did genuinely seek to achieve victory for the party. At times it was quite obvious that Latham didn't like him personally and that he particularly distrusted Rudd's political views. Nevertheless, Rudd worked hard on what he thought was the right thing to do.

His assiduous attention to detail, and self-promotion, were beginning to pay off. The media appearances got him noticed. Rudd knew he needed to reach two very different audiences. He could always speak to those interested in politics through the ABC and broadsheet newspapers, but he needed to broaden his appeal in the popular media.

Most particularly, as a means of expanding his reach, Rudd made himself available to morning television. Channel 7's breakfast-television program *Sunrise* responded positively.

Rudd began appearing on the program in July 2001 along with Ross Cameron. The two would engage in some of the lightweight sparring that was ideal fodder for the breakfast-TV audience. Back then it was Georgie Gardener who would wrap the two up with words like, 'Yes, a big week ahead. Kevin Rudd, Ross Cameron, always a pleasure to talk to you. Thank you.'

By 2004 the program had new presenters, David Koch and Melissa Doyle. Their new format pitted Rudd against Small Business Minister Joe Hockey. The minister was jovial, although few Canberra observers put him in the same intellectual class as his opponent. 'Howard obviously never watched the program,' says a Labor parliamentarian who did. 'It was like a Punch-and-Judy show. And there was never any doubt about who was scoring all the hits.'

Doyle would introduce the two politicians for a sparring session with words like, 'Let's bring on the Monday All-Stars.' This provided much more of an opportunity for the two politicians to directly debate the issues of the day. The format allowed them to range widely while also offering the program an opportunity to dip into the political debate without alienating other viewers who were far more interested in celebrities and sport.

It was never too difficult for Rudd to bat away questions. For example, he was asked about the future of the then Tasmanian governor, Richard Butler. Not only was Butler a prominent Labor identity, he'd also served in Foreign Affairs at the same time as Rudd. But, sensing unwelcome exposure if he discussed the issue, Rudd dispatched the question quickly. 'Matter for the Tasmanians,' he said, decisively. 'Giving advice from 2000 miles offshore to a different place, namely the island of Tasmania, is fraught with danger. Let them sort it out.'

Hockey couldn't resist leaping in for the opportunity to kick an own goal as well as to provide gratuitous advice, only to immediately qualify it. 'They have to get rid of him, if that's their choice. I mean, this (Butler) is the same guy who said there were weapons of mass destruction before the invasion of Iraq and afterwards changed his view. I mean, you know, is he the right person to have ever been governor?'

No one needed to mention that it was, in part, Butler's reasoning that the government had relied on in taking Australia to war in the first place.

***

As 2004 progressed, Latham's leadership slowly disintegrated. At times, things would pick up, but then the overall downward trend reasserted itself. Rudd supported the leader; however, he always managed to make it clear to journalists, off the record, if he disagreed with Latham. Those on Latham's staff suggest there were continual frictions between the leader's office and Rudd. On the other hand, Rudd made sure these disputes didn't surface to disrupt the façade of unity that was being portrayed.

Rudd spent his time working. He kept travelling, putting out the message, speaking to and meeting people. Meanwhile, Latham focused on domestic issues, and the media focused on Latham. He was far more interesting than the Foreign Affairs spokesman. Rudd was left pretty much to do what he wanted.

At first, Latham's unusual tactics cut through the dominance that Howard had established over the political process. But it didn't last. Although Latham had been knocked badly off-balance by the beginning of the election campaign, many still hoped success would come.

Enough voters remained undecided, almost to the end, for Labor to still have a chance of winning. When the election was called, many had not yet made up their minds and the result was still far from a foregone conclusion. But although the voters hadn't made a final decision, they were certainly inclined to vote for the government. Labor poured $12 million into advertising—not because they were desperate to stave off defeat, but because there was still a chance, however small, that a victory could be seized.

'Latham dragged us back from what had been looking like an absolute disaster,' says Daryl Melham, a Labor MP in western Sydney. 'Not enough people recognise his contribution to the party, because of the way it ended. He dragged us back off a much lower base than he inherited.' But it still wasn't enough.

'You can talk about swinging voters,' says Melham. 'But I mainly lost Labor voters, blue-collar Labor voters, who were attracted to Howard's rhetoric—people who were anti-Muslim, anti-immigration and, sure, some of them were prejudiced. But they are still voters.'

Melham reckons the Liberals spent $300,000 in that election, trying to take his seat. 'They'd never tried this before. They managed to get a swing towards them but, because I was the sitting member, I was able to survive.' In the neighbouring western Sydney seat of Greenway the result was very different.

'It was an open contest,' says Melham, 'because our sitting member, Frank Mossfield, had resigned. As a result, we lost. By 2007 a redistribution meant that Greenway was to become a *much* safer seat for the Liberal Party.' Despite arguments from Labor, a large conservative stretch of the foothills driving up to the Blue Mountains were folded into Greenway. This has meant that the safety margin for the seat rapidly jumped from 0.7 per cent at the last election to 11.4 per cent today. Now the the Liberals have turned it into a virtually unassailable seat.

Hope disappeared as the campaign wore on. Instead of the edgy energy that had infused the early period of his leadership, Latham began looking tired and uncertain. His relationship with many of the vital backroom operatives broke down during the campaign. He was willing to accept advice, and a small team of helpers tried to push him along; but every time they did, it seemed to sap something of his own energy and enthusiasm.

Although Labor's polling had been weak for some time before the 2004 election, the final collapse came as a shock. Subsequently, the anger coalesced around Latham's decision to try to save Tasmania's old-growth forests by preventing logging across a large proportion of the state.

The problem wasn't the strategy; it lay in the execution. The images from the visit proved disastrous. The Tasmanian premier, Paul Lennon, could barely manage to treat Latham with civility; the timber workers didn't even bother trying. Small contractors led their members in massive protests. Then, three days later, they enthusiastically embraced the prime minister. The union began endorsing Howard's forest plan, rather than Latham's.

The large physical presence of Tasmanian Labor parliamentarian Dick Adams gave legitimacy to their revolt, when he proclaimed that he 'would not blame Labor supporters if they now voted for another party'. And he didn't mean the Greens. 'Howard played Latham for a sucker,' he says. When it's put to him that after the forestry decision he effectively campaigned for the coalition, Adams responds emphatically. 'I never went up on the stage with Howard—I'd never do that.'

Adams defends his stance at that time. 'Latham would have wiped out 4,000 jobs in my electorate, but he wouldn't have saved one species. We had warned him, but he wasn't listening. He took no notice. He was just trying to get a big swing in the mainland, and that was appalling.'

Labor accepted that there might be some negative reaction to the forest decision within the island state itself; however, the party was confident that the negatives would be outweighed by positive coverage engendered on the mainland. That didn't happen. Instead, viewers saw Latham besieged by timber workers and received frostily by Premier Paul Lennon. As many voters entered the polling booths, many must have reflected on the recent images of anger that had been stirred up as a result of Latham's policy announcement.

The electoral analyst Malcolm Mackerras later spent a long time drilling down into the numbers to find out what had really happened on the day of the election. Although there were two losses in Tasmania that could be blamed directly on the timber vote, the result could also be explained in a different way.

Mackerras slowly realised that to understand what the vital issue had been, it was necessary to view the results through a different prism. He asserted that Latham's mis-step on the forests had simply reinforced a more general mood: it legitimised a feeling that had been growing in the electorate, forming part of a pattern that had been reinforced by Liberal advertising. This gave people permission to cast their vote the way they were already leaning. The government had earlier created a persuasive frame of reference for voters by successfully portraying Latham as 'flaky'.

They had suggested he was not the sort of person you would trust with money. In particular—and this was the key—he was not the sort of person you could trust with your mortgage.

In 2004, Labor actually seized four seats from the coalition. One of them, the seat of Richmond, stretching along the New South Wales north coast, was even held by a government minister, Larry Anthony. Incredibly, in the midst of the government's triumph, this prominent figure (himself the son of a former deputy prime minister) was unseated.

On the night, as the experts cast around for an easy explanation, everyone jumped to the obvious conclusion: it was the 'sea change' seat. Trendies from the city had flocked to the beaches and hinterlands, irrevocably altering the demographic.

But there was another explanation, which only become obvious much later. This was that fewer than 20 per cent of people in this region were paying off their mortgages. This meant that the coalition's threat that Labor could not be trusted to keep interest rates low didn't have nearly the resonance here that it did in the mortgage belts built around the big cities.

Extrapolating his figures, Mackerras arrived at a startling conclusion. The four seats that Labor took from the coalition had one thing in common. As in Richmond, very few of the people who lived in these areas were still purchasing their homes; most had already paid off their mortgage. The Liberal threat of rising interest rates under Labor was relatively ineffective in all four seats.

By contrast, in those seats that swung over to the coalition, the danger of an interest-rate rise meant everything to the voters. They didn't want to mess with the economy. Their attention had become firmly fixed on this single, key issue. Polling done by Mark Textor for the Liberal Party had quickly identified this as the major concern whenever people thought about which party they'd be voting for. That's why the Liberals began the campaign highlighting their own economic credentials, and emphasising uncertainty over the direction of interest rates under Labor. The party's federal secretary, Tim Gartrell, says polling conducted just before the election showed how vital this strategy was. The swinging voters in the seats that mattered decided they just couldn't take the risk that interest rates would go up.

The polls told a simple story. After eight years, many voters were tired of Howard's government. Suddenly, after Latham took over, it looked as if there was an alternative. But, after looking Latham up and down, most people decided they weren't prepared to risk changing.

'In the immediate aftermath of the election, everyone pulled together,' says another MP, who quickly began to doubt that Latham would continue as leader. 'But there were an enormous number of disputes, simmering just below the surface,' she quickly adds. 'It was a very tense time, with angry parliamentarians who were quick to snap whenever something went wrong.'

***

On the hot afternoon before Election Day 2004, a huge blaze destroyed eight houses in Toowoomba and a banana plantation north of Brisbane. By the time dawn broke the next morning, a cool change had extinguished the fire, and the last whiff of smoke had vanished from the horizon. The fire that had reinvigorated Labor after Mark Latham had acceded to the leadership was about to be similarly extinguished.

Rudd was up early that morning—he always is. It's as if he feels hard work and enthusiasm can somehow create something real, where previously there has only been emptiness. Because of his media profile, Labor members had been asking him to campaign in marginal seats across the country. As he spoke to voters, Rudd must have realised that any hope of victory was quickly evaporating. By the morning of 9 October, internal Labor polling showed that the party had no chance of forming the next government of Australia.

Rudd was back in Brisbane. He never stopped working his south Brisbane electorate of Griffith. He'd won the seat by just 3,858 votes in 1998, but at the next election in 2001 he'd increased his safety margin to 9,494. Still, he wasn't the sort of person who would take success for granted. As it happened, later that night he'd find his majority had increased once again, this time to 13,898—and, in achieving this, Rudd had received a remarkable 48.7 per cent of the *primary* vote. But this sort of achievement only came through hard work, continuously getting out and about, and speaking to voters. That's what he planned to do again that day—being prepared to take on board what they told him about their needs, understanding them, and finding answers to their problems. For Rudd, being a good local member was not merely a way of achieving power; it was vital.

As Rudd moved through the electorate on polling day, he continually transmitted his charm to people, especially through physical contact—extending a firm handshake while looking directly into people's eyes; clapping someone's shoulder, just enough to confirm mateship but not over-familiarity; placing an arm around another campaign worker. Rudd demonstrates an easy affinity while talking with Australians. Chatting casually, lightly, and moving on, he never gets too deep, leaving each conversation with a smile and in a casual and easy manner.

It wasn't always like this. 'I remember being at a barbecue where he was meeting and greeting the Labor faithful back in 1998. He was hopeless,' comments a party worker at the time. 'We'd been standing round talking about the rugby and so on when Kevin walked up. There was a momentary pause in the conversation. So, he suddenly starts talking about how closer links with Asia will boost manufacturing exports and help Queensland. Absolutely right, of course, but talk about yawn. Everyone's eyes just glazed over. Soon people began to shuffle away, you know, to get another drink or a bite to eat. He's changed quite a bit since then.'

Another person, who's since moved on from Brisbane, doesn't doubt that Rudd's change is genuine. 'He's an intellectual, and he doesn't seem to have a lot in common with ordinary people. But I think he realised this was a problem. And so he's managed to find a way of making ordinary people—and that includes you and me—interesting puzzles for his mind to keep busy with. That's what's made the difference, because he's become intrigued with us now. He's become engaged.'

For the previous five weeks of the election campaign, Rudd's normally hectic schedule had gone into overdrive. The feedback he'd received about Labor's chances while he was out and about had been mixed. Labor's national secretary, Tim Gartrell, commissioned a quantitative poll just before the vote that confirmed fears the party was facing a disaster. The swinging voters—the people who would decide the election result—had decided to stick with the government.

The morning before the vote, Labor leader Mark Latham had given Howard a bone-crushing handshake at the ABC radio studios in Sydney. These images seemed to confirm their worst fears about the opposition leader's recklessness: the crucial voters weren't going to risk their mortgages with someone like that.

Nevertheless, as Rudd toured the polling booths that day, he received some positive news. The voters in his south Brisbane electorate of Griffith were reacting positively to the volunteers who were handing out Labor's how-to-vote cards. That had happened before. In 2001, the Tampa election, the party's vote nationally had gone backwards by 2.3 per cent, but Rudd had increased his personal following by 4.4 per cent. It just seemed to show that you couldn't predict the result until all the votes had been counted.

But Rudd's mask of hopeful optimism vanished quickly that night. The veneer began falling the moment the first results started to come in. Because Tasmania had already switched to daylight-saving time, polls there had closed an hour earlier than on the mainland. The extent of the debacle on the island quickly became apparent. The party hardheads had already accepted that Labor would lose the votes of people working in the timber industry. This was confirmed as the very first results came in from the small country booths in northern Tasmania. It wasn't a surprise that towns where people depended on logging for their livelihood were voting for the Liberals. However, it didn't take long before a far more worrying trend could be observed. A large Launceston booth that Labor had held in the previous election was now voting for Howard. The size of the swing meant that the opposition would lose two seats in Tasmania; Labor would have to win two extra seats on the mainland to compensate for these losses. But, just after seven o'clock, as the nationwide results began to come in, it became apparent that Labor was going backwards. The result was a disaster.

Across Australia, pro-Labor election parties that began in hope quickly broke up in despair. 'I could probably be expelled from the party if people had heard what I said that night,' said one politician about his feelings at the time.

At their party, Rudd's campaign workers were savouring a similar taste, although theirs was curiously mixed. Just as in 2001, nationally, the party seemed to have become locked into reverse gear. In Griffith, however, Rudd's personal first-preference vote increased by 3.2 per cent. Even after preferences were allocated, he was still up by 2.5 per cent compared with three years earlier. By working hard as a local member, he'd managed to increase his total vote by 5.7 per cent in two elections. As had been the case ever since he'd become the sitting member, Griffith had been one of the ten best-performing electorates for Labor across the nation. That personal commitment to his home territory was paying off in spades.

***

After the experiment with Latham, the party was reluctant to depose the leader immediately. Certainly no one—apart, perhaps, from Kim Beazley—had the numbers to even attempt a lunge for the leadership at this early stage. Yet Beazley seemed to have accepted, quite genuinely, the fact that he'd missed his last chance at the prime ministership after Latham had defeated him in the fractious internal party ballot the year before. This election, Labor had been so badly knocked around that it couldn't even manage to tear itself apart.

Mark Latham's supporters were still backing him — at least until another contender was thrown up from this group. Those who had previously supported Beazley were still looking round, each weighing up their own chances of getting the top job.

Parliament broke up for the Christmas of 2004, and Rudd went back to his family in Brisbane. The mood at the end of that year was hardly festive. Some were even beginning to wonder if Labor could ever return to power. As it happened, Latham would leave sooner than anyone had expected.

***

Christmas had always been an important time for Rudd, but this was to be the first year that he'd be spending the festival without either of his parents. His mother had died earlier that year, and he'd felt the loss intensely. Nevertheless, the holiday provided an opportunity for his family to come together once again. Since he'd begun shadowing Alexander Downer as Foreign Affairs spokesman, Rudd had hardly had a chance to see the family. This time was very precious to him, particularly as he now faced another three years dragging himself to and from Canberra, as well as travelling overseas. Spending time working back in Brisbane was almost beginning to seem like relaxation.

Then came the first news of a terrible tsunami erupting after an undersea earthquake off Indonesia in the early hours of the morning. It took days before the extent of the tragedy became apparent. Slowly at first, the details filtered through. The first reports were from resorts in Thailand, where thousands of

Australian tourists had been affected. Eyewitness accounts and good communications ensured that their stories dominated the news. At about the same time, other stories from Sri Lanka and India demonstrated just how bad the waves had been. The devastation was widespread. But there was an initial ominous silence from the Indonesian islands that had been closest to the epicentre.

When the news came it was almost unbelievably bad. It was difficult to understand how water—a flowing liquid—could have had such an effect on land and houses. But what this under-estimated was the tremendous power that accompanied the surging water as it smashed onto the land. It had swept everything away. The face of the earth had been changed. More than a quarter of a million people had died.

By early January, as soon as he became aware of the extent of the disaster, Rudd had decided to travel to Indonesia. For some time now, his focus had become firmly locked on Australia's nearest neighbour. Not only was this the site of some of the worst destruction that the tsunami had caused, but Rudd believed the bilateral relationship was vital. It was important not merely to make a statement—Prime Minister John Howard and Foreign Affairs Minister Alexander Downer had done that immediately—but also to go and do something himself. Downer announced he'd be travelling to Indonesia on New Year's Day. Rudd decided that, although he would not be able to achieve a great deal personally, by going to the region he was showing how concerned he was about the situation. He felt he was demonstrating something very important, not just to the Indonesians, but to Australians as well. By standing in the middle of the devastation, he would be making a personal statement about just how concerned he was by the disaster. He knew the Javanese politicians would be carefully watching to see how other countries reacted to the tragedy and what they did to assist.

His decision to travel was to become critical over the next few days. He was doing what was necessary for the country and for Labor, but this meant that he'd find himself unable to capitalise on anything that was happening politically back at home. Rudd wanted to take advantage of any opportunity for media exposure, and to fly Labor's flag. By going there and being on the ground, the media would naturally gravitate to him, and not just rely on Downer for interpretations of the disaster. The devastation caused by the tsunami was the only story that was getting a run in the news cycle. Rudd would be able to articulate, in the short grabs that are loved by the electronic media, exactly what Australia was doing to help with the situation. For a brief period, it almost seemed as if Rudd himself was directing the relief effort. He was careful not to get in the way of any of those people who were genuinely co-ordinating what was going on—and yet, by hitching rides on defence helicopters, speaking to the commanders, and using his contacts within the Indonesian government, Rudd subtly inserted himself into the story of the rescue effort.

His personal anguish at the horror of the situation should not be underestimated. Military personnel were co-ordinating much of the relief effort that Australia was providing at the time. One of those officers later said, 'I was very impressed when I saw him. Kevin wasn't just another "disaster tourist", travelling around for a photo opportunity. He seemed to really want to help and not get in the way—which is what we were all afraid of, when we heard a politician was coming.'

Rudd must also have been aware that the television coverage would not hurt his positioning with his colleagues, particularly those on the left of the party. Normally it had been these people, carrying their hearts on their sleeves, who'd been associated with assistance and relief after natural disasters. Now they were watching as normally conservative institutions like the defence forces became a vital part of the relief undertaking.

Having already spent nearly a decade as a Foreign Affairs diplomat, Rudd knew exactly how things would be swinging into action. This meant he could make sure that he was in the right place to see not only the extent of the devastation, but also whatever attempts were being made to assist the survivors. Nevertheless, he had never seen anything like this.

Rudd later described the scene he'd witnessed as he flew across the island in a navy helicopter. The enormous wave had swept everything away. Everything. 'There is nothing left. It is as though you are looking down on an archaeological site of some millennia ago,' he said. 'There is nothing left but the imprint of the foundations.' Emptiness stretched for up to a kilometre or two from the water's edge. 'That is why most people died, not by drowning but by being crushed by the sheer force of the wave. The locals said when the wave hit it was the height of two coconut palms—20 to 25 metres.' Rudd points out that even for Australians who regularly go to the beach, 'this is beyond our imagination'. At the time he was there, the Indonesian military was facing the extraordinary task of burying 120,000 bodies. The crushing impact of the wave had killed most people immediately. A smaller number died afterwards by drowning.

At a hospital in Banda Aceh, Rudd found a little boy, just eleven years old, sitting and staring silently on a bed. Every member of his family had drowned as the huge wave had swept across the beaches, smashing the ramshackle houses into sticks. This boy was just one of 11,000 orphans who had been registered so far by UNICEF, but Rudd said that the figure was expected to rise to thirty-five thousand. He pointed out that the wave had killed 'probably at least 300,000 (people) and maybe more'. This meant it had become the third greatest natural disaster—in terms of the number of lives lost—in over a hundred years.

Rudd had also been particularly impressed by the way

that Australian medical teams got straight down to work. He joined soldiers handing out bottles of water to an endless line of refugees. Rudd described the way the digger next to him turned and said, 'It feels good, mate, to do something practical and see a smile on the locals' faces when, mate, there's not much to bloody smile about, is there?'

***

When Rudd returned from Indonesia, the party was consumed with trying to find a replacement for Latham. Rudd's activities at this time are described in the prologue. There were, however, some other politicians also aspiring to the leadership of the party. The time when such things were sorted out by backroom boys was well and truly over. A former faction chief agrees with others who say the rigid factional discipline of the past has now broken down. 'People will vote for the person they believe will best do the job. End of story.'

Carmen Lawrence spoke to all the potential contenders, including Rudd, to encourage them to stand for the leadership. Her argument was crisp and sharp. 'Mark Latham's gone. We can't ask Kim to go through everything again, after what he's been through for the past couple of years.'

'I urged Kevin to consider running,' she says, 'because it would represent a clean break with the past.' It seemed to her that it was now time for the next generation to articulate where they wanted to take the party. 'In my view,' she says, 'he was the best contender; however, no one was really counting the numbers.'

That's not completely true, because a number of people were counting those votes quite precisely. Very quickly, the person counting for Rudd found that he needed the fingers of more than two hands to do so. 'There was considerable interest,' he says. But, at this stage, there were also no other candidates.

Stephen Smith and Wayne Swan both began making telephone calls to try to gauge the level of support they'd be able to command in a ballot. These were in the nature of general discussions rather than specifically canvassing for votes, but one MP says he has no doubt about what the calls meant.

Smith and Swan knew that any public fight between Beazley, the old warhorse, and younger politicians who offered a new direction would emphasise his age, damaging him irretrievably. They were unwilling to do this, and instead gave in to Beazley's appeal to them to give him one more chance to drag the party up from the depths of electoral despair, the same place he had found it in 1996. With Smith and Swan throwing their weight behind Beazley, the former leader realised he might get the numbers to win. This decision was to cost both of them personally. One of their supporters later admitted, 'When Smith and Swan decided to support Beazley, they did it for the right reasons. But, in retrospect, those actions for the good of the party certainly didn't help them later on.'

'The first real people who had the ability to understand what the numbers meant were Smith and Swan,' said one of those who was counting. Another came to the same conclusion. 'They knew they couldn't win without Kim's support,' he claims, 'so, basically, Swan and Smith just had to fold.'

The NSW premier, Bob Carr, was normally one of Rudd's supporters. But privately he'd offered Rudd some surprising advice. 'The danger was that Kevin would get the leadership too early, while Labor was still sunk in this trough. In other words, his best efforts would be wasted,' says Carr now. As soon as it had become obvious that Latham was definitely going to resign, Carr had spoken to the media. 'Beazley is the obvious choice for leader,' he said then. But this was before he'd spoken to Rudd.

Once he knew that Rudd was interested, Carr's language subtly changed. By this time he was more carefully suggesting that either man would be suitable for the top job. 'I've got a sense in my bones that Kevin Rudd will be prime minister of Australia one day,' he said. But the obvious question was—when?

It turned out that Rudd wouldn't become opposition leader in 2005. But if he had decided to throw his weight behind Gillard, there was a real chance that a new leader could have been elected. However, other factors militated against this possibility. First, Rudd had no doubt—absolutely no doubt—that he was the right person to lead the party. This self-confidence was complete.

Some observers felt that, added to this personal conviction, there were other concerns about the social conservatism of Australian voters. In other words, some people wouldn't vote for a single woman or would use this as an excuse not to support her. This was the extra baggage that Gillard found impossible to shed. Former Victorian premier Joan Kirner later exploded when she was asked about the issue. 'What's wrong with the media that you keep asking this question?' was her sharp riposte.

'No one wanted to take the chance of installing our first-ever single, young, female leader at a time like this,' says a member of caucus. The real problem was that there was absolutely no way of countering the implied smear that Gillard was somehow 'different'. Her support was rock-solid, but she never had enough of it to win.

'What clinched it was the New South Wales right,' says one of those counting for Gillard. 'The state secretary, Mark Abib, is young, but very smart.' This is a surprising tribute, because Abib was not on the same side as the number-counter at this time. 'He was clearly of the view that the party needed stability,' says Gillard's ally. 'That meant Kim.'

As the situation built to a crisis in the final week of January 2005, Beazley flew to Melbourne to meet Simon Crean in his home. It was to demonstrate that he'd be inclusive. Another person supposedly scheduled to be at the meeting just didn't believe Beazley would ever change. He went fishing instead. The negotiations, aimed at trying to slip Gillard into the deputy's job, went nowhere. She tried every trick, but still came up empty-handed.

A number of people saw her as the future answer to the leadership question. Many in the party both liked and respected her, and felt that she was very definitely part of the unfolding direction of Labor. But not everyone felt this way. Some were concerned about her personality; others, about her political judgements. She would need to overcome these reservations before aspiring to the leadership.

Although Gillard could get solid support in caucus at around 30 votes, she couldn't move to the 44 votes that she needed. On Wednesday 27 January, Gillard also withdrew. It appeared that in order to get Jenny Macklin's support for his candidacy, Beazley had done a deal to make her the deputy.

Rudd had also learned that he could not, at this stage, win a contest with Beazley unless Gillard was out of the equation. Even then, the numbers would be too tight to guarantee victory. Although many liked him, by itself this would not be enough. If Rudd was ever to aspire to the top job, there had to be important changes. First, he realised he would need to continue scoring significant 'hits' on the government in his Foreign Affairs portfolio. But it was becoming obvious that that, alone, would not be enough. Rudd needed to broaden the way people saw him. He needed to escape the box he was increasingly being slotted into as someone just concerned about international policy.

At the next caucus meeting, Beazley was elected unopposed.

***

'Anyone who didn't consider Kim to be the answer to the leadership question was treated like a heretic,' a frontbencher says of this time.

But it's important to realise that Beazley did not merely return to the leadership because no one else could get enough votes to topple him. Labor had made a real choice to embrace him as leader. He was the one person who could unite the party, everyone respected his experience, and he'd taken the party back from the brink of electoral oblivion once before. What's more, Beazley promised he'd changed, that he would be a more inclusive leader and more aggressive, and they'd taken him at his word.

Even one of those urging Rudd to stand admitted that the majority view conceded the need for a calm, settling influence. And that was exactly what Kim was. That was the role he'd already begun to play in the party in the immediate wake of the defeat. 'In the aftermath of Latham. there were a lot of people in this place who were just bruised,' says one parliamentarian. Although he was not an initial supporter of Beazley, he went on to say, 'It was like, I know Kim. I trust him. I'm comfortable with that.'

Afterwards, Bob McMullan spoke to Rudd, telling him that it was a mistake to have pulled out of the ballot. As far as he was concerned, returning to Beazley was a defensive measure, and he didn't feel this was appropriate. There was also a chance, however small, that Rudd might have won. He was also angry about the way the debate had been short-circuited. 'There are too many people in the Labor Party who try to do deals to avoid having a ballot,' he said. 'Ironically, I think that's usually a sign of your weakness rather than your strength.'

Others couldn't believe that Beazley was really prepared to put himself through the pain and suffering again. When Beazley telephoned Bob Carr to say he was again shouldering up for the task of leading the party, the premier asked him,

'Kim, do you really want it? Do you *really* want it?' There was a note of incredulity in his voice.

As it happened, Beazley would again provide the vital psychological break by taking over from a Labor leader who'd been rejected by the electors. Under him, the party could regroup. This time, Beazley did really want it, as he'd tell anyone who asked. He wasn't just putting himself forward to hold the line as a stopgap leader. He wasn't casting himself as a forlorn hopeful whose task was to hold the breach as part of a desperate effort to gain time while others regrouped behind him. Beazley believed, absolutely believed, that he could carry the party to victory. As he telephoned around, trying to build support for his renewed tilt at the leadership, he borrowed Carr's line, asserting, 'This time, I really want it'. Sceptics wondered if that meant he hadn't *really* wanted the job the last time. Or whether it would have made any difference if he had. Or what 'it' was.

CHAPTER SEVEN

Positioning

2004–2006

> 'Now it is high time to awake out of sleep: for now is our salvation nearer than when we believed. The night is far spent, the day is at hand: let us therefore cast off the works of darkness, and let us put on the armour of light.'
>
> –St Paul's letter to the Romans, chapter 13, verse 11

After Mark Latham left Labor, the party was reeling like a punch-drunk prizefighter. 'We just stood there shell-shocked,' says one Labor frontbencher. 'When Mark took over as leader, many of us had been absolutely 100 per cent behind him. We really thought he could do it. But by this time the mood was just the same as it had been in 1996.'

Once again, the result in Griffith was one of the ten best Labor managed to achieve anywhere in Australia. Rudd quickly settled back to work. He always had an eye to advancing his position, but the contest that had proceeded Beazley's accession to the leadership had revealed the fragility of Rudd's support-base. Only perhaps 15 per cent of the parliamentarians were prepared to fully back him for the top job against his rivals. Others didn't like him. He was perceived as being arrogant, a ponce, and an intellectual snob. He was seen as a specialist in foreign affairs with no broader appeal in the wider community.

Somehow, Rudd managed to turn these views around over the next two years. His ability to do this was remarkable. In part, it was due to the way he threw himself into his work, but there was also much more to it than that. Rudd took advantage of every opportunity to push himself forward: in parliament, amongst the wider community, and particularly by cultivating opinion-leaders to advance his credentials for the leadership.

Rudd was always searching for linkages, and was keen to publicise them. For example, when parliament returned in 2005, Rudd spoke about how he'd been able to inform Indonesia's foreign minister, Hassan Wirajuda, about local fund-raising efforts in 'the little country town of Coolum on the Sunshine Coast' for the tsunami victims.

By quickly travelling to Indonesia, Rudd had made an important point to both the Indonesian media and government: Australia was concerned about the devastation. He knew how important personal contact could be at such times. Not even the conservative government suggested there was any 'grandstanding' involved in this trip; it was a genuine and pivotal engagement with the Indonesians. Efforts like this went some way towards overcoming lingering resentment over East Timor. Rudd saw this as 'a remarkable opportunity' to rebuild the relationship between the two countries. He implored the government to seize the chance 'with both hands, because our country's future and our security in this region depend on the strength of our relationship with Jakarta'.

The government, of course, had been the primary actor in the relief effort. But Rudd always wanted to go one step further. He wanted to develop the compassionate response that

Australians had immediately displayed as they opened their hearts (and wallets) in response to this tragedy. In parliament he asked for the same sympathy to be extended 'to the silent, non-telegenic, non-dramatic poverty that today afflicts 1.4 billion people across the world'.

Beazley worked hard through 2005, but it was an uphill battle. He believed an experienced leader was vital to the party, particularly now that it had sunk so low. Nevertheless, a person who knows him well says that Beazley had also become trapped by this time. He was imprisoned in the stereotype that Howard had formed when he made he claimed that the Labor leader lacked 'ticker'. 'Nothing had hurt him more than this,' says this person. 'It wasn't true, but people believed it. That just made Kim angry. In the end, he would fight on ridiculous issues, just to prove that he really did have ticker.'

The other serious problem was speculation about his health. A senior labour frontbencher says, 'Sometimes we'd be in shadow cabinet and he'd forget a name. The first time, no one really noticed, but then it happened again. You start to wonder if, just perhaps, it's ...?' He trails off, and the question is left hanging.

When Beazley came down with Schaltenbrand's syndrome back in March 2004, most people had to go to the medical dictionaries to find out what it was. There are, in fact, no associated psychological links to this leakage of fluid around the brain. But illogical suspicions are easily aroused in an electorate that always seems to want the perfect answer—even when the perfect only exists in our imagination.

There were other problems that worried Labor members, too; things that Beazley would not have control over. The main issue was the broader Australian setting. How would voters react to Beazley, and what would they think of him compared to Howard? The voters had made their choice on this before, and no one knew if they changed their minds. Beazley had nearly achieved victory in 1998. The party mythology insisted he had only been denied triumph in 2001 by the arrival of the Tampa. Perhaps it would be a case of third time lucky.

***

Rudd enthusiastically engaged in parliamentary debate. But for him this meant much more than just focusing on the main political issue of the day. He still found time to engage with the issues that were close to his heart. On Valentine's Day 2005 he spoke, condemning the continuing detention of Aung San Suu Kyi and repression of pro-democracy supporters by the Burmese military junta. 'The Burmese regime is one of the most corrupt, incompetent, and oppressive regimes in the world,' he said. 'We do not pretend on our side of the House that there is a simple or obvious solution to the question of how to bring effective pressure to bear on the Burmese regime,' Rudd admitted.

He may have been aware there were no easy answers, but at least he was trying to address the issue in any way he could.

In November, Rudd's frustration with the government was palpable. 'If there is one word that characterises the political culture of the Howard government since the election,' Rudd asserted in parliament, 'it is the word "arrogance".' He went on to accuse ministers of dripping with arrogance, attacking Peter Costello as 'Captain Smirk himself'. What quite genuinely angered him most of all was the government's attitude to the Asia-Pacific region. Mining the economic data, he could see that China's economy would become bigger than Germany's by 2010, greater than Japan's by 2015, and larger than that of the United States by 2039. Rudd felt that Australia was missing out on the opportunity to engage with this dynamic change that was fundamentally altering the economy.

But, as ever, security questions fascinated him. He was

concerned that festering issues needed only a brief wind to ignite and destroy the peaceful region in which we live. He listed problems such as the military division of the Korean peninsular and tension over the Taiwan Strait, together with the 'unresolved challenge of Islamist terrorist organisations'. When Kim Beazley was defence minister, cartoonists had made fun of his obsession with military hardware and equipment. Nevertheless, there was always a grudging respect and understanding that he understood these issues. Rudd addressed them from a different perspective. Instead of a strategic background, his was located in a comprehension of the broader, grand sweep of history.

Rudd isolated specific instances of government failure, so he could hammer them mercilessly. One example at this time was the 'Howard doctrine of military pre-emption', announced (off-the-cuff) by the prime minister. Rudd said that this 'basically says to your neighbours, we reserve the right to one day launch a military strike on your territory. When I read the textbooks, that equals war,' said Rudd. He pointed out that it would be outrageous for any foreign government to attack Australian territory—even if there were opposition groups training in, for example, the Kimberley. Rudd's speeches were constantly concerned with these sorts of issues.

What really frustrated him was the sort of statements that Howard knew would play well to a domestic audience, but which were inappropriate as a basis for sound policy. There was an almost palpable frustration in Rudd's words about the way the media, in particular, allowed the prime minister to get away with tailoring his message to different audiences. Rudd was angry that Howard was not forced to account for inconsistencies in his positions or for his shameless appeal to the electorate's prejudice.

Journalists were bemused by this attitude. Surely Rudd understood the news business, they thought. Their focus was (almost) exclusively on the next day's paper, that night's bulletin, or the hourly news. Many sympathised—not with Labor, but with the points he made. But no one person had the power to individually change the 'news agenda'.

The validity of Rudd's views was not in doubt; however, they remained, effectively, academic. It was not that no one cared; it was rather that they did not fit in to the formulaic responses that the journalistic trade insisted upon. As a result, nothing happened. Although Rudd may have won little altercations, the debate always seemed to have already moved on to new territory. He was trying to turn around an issue that was going all Howard's way.

His speeches provided examples of excoriating attacks that blistered the government's fragile defences, yet they had no practical effect on policy. The government, secure in its majority, ignored the assault. On the other hand, while his performances may not have been widely reported, they demonstrated his fluency in prepared debates. The format allowed him to display his strengths. In parliament, the arguments had the power of a wrestler who first knocked his opponents to the floor before pinning them down so they couldn't escape.

Even here, though, not every post was a winner. Because Rudd was a key frontbencher, Beazley provided him with numerous opportunities to shine in debate. But a government controls the way parliament works, and so significant issues can be easily dismissed with impunity. Fascinated with the issue of pre-emptive military strikes on neighbouring countries, Rudd continued to worry away at the government by asking questions on this issue. But the terrain was Howard's.

The prime minister would often banish Rudd's carefully crafted questions with disdain by referring to public opinion. 'I think the overwhelming majority of the Australian community well understand that as a last resort any nation has a right to act to protect itself.' In such a way, a swiftly delivered sentence would dispatch a significant question. Tactics like this prevented the opposition from achieving media exposure. If allowed to tackle an issue with a head-on debate, Rudd could win. But it was much harder when playing by someone else's rules.

Rudd was absorbed with the international debate, and found it difficult to believe that other people were not equally fascinated by what was going on outside Australia. One of Beazley's staffers says, 'He was always promising that if he got the chance to really interrogate the government, he could get them on the run. But we couldn't afford to waste our bullets. Somehow the government would always find ways of escaping Rudd's attack. So we had to keep the number of questions he would be allowed to ask relatively limited. Aside from anything else, there was a small attention-span for these foreign issues. The main game was always going to be what was happening in Australia.'

When he was cut out of verbal debate, Rudd would engage in a written assault. MPs submit questions in writing to ministers as well as using question time. Rudd regularly grasped this opportunity to interrogate the government, although he would normally have to wait months for a reply. These were often just as dismissive as the verbal answers provided on the floor of parliament. For example, it took three months for two detailed questions of his about the security treaty with Indonesia to be answered. When they were, it was only for them to be discarded with a cursory, one-sentence reply: 'It is the long-standing practice of successive governments not to comment on internal discussions or negotiations with foreign governments.'

Occasionally, Rudd's immersion in the policy arena would leave colleagues wondering if perhaps he hadn't become a bit too close to the action. In a speech about national security, for example, he'd approvingly quoted the strategist Aldo Borgu, who'd been working at the Australian Strategic Policy Institute. As it happened, Borgu had previously worked for defence minister John Moore and was soon to return as a specialist adviser to Brendan Nelson. Rudd sometimes appeared more focused on achieving the correct policy, rather than engaging in political opportunism. This occasionally disconcerted other politicians in the Labor ranks.

Rudd would always take an opportunity to speak, and would sometimes draw on tenuous links to edge his own interests forward. For example, when a controversy erupted about the contribution made by John Simpson and his donkey in rescuing wounded soldiers at Anzac Cove, Rudd was determined, just like a digger, to fight for every abutment and every redoubt in the debate. This was a reflection of the fact that the most iconic piece of Australian ground is not in this country at all; instead, it is halfway across the world, on the shores of Gallipoli in Turkey. The conservative parties have always attempted to harness the legend of Anzac, but Rudd was determined to address the issue in his own way. After briefly relating the story, he got to his real point: Simpson and his beast were now the official emblems of the Gallipoli Research Foundation, located in Brisbane. He then congratulated the researchers at the institution, who were investigating the health of veterans, as well as of the community more broadly.

This subject appeared a long way from the torn soil of Shrapnel Gully and whether or not Simpson should have been awarded the Victoria Cross, but the incident demonstrates something important about Rudd. He believed in the work of the foundation, and he wanted to do what he could to publicise this. Everything is personal for Rudd. Enthusiastically, in his own way, he attempted to do all he could to advance a good cause.

When in parliament, Rudd appeared to positively enjoy the opportunity to occasionally act as if he was back at school—and still the smartest kid in the class. A debate about 'truth in government' would lead through a consideration of the erosion of accountability in government to a disquisition about Louis XIV, the French 'Sun King' who famously declared to the Parliament of Paris, 'L'État, c'est moi.' Using techniques like this, Rudd managed to compare Howard to a French monarch who believed in the divine right of kings to rule as they saw fit. But then his frustration would suddenly bubble over into real anger. 'Foreign Minister, you have form when it comes to telling the truth to this parliament. You have genuine form.'

Alexander Downer described that particular assault as 'Groundhog Day'. Seemingly unaware that the government's apparent sense of inherited privilege was exactly what Rudd was complaining about, Downer continued his response with the words, 'My father was a member of the House of Representatives.' Or perhaps Downer was just attempting to bait the fatherless boy from Nambour.

Rudd rapidly dispatched commentary from the ill-informed, like a cricketer slogging a ball to the boundary. Peter McGauran attempted to intervene in a debate with Rudd by throwing a general question around the chamber. 'Can anyone understand what he's saying?' demanded McGauran. Rudd rounded on him in a stinging attack. 'Minister at the table, I am glad you opened up at this point, because nobody in this parliament understood a word you said yesterday. The panic, which broke out on your front bench and your backbench, was extraordinary. You had not even bothered to read your brief.' The next time McGauran interjected, the deputy speaker told the minister to 'restrain himself'. Rudd had effectively managed to silence one critic.

Members are allowed to make a personal explanation to the house if they claim to have been misrepresented. This is intended to offer the opportunity for members to make a brief statement to correct the record. Rudd would do this; but he also tried, wherever possible, to slip in a further rebuttal of the government's position. It was a smart way to needle his opponents, but he didn't always get away with it. Occasionally, even Rudd would find himself called to order by the Speaker and told not to debate the point.

By making efforts to comply with the letter of the rules, even if not their spirit, Rudd would always attempt to get a few extra words incorporated into the record of debate. He was diligent in making his point wherever possible.

As 2005 finished, Julia Gillard compared the year in which Beazley had taken over the party's leadership again to a film. Nevertheless, it was 'not a blockbuster', bearing more resemblance instead to a B-grade Hollywood movie. She continued the analogy on the floor of parliament. 'Every Hollywood movie has to have a villain and that brings me to the leader of the house, Tony Abbott.' Julia admitted that she found him easier to get along with outside the chamber than inside, but quickly drew the bonhomie to a close. That is 'the limit of the compliments', she insisted.

***

Yet, in some way, none of these debates mattered to Rudd. Unless he could build up more support he would never become leader. The problem was that there was no obvious group of people within the party that he could win over to help him take his ambitions further. His natural policy inclinations meant that he could never expect those on the left of the party to switch to him en masse. In any case, a number of these people tended to support Gillard, who had her own leadership aspirations. Others from this faction backed Beazley. The right was also divided in its allegiances, with most MPs backing Beazley. And if (or when) he failed, it was more than likely that Swan would assume the mantle of leader of this group.

The centre was far too small and fractured to be significant. There was no readily apparent means by which Rudd could achieve his ambition.

Hard-headed political analysts didn't really believe that Kim Beazley would take Labor to power. The defeat in 2004 had been so devastating that no one could envisage there'd be any possibility that the party could win the next election.

After watching Latham slowly fall apart, everyone understood the incredible intensity of the job. And Beazley began well. 'The advantage of going back to Kim was that, in a period when there wasn't a lot of hope for Labor, he could cop the tough times,' said one frontbencher. But Beazley had forced himself back into the leadership role. He had levered himself in by arguing that he was the only person who could restore the party. The question of victory was left unaddressed.

Beazley had thrust himself ahead of a new crop of younger people who were also ambitious to lead the party. A few felt that he'd already had his chance—and blown it. They felt it was their turn, and wanted the chance to try a new approach. Others didn't trust Beazley because of the turmoil that had engulfed the party when Crean was deposed as leader. By taking the reins again, Beazley had placed himself in the way of change. To begin with, at least publicly, everyone had only good things to say about him. But that support would evaporate the minute he began to slip up.

Beazley did what the New South Wales branch told him to do, and established a home in Sydney. They hoped that this would lead to an entirely new mindset. There was a feeling he was too detached over in Perth and that he needed to begin looking at the world in the way that the new 'aspirational voters' on the east coast did. He appointed new staff, because there had been a feeling that he wasn't consulting enough. And Beazley worked on rolling out policies early, rather than hoarding them up for the election campaign itself.

But there were always lingering suspicions about his commitment to changing his style. Scepticism grew as he seemed to retreat to the same old closed group for advice. 'It was no one individual thing that he did—apart from the Victorian pre-selections, of course—but it was a general mood in caucus,' says one of those who'd become disillusioned with Beazley's leadership.

The Victorian pre-selections—the occasion on which party members had to choose a candidate who would contest the next election in that particular seat—had come up just over a year after Beazley regained the party's leadership. This is always a time of tension, especially for sitting members. All politicians have learned to be alert and watchful about encroachments on their support-base, and it is those who hold safe seats who are always on the lookout. They know it's much easier for their rivals within the party to attempt to grab control of some local party branches than it is to wrest a marginal seat away from the other side.

In Victorian Labor, some members noticed that the 'stack' was on. Numbers of new people were suddenly joining up in particular branches within their own electorates. This could only mean one thing: internal machinations had begun to throw out a number of sitting members and replace them with new candidates.

The problem was that some individuals who thought they were powerbrokers overplayed their hands. For some reason, those who were behind the stacks thought they could achieve a clean sweep in a number of electorates. In particular, they targeted the seat that was held by the former leader, Simon Crean. This was not so much arrogance as stupidity. It assumed that Crean would simply roll over.

Crean, like Beazley, was the son of a former Whitlam government minister. However, it was a mistake to assume that he'd become party leader simply because he was Labor aristocracy. He fought back, routing those who sought to destabilise him. And he didn't forget.

Beazley had always attempted to maintain neutrality over internal party battles. Years before, he had failed to properly back his own chief of staff, Michael Costello, when he was attempting to grab the Sydney seat of Lowe. He didn't get involved this time, either.

But remaining non-partisan wasn't really a possibility. By appearing disengaged, Beazley allowed events to cascade away from him. It seemed as if he was either irrelevant or, even worse, playing a double-handed game. The polls went into free-fall as bitter divisions within the party resurfaced. No politician wants to see internal disputes played out on the daily news.

In a play that could also serve as a guide for aspiring politicians, Shakespeare reveals Macbeth pondering an assassination he is about to commit. 'If it were done when 'tis done, then 'twere well it were done quickly,' says the Scots king. Labor's would-be executioners hadn't read the script (although, to be fair, it must be said that Macbeth did come to a bad end). Not only did Labor's drama play for far too long in the media but, much worse for the plotters, the attempt to topple Crean failed.

Beazley could not expect any support from Crean if another plotter eventually decided to turn on the leader.

***

The tactics group is a tight network of politicians and staffers who meet daily in the leader of the opposition's office. They determine where to focus the opposition's main effort in order to gain the most reward—ideally, by generating anti-government stories that lead the television news that night, and that attract headlines in the next day's papers. It's all about creating momentum and making the government look as if it's on the ropes.

Colin Campbell was Beazley's press secretary at the time. He remembers, 'Kevin would always come in with ten, no, eleven questions, and they'd always be deeply researched. It would be new stuff that would really push the argument forward. He was indefatigable.'

Another person has a very different take on this enthusiastic effort. 'I only attended a few of the meetings—I wasn't part of the normal group—but I was amazed. Kevin would come in with a long list of questions. Swannie would have three good ones and someone like Smith would probably wait to see what came out of tactics before he went back to dig something up.'

'Kevin was always trying to hog the limelight,' he says.

But it wasn't just Rudd's determination to stand in the spotlight that drove him at this time. He was obsessed with the horrifying string of policy failures that led to what became known as the 'AWB [Australian Wheat Board] Affair'. He felt the government had destroyed the wheat industry because it had allowed kick-backs going to Saddam's regime to continue unchecked. Rudd believed the government should receive opprobrium for its actions. It focused his ire; soon he was calling it the 'wheat for weapons' affair. He insisted that the case the government had constructed in its own defence had collapsed, because Foreign Affairs would not provide the inquiry set up to examine the issue with access to its electronic files. He insisted it proved three things: gross negligence, an attempt at a cover-up and, perhaps most significantly for Australia, a harsh cost for the wheat farmers and the community in general.

However, the government could always fall back on the previous election result as its ultimate defence. This, at least, was no lie. 'The Labor Party got 16 per cent in my electorate at the last election,' Downer asserted, while Rudd was left interjecting into thin air. Even the foreign minister could occasionally strike a virulent blow, as he did by switching his attack to target Kim Beazley.

'The leader of the opposition used a sentence describing the Iraqi situation which was 106 words long,' said Downer, who was keen to demonstrate he was so unconcerned by Labor's attacks that he could spend his time counting words. 'Just babble, babble, babble: 106 words,' he said, proceeding to compare this with Abraham Lincoln's famous Gettysburg Address—which Downer claims only contained 244 words.

The exchanges with Downer across the chamber continued. Angrily, Rudd asserted that the government was a 'cocktail—one part incompetence, one part arrogance'. He couldn't stand the way the government was able to paper over its lack of foresight by using the massive machinery at its disposal. 'In the budget in May,' said Rudd at this time, 'there was no mention of the drought, but, whoops, by June, suddenly there is one.' He seemed utterly frustrated that the government wasn't being called to account for its failures to anticipate events.

He attacked the Cole Inquiry into the AWB by dissecting the constrained terms of reference it was given by the government. Rudd noted that 'the commissioner was not asked to make determinations in any respect in relation to the incompetence or negligence of ministers'. Exasperated that $300 million had been filtered through to Saddam Hussein, a dictator with whom the government was on the point of war, Rudd detailed the warnings that the government had ignored. He identified 25 specific warnings that had been received by the government before the war, and a further ten before the the full exposure of 'the tawdry scandal, the largest corruption scandal in Australia's history'.

This strong attack, into which Rudd put much work, was not wasted. Although the government remained relatively unscathed in the polls, his own side could now see clearly that Rudd had been one of the few frontbenchers to force the government to fall back on the defensive. He had not secured any knockouts or ministerial scalps. But defence and trade were both meant to be areas in which the government would always triumph over Labor. Gradually, but inexorably, Rudd had turned this around. He had clearly demonstrated a mastery of the parliamentary process, and an ascendancy over Downer. A feeling of hope infused the party. Some members began a whispering campaign aimed at drafting him to the leadership. 'If Kevin is achieving this sort of success in an area that was supposed to be Labor's weak point,' they murmured, 'imagine how good he'll be if he's leading the main attack.'

Out in the broader electorate, some interest groups were less excited by the success Rudd was achieving. The independent MP Peter Andren says some of the wheat farmers in his country electorate were not happy about the underlying ideas motivating Rudd's attacks. 'I'd describe him as an economic rationalist,' says Andren, 'although I'd hope he'd be more flexible if he ever got into power. He's got to understand we need fair trade and not just free trade.'

'Just getting rid of AWB won't help anyone,' Andren adds. 'Rudd's got a far more inquiring mind than that. It's up to him to come up with a real solution to this long-term problem.'

***

Almost from the minute that Beazley had taken over, one MP in particular had begun putting out leadership feelers to Rudd. He encouraged Rudd to broaden his outlook beyond foreign affairs and the Iraq war. 'He was fixated with the war and the AWB. I said just get out and understand the local members,' this person said. 'Talk to them about what they're doing and that way you'll find out the mood of the electorate,' he advised.

'Just have a coffee with them and talk. Talk about what it's like out there, and that will give you a composite picture quite quickly.'

The counsel came with good intentions, and Rudd appeared to accept it as such. However, he was, almost certainly, far more politically sophisticated by this stage than that particular parliamentarian would ever be. Nevertheless, the fact that Rudd accepted even this sort of naïve advice suggests that he was working hard to get on with members of caucus. Another person says of this period, 'Kevin certainly appeared to make a greater effort to get on well with a wide cross-section of his colleagues than some of those other people who'd been talked about as the "next generation". It looked to me pretty much as if they were just waiting for Kim to fall in a heap after the next election, so they could move in and collect the prize.'

But not all backbenchers are destined to get to the top; reaching for the stars requires a lot more than just dropping in on people and chatting to them. Rudd knew he'd require three things to happen if he were to achieve the goal he'd set himself so many years before. The first was completely within his control. He worked like no one else, putting in a 100-per-cent effort. Then, because that might not be enough, he'd reach into his reserves to find that little bit extra. Rudd also began networking with intensity, and not just with backbench MPs. But he still knew that this combination of work and contacts would not alone be enough to push him to the apex of party leadership. This is where the third factor—good luck—would enter the equation.

Rudd decided to manufacture his own. He made sure that he would always be ready to grasp any good fortune that should happen to come his way. But he also realised that sometimes you just can't wait for luck to fall into your lap.

A parliamentary disciple (also a member of the Christian Fellowship) went to work encouraging other MPs to drop in on Rudd, staying for tea and a chat. As time wore on, Rudd became increasingly sure that something was about to change. He continued enthusiastically traversing the country. Assiduously, he'd court any MP who was prepared to have him come and speak to the party faithful. A year went past. The polls revealed the story of Beazley's declining leadership.

Any politician who proclaims that 'the only poll that counts is the one on election day' is only half-right. Everything is geared up for that one, brief moment. But, in the meantime, the political agenda is informed by the results of polling that punctuate the real news. It's the only 'real' feedback that can be used to track what's happening out in the electorate. Whenever a politician does something, he or she has one eye on the polls. It's a circular feedback loop. Politicians know that, with a 3-per-cent margin of error, the detail can't be trusted. But the polling can measure general 'feelings' amongst voters with a degree of accuracy. For example, watching the two-party-preferred tallies might offer a good guide as to how people will vote. However, looking at a leader's satisfaction rating—or, more particularly, their dissatisfaction rating—will give real clues as to what factors could be holding back support for the party.

This was the dead weight that Beazley continually had to carry around with him wherever he went. He did manage to stabilise the party relatively quickly. But the plane kept taxiing around; he couldn't get off the ground. He received support from an unlikely source when Bob McMullan made a speech during the grievance debate in parliament.

McMullan said that people were misreading the polls. 'The view was that Howard was absolutely dominant, and we were uncompetitive. This was wrong. Quite wrong. People had formed the view that Howard would win, so they were interpreting the polls through that prism.' A political professional, skilled in the interpretation of polling figures, McMullan felt journalists in particular were ignoring information that was right before their eyes. He, of course, emphasised the two-party-preferred results, which showed that Labor was still very much in the game.

However, this was the old political professional speaking out—a person who didn't have any urgent personal need to destabilise the leader or to spin the results one way or the other. By this stage of the cycle, McMullan felt the party had probably missed the opportunity for a leadership change. He was trying to assist the Labor Party by helping Beazley. But events were about to move very quickly.

It's difficult to overestimate the degree of energy and work that Rudd was putting into establishing himself. It wasn't just inside the party, or talking on the ABC's *AM*, *7.30 Report*, or *Lateline* to the political cognoscenti. By this stage, Rudd was also such a regular fixture on Channel 7's breakfast program that people were beginning to think he was everywhere.

'There was a process by which he pulled himself ahead,' one colleague insisted, 'and it was all that assiduous work. I don't think, after a point, it was worth the effort. But he kept doing it.'

The fact is, Rudd knew that voters in the key electorates often don't get their news from the broadsheet newspapers. The Labor Party did some detailed polling in the by-election that followed Latham's resignation from parliament. This showed conclusively that people in these areas received their political news from FM radio and Channel 10.

Even the role of tabloids like Sydney's pro-government *Daily Telegraph* appeared to be overblown. The polling suggested that the paper goes too far in pushing one particular line. The result is that no one trusts it as an unbiased source and, instead, they assume the paper is just 'skylarking'. Readers enjoy it, but they don't believe it. A highly experienced political analyst says, 'Although the newspaper is reaching lower-income groups, the letters pages are dominated by "right-wing nuts". No one assumes it is representative of what the community feels.' By contrast, the analyst asserts, 'Members of the inner-city Green Party dominate the broadsheet newspapers. You can't believe everything you read.'

***

'I've known Kevin for a decade now, I suppose, and although I'd say we are friends, I wouldn't say we are personally close,' says a colleague. 'He's a professional in the way he approaches everything. He really is genuinely interested in these sorts of issues. Completely, obsessively involved in them almost to the exclusion of everything else. Maybe,' he speculates, 'this is to do with the fact that his father died when he was young.'

Another person has a slightly different perspective. 'If you cross Kevin, well, then you're a cunt and will be killed.'

There came a time when his self-promotion finally pulled him ahead. Bob Carr claims it was a feature by Peter Hartcher of the *Sydney Morning Herald* that brought Rudd out of the ruck. By positing the idea that he had a chance—even a ghost of a chance—of standing as a rival to Beazley, Rudd was charging ahead. He was saying that he had supreme confidence in himself as the best person, the only person, who could lead Labor to victory.

It was all the little things that made the difference—all the appearances on the media that build momentum, until, suddenly, a politician is noticed. Carr remembers one day a person suddenly made a comment: 'That mate of yours, Kevin Rudd,' he observed as they were gliding through the traffic, 'he went very well speaking on that drive-time radio program today.' Carr fed the information back to Rudd. 'All those interviews you do,' he said, 'they've made you a name.' Rudd responded by trying harder, pushing himself further, and working like a demon.

Traversing the country; assiduously courting the media; working in parliament; maintaining his support in the electorate—which was the real Rudd? The question of motivation is obviously the key to understanding the man. 'Kevin is not some sort of apparatchik who will do anything to get into a position of power,' says one of his supporters. 'Kevin is not like that. He's working for the party, first and foremost.'

His staff displayed complete dedication and remarkable professionalism. This support allowed Rudd to crisscross the country, cultivating endorsement from others.

***

If someone had worked out a detailed plan to snatch the Labor leadership from Beazley, they couldn't have done a better job than Rudd. Every base was covered. He could tick off his specific portfolio—foreign policy—with his total command of the portfolio in parliament. He developed those credentials with the 'opinion makers' by appearances in the broadsheet newspapers and on the ABC. The 'soft' media (particularly appearances on the *Sunrise* program) brought him to the attention of a large number of ordinary voters.

The only thing missing was the establishment of a wider audience. Rudd needed to give himself a profile and ability to talk about domestic social issues. As mentioned earlier, both Latham and Beazley had refused to give him Treasury to shadow. The reason for this should have been obvious. As the person with the money, the treasurer has his or her fingers in every pie. This means that incumbents can, quite legitimately, range across a number of portfolios, occasionally poking their oar in (to the ire of the shadow ministers involved).

Somehow, Rudd had to carve himself a space to insert his commentary into the domestic political agenda. The victory of Family First in the Senate represented an obvious threat to Labor. So did the 'evangelical vote' that was helping the Liberals on Sydney's north shore. The assumption that the conservatives had a mortgage over Christian voters was a growing political problem that needed to be addressed. Rudd decided to tackle this head-on.

Doing so had a number of ancillary advantages. First, no one could question his Christian credentials; his faith was its own armour in this struggle. Second, the terrain was vacant. Rudd wouldn't be stepping on any Labor toes or causing any demarcation disputes to suddenly erupt around him. Finally, and probably most importantly, this was a vital social issue that directly affected Australian life. By articulating his views on these issues, Rudd was emphasising his credentials for the leadership. This was not an academic debate for him—it was an urgent and vital issue.

Rudd began by reflecting on the Christian variants of ways of engaging in politics. He gave a speech at New College at the University of New South Wales. Perhaps significantly, this was not the hall of residence on the campus that is influenced by Opus Dei. In his speech, he simultaneously tried to defend the use of religious values in politics while questioning whether some politicians were simply using Christianity as a veneer to get votes.

'If the churches are not allowed to participate in the great debates about values,' he asserted to a receptive audience, 'then we have reached a very strange place indeed.' Instead, Rudd outlined his own model for religious engagement. He emphasised that the Bible had both spiritual and social dimensions. 'And if it is a social Gospel then it is in part a political Gospel because politics is the means by which society chooses to exercise its collective power.'

This carved out a significant role for the churches in the policy arena, although Rudd insisted there could be no 'automatic mathematical formula for determining every item of social, economic (or other) question before government'. Nevertheless, he believed there was a significant and necessary role for Christians who wished to insert their views into policy debates—with limitations.

'Sometimes you encounter in the broader Christian community the view that a Christian view on policy should always prevail no matter what. I respond by saying that's terrific, but we don't live in a theocracy,' he argued. 'We live in a democracy, which by definition is secular. If you want a theocratic form of government then you're several centuries too late. But if you want to live in a secular democracy you are in a contestable polity where views will be distilled through the ballot box.' This formulation was designed to provide reassurance to the many agnostics and atheists in the party.

With this argument, Rudd clarified his own position, reconciling it to that of the broader labour movement. In other words, the religious view was necessary to guide the individual. However, society was ruled not by the Bible, but through a democratic form of government. Indeed, he also pointed out that the number of Australians declaring that they believed in God had declined to just under 70 per cent, 'although the trend-line has been in one direction'. This way, Rudd could justify arguing his own Christian perspective in the hope that it might prevail, but still accept the result if it didn't.

Rudd was insistent that the Liberal Party needed to be challenged to prevent them from claiming the churches as a 'wholly owned subsidiary group'.

Rudd then chose to write two articles for *The Monthly* magazine, demonstrating his usual careful placement. He engaged with the right audience, in the correct political space. The magazine appealed to a progressive readership. He could engage with thinking people, reassuring atheists that he was not some sort of proselytising evangelist, while at the same time appealing to Christians who were demanding a religious dimension to political life.

Perhaps even more importantly, the magazine had a wide circulation but not a massive one. Most of the influence of the two articles he wrote tended to come from the fact simply that he'd bothered to address the issue. A lot of people were unaware of exactly what distinctions Rudd had been seeking to make; nevertheless, they admired the fact that he'd sought to engage in the debate.

One of those who did read the articles, the Victorian Labor warhorse and party elder John Button, wrote to Rudd after the first essay was published. He contended, 'This will do you, and the Labor Party, a lot of good.' He insisted that, as a humanist, he could not find any fault with Rudd's position. 'The essay stands up for something that represents a contrast to the unattractive, ambitious, individualistic ethos that has grabbed Australian society,' he said. Later, after Rudd became party leader, Button was fulsome in his praise. 'There is a new feeling that's been injected into the party,' he said, 'a feeling that it can win.' He mourned the fact that Gavin O'Connor had been 'the last Labor farmer in Canberra—but at least Kevin was a farmer's son'.

Button thought that at least Rudd was articulating a vision of the future. This was a big contrast to the past. 'Before the ascension of Rudd and Gillard, I wouldn't have voted for them. But the combination of the two of them works. There is a new feeling that Labor can win,' he reiterates.

On the last day of October 2006, Rudd launched the Jesuit Father Frank Brennan's book, *Acting on Conscience*. His decision to do this demonstrated the way that Rudd would establish his own path through the religious and social debate. The former prime minister Paul Keating had once accused Brennan of being a 'meddling priest'. This was probably a subtle reference to what King Henry II had said about Thomas

Becket, Archbishop of Canterbury. Shortly afterwards, that priest had been murdered in front of the altar of his own cathedral by the king's knights.

Health Minister Tony Abbott—who is also an overt Christian—was present at the launch. He'd previously accused Rudd of attempting to 'recruit from the pew'; however, the debate did not continue along political lines. Rather, it concentrated on the issue of how individual Christians should engage in the public arena. This was an issue that Rudd had given a great deal of thought to.

Brennan observed that 'those who have recently held the highest political office in the land have had occasion to tell religious people to butt out' of the political debate. No one could be sure whom Brennan meant, because politicians of every hue had said the same thing—particularly when they were in power. He said his book represented 'a plea for a rightly circumscribed place at the table for religion in public deliberation about law and policy'. Brennan hoped he had 'set out rules for engagement which apply equally to me, Sheik al-Hilaly and Archbishop Aspinall, the Anglican Primate.'

Rudd said, 'Australia's founding fathers had got it absolutely right, that there should be a separation of church and state in Australia.' But, for him, this did not mean that religion would not have any influence on government. 'What this meant was that there should be no established religion in Australia as the Australian state religion,' he said. Christianity had never been a privatised faith, but rather offered 'a range of social teachings from the sanctity of life through to a deep commitment to social justice and the doctrine of a just war'. But, in the parliamentary forum, Rudd couldn't resist a sideswipe at Tony Abbott. 'Criticising me for trying to recruit from the pew' had missed the point, he said. God 'is neither Liberal, Labor, nor even Family First'.

However, in politics, while beliefs represent the foundations of success, they will never be enough in themselves to help a person into the leadership. This requires solid parliamentary work, an ability to engage with ideas and, crucially, good relationships with other members.

In September 2005, Rudd's Christian Fellowship colleague Quick was rushed to hospital and put in intensive care for pneumonia. The next morning, Rudd stopped one of Quick's staff members as he was walking into the office. 'What sort of things does he read?' Rudd asked. Walking into his office, Rudd began going through the bookshelves. He took one book down, considered it, and then took down another, before pressing them both firmly into the hands of Quick's staffer. 'I can't get away see him,' said Rudd. 'There's too much to do; it's just impossible. But here, give him these. Do you think he'll read them?'

At this stage, Quick was secretary of the parliamentary Christian Fellowship, so the choice of a massive volume entitled *A History of American Churches* was an unsurprising choice, if an uninspired one. But the other book, much more to Quick's anti-war taste, was about the failure of the American engagement in Iraq. 'Harry was tickled pink to receive the present,' says the staffer who delivered it.

Quick had earlier pointed out to Rudd the danger of remaining too focused on policy. 'Coming from the background that he does gives him incredible drive,' says Quick. Nevertheless, he believed there was a need for Rudd to balance his own convictions with an understanding of others.

'Religion is a rock,' he says. 'It can provide you with a moral compass, although it doesn't explain what motivates other people,' he adds. 'To get your act together you need to find a religious basis, then read the philosophers, and finally pull all of it into a framework. But this is only one part of the key to electoral success. People will support you because of the person that you are, not because of your political persuasion,' he says. 'But then work your electorate and work it hard.'

Rudd was doing exactly that.

CHAPTER EIGHT

Crisis

December 2006

> 'Kim Beazley has had my consistent support since his return to the leadership in January 2005. There is no change in my position. My support continues for him as leader. Like all Labor members I am working hard for the election of a federal Labor government.'
>
> –Kevin Rudd, 21 November 2006

When Beazley had begun actively campaigning for the leadership before Latham resigned, he'd left a message on the phone of a Gillard supporter. 'It was the first time that he'd spoken to me—the first time that he'd been bothered to even try to contact me. He said, "I know you won't vote for me, but listen, this time it will be different." Well, I thought, let's see. Can the leopard change its spots?'

'I've heard the suggestion that Kim wasn't listening,' says one of those who later helped to overthrow the leader. He hesitates. 'I know who's been saying that—but, basically, it's not true.'

The problem was that no matter how hard Kim Beazley was working, it wasn't reflected in his personal polling figures. In his first time as leader he'd had an exceptionally healthy poll rating. Bob Carr noted, 'I used to think that I was doing well as opposition leader if I received a 44-per-cent approval rating. Then it would fall back again to 38 or 39 per cent. You are always in that sort of range while you're in opposition. But back in 1998 Kim managed to get up to 50 per cent, and that was very, very high.'

Even today, those figures are stratospheric by comparison to the recent crop of state opposition leaders around Australia. Unfortunately for Beazley, there was no recurrence of the good polling results in his second period as leader. Australians seeemed to have moved on, even if Labor was still stuck in the past.

The journalists still thought he looked like the old Beazley. They thought he sounded like the old Beazley, too. Yet when he tried to change, the journalists attacked him. 'That's not our Beazley,' they thought. 'He's trying to pretend he's something he's not.'

'The reason he didn't manage to cut through,' says Bob Carr, 'is one of those hard-to-assess elements of political communication. If he'd been prime minister in 1998, as he deserved to be because he got a majority of the votes, I think the country would be a better place. But you can't rewrite history.' A federal parliamentarian says, 'The real problem was that everyone thought they already knew him. They thought they'd heard everything he had to say before. Every time he came on the TV at night they'd mentally switch off.'

Some Labor parliamentarians remained depressed about the lack of progress. 'Kim was like the ruckman in a country football team,' says one. 'He was a fantastic player—he could have played in the AFL. But every time the team ran out, you have to make sure that one of the players was designated to wack him around the ears to keep him "on focus". It wasn't good enough.'

The feeling was that Beazley had become institutionalised. 'After fifteen years in this place, that's what you become,' says another Labor member, looking around at the walls of his Parliament House office. 'When you saw him, it was like watching a long-term inmate spending his time in jail. Kim was actually looking comfortable,' he adds. The trouble was, the capacity for forgiveness had worn out amongst other members of the party. They urgently needed to win. 'Kim may have been a Rhodes Scholar, but perhaps that was part of the problem. He'd forgotten what it was like to talk to people.'

The Roman writer Plutarch quotes the politician and general Fabius Maximus (the person made famous by Russell Crowe in the movie *Gladiator*) as saying, 'To be turned from one's course by men's opinions shows a man is unfit to hold office.' But this is not the way of modern politics. The mood is set by the impressions of others.

Opinion polling is vital in establishing dominance in the political debate. The polls are watched very carefully by the entire political class: not only the politicians themselves, but also those who get their food from politics—the backroom boys and the apparatchiks. 'Nobody wants to be part of the losing team,' says a close observer. 'Their future is on the line as well. People want to be winners.'

There are a lot of different ways of interpreting the polls. The most simplistic (and therefore the one that the media tend to focus on) is the two-party-preferred result. Everyone likes to tell you what this means because it's easy to understand: there is a winner and a loser. The poll appears to sum up the way voters (or at least the people who have responded to the questions) feel about political parties. In its way, it does. But that doesn't make this result useful to the people who want to change its outcome.

They find the question is so general it doesn't tell you what you need to know, which is *why*? And because the polls are taken (normally) over a particular weekend, they present a snapshot of how people are feeling, rather than a long-term indication of the changing mood in the electorate. However, the cognoscenti use polling very differently from the way ordinary media consumers do. By mining the results, party-workers can excavate the information that is key to a lot of the decision-making that will go on behind the scenes.

One of the questions asked by Newspoll is how satisfied people are with the leaders of particular parties. Those in the know don't bother comparing the prime minister to the opposition leader. That figure is useful, but it's not the most important when trying to work out who is the right person to lead the party. For this task, the vital figure is not even the percentage of people who are satisfied or dissatisfied with a leader—it's the margin between these two results. If more people are satisfied than unsatisfied, the margin will be positive. If a leader alienates a larger number of people than those who are happy, the satisfaction rating turns negative. A negative rating is never good, but a small one doesn't really matter. However, the moment the margin goes to minus 10 per cent or worse, the situation becomes critical. If it remains there, the leader is on life support and can expect the party to turn on him at the slightest provocation.

Immediately after Beazley took over as leader from Latham, Newspoll reported that 40 per cent of people were satisfied with his performance and 22 per cent were dissatisfied, leaving him with a positive margin of 18 points. By early April 2005, people were again feeling comfortable with Beazley as opposition leader, and the margin rose to 24 points. Those who had supported Beazley as the obvious choice to reunite the party felt vindicated. Less than a year after the election and just months after he had taken over as leader, everything was looking good. But, as it turned out, that was the best figure he ever managed to record in his second stint as leader.

By early July that same year, Beazley slipped over into negative territory for the first time. The problem was that, instead of stabilising, the margin continued collapsing. By the end of August, although Beazley could still manage to attract a satisfaction rating of 32 per cent, the number dissatisfied with his performance had climbed to 50 per cent. The key figure to emerge was a disastrous margin of minus 18 per cent. This steadied, but it didn't change direction. For the rest of that year, the margin bobbled along around minus 16 per cent.

Labor voters may have loved Beazley (and may still have been embracing him when he was out and about in shopping malls), but the older party members remembered the effect Whitlam's leadership had on the party. After the disastrous defeat in 1975, Whitlam remained party leader. He then led the opposition to another terrible defeat at the next election in 1977. Although the party faithful, who could never forgive Fraser for blocking supply, loved him, the rest of Australia had absolutely no interest in ever giving Whitlam another chance at government. It was only after he retired in 1978 that the opposition finally began to make up ground.

Given this background, the amazing thing is that Beazley was able to remain leader for so long. Soon a rating of minus 16 didn't look too bad. On the second weekend in March 2006, the margins hit minus 33. In April, it was down to minus 35. The satisfaction rating hadn't changed too much; the problem was that the more people thought about Beazley, the more they decided they didn't like what they saw. In the early-April poll, 26 per cent of people still said they were satisfied with Beazley's performance. By then, though, the number dissatisfied had grown to a whopping 61 per cent of those polled.

Beazley's team was incandescent over the internal emphasis being given to these figures. 'These people should learn how to actually read the figures,' one of his supporters says. 'Those figures don't reflect whether someone will be elected or not. It's the two-party-preferred results that are vital, not leadership,' she says sharply. This remained the core of Beazley's argument.

But it didn't convince the doubters. The continuing coda set the background music to the political score. There's no need to wander through the figures in detail; suffice it to say that not just Rudd, but more particularly those who were later to approach him about the leadership, became attuned to this constant drumbeat of despair. The margin did pick up after plumbing the depths in April 2006, but only just. The negative rating never improved above minus 15 and was often in the low minus 20s. Those who could read the polls felt like slashing their wrists.

But another Beazley supporter fingers the real problem. 'He wasn't doing well enough in the polls. That's it. It was no good him saying, "But I'd still win an election." Beazley had a number of real enemies in the party, and there was no way they were going to cut him any slack.'

And that wasn't the only frustration that people began feeling. Slowly, Beazley seemed to become more remote. Some politicians felt he was again becoming surrounded by a small coterie of advisers, and that he wasn't as open as he needed to be. One opponent called these people the 'Secret Seven'; others used the old word, 'roosters'. They felt that not enough was being done to get other people to contribute.

Increasingly, the feeling grew amongst parliamentarians that they were being set up for another mediocre outcome. Many liked Beazley, but there was a feeling that somehow he wasn't doing enough.

'Kim pointed to the way he had changed, but everyone in the real world just shrugged their shoulders,' says a parliamentarian. 'They weren't listening to him.' Gradually, the (unfair) perception grew that he wasn't developing any new policies and didn't have anything new to say. Critics pointed out he didn't work up a whole new approach to health, or a 'Labor' way of dealing with the economy.

Beazley just didn't seem able to 'cut through'.

'The sad thing is, for all the talk and criticism of Kim waffling, his language was actually incredibly sharp,' says Tony Burke, an MP from the NSW right of the party. 'The problem is the public wasn't listening to Kim anymore. The government's smear campaign had worked. Your starting point has to be that the public is right. That was the seed.'

'I'd come down here to parliament, and hear Kim, and think we're going to get there,' he adds. 'Then I'd go back to the electorate, but none of it was being heard.'

'Our theory in the past was always that we had our issues and they had theirs,' says Tony Burke. 'Ours were health and education; theirs were the economy and national security. But this meant we had to convince the public that bringing us to government was all about our issues. That strategy was always wrong.'

'The public was never going to believe that an election had nothing to do with the economy,' says Burke. 'If you vacate the field on some issues, you concede the ground.'

'The other thing that was essential was that people had noticed that John Howard had started to change,' continues Burke. 'This opened up a chance for us. Every other election we've said, "He's a 1950s' man." There is a key problem with that. We were telling people they'd got it wrong for the past four elections, which is a pretty arrogant way to approach an election campaign.'

'The real strength of this argument now is that it's true. He has changed. There's a hard edge to policies, and in more recent times he started to make mistakes.' Burke won't mention age directly, but that's the implication. 'He's not the same bloke that people elected.'

Much later, after Rudd became leader, Burke added another thought. 'When the government tries to attack Rudd over current issues, they demonstrate they're not participating in the debate on the future,' he says. 'It's a big mistake.'

***

Beazley's backbench was restless.

'These are serious people,' says a politician. 'You don't go into politics and do all this work just for the adrenaline rush. The personal cost is too high. This is all about core values.' He gets quite worked up as he is speaking. 'This is, most of all, about what you believe in — there's no point in coming to Canberra just to sit in comfy seats, because that's not what it's about. We've got to make a difference.' And then he utters the clincher: 'You can't make a difference from the opposition benches!'

The politician continues, 'There was no way we were going to sleep-walk into another electoral catastrophe. This is not some type of amateur hour, where everyone gets their chance to sing their song. It's not a middle-class parlour game that we are playing here. This is about deciding the future.'

This was the conclusive argument advanced as the reason that Beazley had to be dropped. But the polling wasn't enough by itself. Anger eventually solidified over one issue that seemed to legitimise opposition to the leader. The flare-up occurred during a pre-selection battle when the Victorian right targeted five sitting members. Not content with just one scalp, the right attempted to dispose of everyone in a clean sweep, including Crean, the party's former leader. Analysing the stoush in retrospect, another Victorian MP says, 'The right went a step too far; it was a strategic error.'

According to one person on Beazley's side, Simon Crean never stopped working against the leader. 'He is a very, very dogged person. He just doesn't give up,' this person said. But that's just one view, emphatically rejected by others. 'He absolutely played the team game—until the pre-selection. His opponents underestimated him. That was a remarkably stupid mistake.'

Another colleague says, 'Simon was never a good enforcer; perhaps that's why they took him on. Remember, he was from Labor royalty. He is thoroughly decent.'

Crean himself says that, after he secured his pre-selection, he telephoned Beazley in a final attempt to broker a peace.

Nevertheless, although this was the noise that was amplified in the media, the real action was occurring elsewhere. It had already been going on for quite some time.

***

In late 2005, Labor's New South Wales secretary, Mark Abib, commissioned some special qualitative polling. The point of this was to understand which issues were really concerning people, along with the things that were likely to change their vote in the coming state election. That way, the New South Wales government could begin to address problems before they exploded onto the political agenda. The ballot was still a long way out, so there would be plenty of time to take action to defuse any significant problems.

As was usually the practice, a few questions concerning federal issues were tacked on to the end of the discussion. They weren't exactly an afterthought, but they certainly weren't driving the research. Basically, the party felt that, if it was going to conduct the focus-group research anyway, it might as well probe people's attitudes as deeply as possible. But the response to these questions was dynamite.

It rapidly became clear that voters had lost interest in anything that Beazley was saying. Two findings in particular shone through like beacons, illuminating the negatives. First, they felt they'd heard it all before. Probing more deeply, it turned out that voters agreed with many of the things that Beazley was advocating. The problem was that they mentally switched off as soon as they saw him on the telly; no one was listening to the message. Second, everyone felt that they knew the real Kim, and most people liked him. But watching the 'new' Beazley—an angry, aggressive man—worried them. They felt it wasn't the person they knew, and they didn't like what they were seeing. Ironically enough, they were reacting adversely to a persona that had been adopted by Beazley to show just how keen he was to become prime minister.

Abib pondered this information. It was the strongest, most consistent message coming through from the focus research. To the extent that there was any overlap of the state government's prospects, it wasn't useful. But that wasn't the reason that Abib decided to do something. He acted because he was worried.

His thinking had solidified by November 2005. He was in a difficult situation. He was young, and it wasn't his responsibility to solve the problem—it was up to federal caucus.

Eventually, he decided that he couldn't hold the information back from the people who needed to know it. By February 2006, the polling results had been shown to New South Wales' federal Labor members. Abib was careful to ensure that nothing leaked. These polling results never appeared in the media, and the details were tightly guarded. But what did slip out, inevitably, was the changing mood in the party's biggest branch. Shortly after parliament commenced sitting at the beginning of the year, Beazley realised he could no longer rely on a solid core of support from New South Wales. Their votes for the leadership were back in play.

The faction had always operated as a relatively disciplined group. Because of this, it had the numbers to make a difference to guesstimates about what the result of any new leadership ballot might be. Additionally, it represented the first crack in Kim's support-base. The fissure was small, fed only by speculation. Nothing was sourced back to any of the backroom players — who were, at this stage, just talking. But that's where the information originally came from, and most in the party could work out what was beginning to happen. The rumours meant two things: Beazley had to lift his game, and he only had a limited time in which to do it.

The other point that the qualitative work revealed was that voters were interested in Rudd. They didn't know a great deal about him, but what little they had seen they seemed to like. He was coming across as conservative — certainly someone who was not a risk. The contrast with Latham was self-evident. But there was more to it than that. The focus groups thought he 'looked okay' and that he had a clear command of detail. They liked this; here was a politician talking about something that he obviously knew about, they felt. People figured that if Rudd knew something about foreign affairs, he might be able to cope with the economy and other issues as well.

When asked today about what made the difference in popular perceptions of Rudd, Abib replies, 'That's easy — *Sunrise*. This proved he could connect with an audience. As well as that, there is not a harder worker on either side of politics.'

Abib realised that the positive comments were coming from people who didn't really know Rudd at all. At this stage, they only had an inkling of the person. Rudd's phenomenal workload ensured that people were getting more of an opportunity to make an assessment about his capability to lead the party.

The leadership was now effectively in play, and it depended on Gillard. She could command a significant number of votes, but not necessarily enough to win. In order to do that, she'd need a wholesale defection from Beazley's camp. However, none of these people were prepared to play second fiddle to her. Rudd had made that very decision at the beginning of 2005, when he'd refused to back her for the leadership against Beazley.

Gillard had to think long and hard about what was in the best interests of the party. Those who had seen her attempt to become leader and then the deputy in January 2005 assumed that she was remorselessly driven by personal ambition. This blinded everyone to the possibility that she could act altruistically, too.

Coinciding with Beazley's early wobbles in the polls in late 2005, one of Gillard's supporters contacted a known Rudd backer. He was freelancing. He postulated an idea that the two could get together. At this stage, neither side appeared interested in the prospect, even though a rapprochement between Rudd and her inside the party would change the numbers decisively.

Another political player who wasn't involved in any of this dealing later tells me, 'You can call this period "The Education of Young Kevin". He is not the sort of person who would appear, at first glance, to have a great deal in common with, say, John Robertson of Unions NSW. But it seems he decided he had to broaden his view of the world.'

It certainly appears that Rudd extended not simply his range of contacts but also his approach to policy. It was good for him to be forced to look for support from amongst groups that he might not otherwise have spoken to. It all had the effect of broadening his outlook. Instead of relying exclusively on the usual detailed academic analysis that he had embraced in the past, he had to incorporate real people, and their needs, into the way he dealt with issues.

It's still too early to work out how significant this has been in determining his overall political direction. But it is certain that the interaction has been vital. 'You'd have to sum up his first approach as very artificial,' says one of those involved. 'But Rudd's learning to think with his heart.'

***

At least until the middle of 2006, the dominant groups remained somewhat ambivalent. The NSW right hadn't yet formally committed to Rudd, and Gillard hadn't switched to him either. Something had to move.

Because Gillard was a member of the left, a quiet underground rumour was sent abroad suggesting that she was planning to change to the right faction after the 2007 election. Whatever the reality of this, the underlying aim was undoubtedly to cast Gillard as simply another ruthless politician. If the rumour was to be believed, it would demonstrate that her designs to become Australia's first female prime minister were implacable. No one could imagine a person like this staying number two to Rudd for long. This line was meant to damage the unity of any potential combination between the two younger contenders.

As 2006 wore on, she decided that winning came in front of personal ambitions. She was also very concerned about the prospect that Labor might lose the next election. She hadn't joined parliament just to ask questions, or to sit and watch while, in her eyes, a government (towards whose ideology she had an almost visceral opposition) tore apart the fabric of Australian society. Gillard decided to throw in her lot with Rudd.

More was required to get a team together than just agreeing on who was willing to be deputy. It meant sitting down together and working out if policy viewpoints could be aligned.

Recent interpretations of politics have focused on the idea that only one side can triumph, and that the other must be left in despair. But this was not the way Rudd and Gillard eventually sat down to discuss the issues. For them, the art of politics became the art of negotiation. First, though, it was necessary to arrange the parameters for the terms of a discussion.

Ironically, a Queensland Liberal, Michael Johnson, thought a pairing between Rudd and Gillard was so obvious that he talked about in parliament at this time.

'He was so ambitious and a strategic thinker,' says Johnson today. 'People just give off vibes. I saw him at a conference on China, and Bob Hawke was introducing him around as a future Labor leader. I'm surprised it took so long,' he adds. 'He is hungry, and desperate to be prime minister. Clinical and forensic as well.'

A Labor politician not involved in any of these moves also says the pairing was obvious. 'Mate, the key thing it required was for Gillard to realise that she couldn't win. It took her two years longer than what it should have.'

'At the end of the day, there wasn't any choice to make. It was a one-horse race,' says Joel Fitzgibbon. 'I would assume that it became obvious to Julia that whilst she had the single most number of primary votes, it wasn't enough to win a ballot. Also, she was well aware it wasn't healthy for the caucus to have that sort of showdown,' Fitzgibbon adds.

It all boiled down to be two crucial factors: votes and timing. As late as May 2006, even with the New South Wales right on his side, Rudd didn't have the ability to win a challenge. And there was only a narrow window of opportunity to change the leader—the brief period sandwiched between the Victorian state election in November and the New South Wales election.

'For a lot of people, it was very difficult to move away from Kim,' notes Abib. 'Everyone knew that if he was still leader at the beginning of 2007 there would be no room for any more destabilisation.'

Rudd didn't have the numbers by himself. He needed Gillard. The approach came as the dry winter was beginning to grip the country. Gillard had never apparently warmed to Rudd, and it seemed implausible that she would now. Ideologically, the pair initially appeared to have little in common. They had to find shared ground. The question was, would it be a forced and brutal compromise urged on the two because of political necessity?

The only way to find out was to talk. Both had been elected in 1998, but that was where the similarities appeared to end. Rudd was from the right; Gillard, from the left. Rudd still thought of himself in some ways as a Queenslander from the country; Gillard was more familiar with law courts and the inner city. He was married with a family; she was single and childless. As frontbenchers, they'd argued. 'There was a forced civility when they talked,' according to one of her supporters.

Perhaps surprisingly, from that first meeting they began to 'click'. Gillard decided to keep the talks a secret from her staff until the last moment. Perhaps no one was more astonished at the emergence of the Rudd-Gillard 'ticket' than one staff member who had invested considerable time and effort supporting Gillard's ambitions. 'I don't know how it happened,' this person says.

Another politician who was involved challenges this. 'Don't forget, these people are professional negotiators. Of course everyone wants to win. But if you can't get your entire agenda up, that doesn't mean you just go home with nothing. It's not just Kevin who is diligent, hard-headed, and experienced. Julia wants to really achieve something in politics as well. They've got an enormous amount in common.

The two politicians reached an agreement. Gillard would fold her leadership ambitions in behind Rudd; she was prepared to stand as his deputy. But there was still not a vacancy, and Rudd knew he would have to be careful not to alienate his new supporters as he waited for a chance to strike.

Three factors were now critical for the success of Rudd's

and Gillard's enterprise. First, Rudd could not be seen to depose Beazley simply for the sake of it—the leader had to fall by himself, by making either a significant mistake or enough little ones to bring his judgement and entire capacity to win into question.

Second, there was a need to ensure that the two contenders could immediately outline an agenda clearly different from the one that Beazley had espoused. Gillard and Rudd both understood that they would be judged not simply by the polls, although these were vital. The new leadership team knew they had to justify their decision to overturn Beazley in ideological terms. It would not be enough to simply assert that they could win the coming election; they also had to be able to justify their actions to faithful party members. This meant they had to propose new policies to differentiate themselves from the former leader.

The final factor was timing. The political debate in Australia shuts down almost completely in the second half of December and the whole of January. If a decision to change the leader were not made by late November/early December 2006, it would be almost impossible to move before February 2007. However, by then there would be a serious concern that leadership turmoil would impact negatively on the New South Wales state election, which was due at the end of March. By April, the question would have become whether a new leader would have enough time to establish himself or herself before Howard called an election.

Rudd needed to lift his profile to ensure he was seen as the obvious candidate, should a vacancy emerge. Rudd spent $35,543 on domestic airfares in the first six months of 2006. Kim Beazley spent $41,530 in the same period.

'Either we did it in December,' says one of the plotters, 'or we didn't do it all.' As it happened, all the skittles aligned themselves just in time.

***

A few politicians are utterly contemptuous of the sort of political analysis that is regularly served up by the media. One says, 'It should have been obvious to everyone that Kim was on the skids. The press is very gullible. Many of the people in the press gallery operate on a drip-feed.' This person is scathing about the lack of questioning of Beazley's position. 'It's as if the gallery is sedated. A golden rule of politics is to talk to people; it's the only way to find out what's going on. The big changes aren't broadcast.'

But it's the media's role to report on what has happened, not to stoke leadership challenges.

In order to establish the sort of crisis where such stories could be run in the media—and run prominently—it was necessary to have significant politicians moving to actively remove Beazley. That led straight back to catch-22, because any dynamic campaign against the leader would be immediately branded as destabilisation. No one wanted to be accused of treachery, so the politicians couldn't move—and there was nothing to report on. The daggers were poised, but no one was willing to lunge forward against the leader.

That's why the situation lumbered on for months after the real point of no-return had been reached in the winter of 2006. At this time, Beazley was tapped on the shoulder and encouraged to take the decision to stand down by himself. The messages were not official warnings that a coup was coming, but they were not casual off-the-cuff comments either. Politicians, attuned to the need to sensitively understand the hidden meanings in conversations, were suggesting to Beazley that his time was up. On at least two occasions, different politicians individually broached the possibility that he might like to hand over the leadership to Rudd.

'No one wanted to tear him down,' says one of those who

spoke to the leader, a member of the New South Wales right. 'He must have known his support was collapsing, but he decided to hang on.'

The simple fact that this particular politician was speaking to the leader about his future should have been enough of an alarm bell to make anyone seriously consider his position. But Beazley decided to tough it out. He seems to have made a crucial misjudgement at this time: that Rudd would baulk at challenging him at the final moment. In fact, Rudd was already being held back by others who were urging him to wait for Beazley to fall over by himself.

Most of Rudd's supporters still hoped that a challenge wouldn't be necessary. They showed Beazley the polling, but he refused to draw the obvious conclusion.

In September, at the conclusion of a sitting week, Beazley had dinner with the political correspondent of *The Australian*, Dennis Shanahan. 'At this time, Kim was staying at University House at the ANU,' says Shanahan. He remembers, as the group of diners were pulling on their coats before heading out into the cold night air, 'There almost seemed to be a touch of melancholy about Beazley.' He noted this later in an opinion column which speculated that the leader 'was missing his wife and family'.

A person working closely with Beazley endorses this judgement, although he warns against reading too much into it. 'Yes, Kim was exhausted. But that was because of the way he'd been working. You just can't imagine — no one can — the amount of pressure on him,' he says. 'The prime minister has burdens, too, but he's got massive institutional support. The opposition leader is just out there, completely on his own.'

Another Beazley staffer is fiercely supportive of his former boss. 'Around this time, Howard's press secretary would always be up in the parliamentary gallery,' he says, 'spinning away like mad. He'd be seizing on any opportunity to say, "Oh, look at this, you can't have this bloke as the PM", and then he'd rush to point out a little slip or some other tiny, irrelevant mistake. A level of scrutiny was being applied to Kim that was never applied to anyone else,' he insists, 'and I particularly include Howard in that comment.'

'There were other times when it was us who slipped up,' he adds. 'At first, we sometimes had Kim scheduled to do morning radio on the east coast, right after he'd flown back from the other side of the continent the night before. Well, it would be 7.00 a.m. in Sydney or Melbourne, but five o'clock or even four o'clock for his body clock.' He shakes his head. 'No one can do that.'

When Labor MPs want to get an unattributable message to their colleagues, they don't use the phone. They use the media. *The Australian* can be a popular choice during non-sitting periods. It's a newspaper that goes right round the country, which lends it power. So it was that one of Rudd's supporters began leaking stories to the newspaper's political correspondent, Dennis Shanahan, because he believed the time had come to shake up the caucus.

There was another reason for Beazley's opponents to be well disposed towards the paper. The editor, Chris Mitchell, had formerly headed up the Brisbane *Courier Mail*, and he knew Rudd well—so well that he'd asked Rudd to be the godfather of the child he'd had with his second wife, Christine Jackman. Although it was well known that journalists at this newspaper tended to have better contacts with the government rather than the opposition, there seemed to be a fair chance that an anti-Beazley story would get a good run in it.

A journalist who didn't work for *The Australian* says at this time that Mitchell appeared extremely confident that Rudd would be leader by Christmas. 'I'd put money on it,' he said.

Then a Newspoll was published in *The Australian* showing that Labor's primary support had plunged to 37 per cent.

This was deadly territory. The last brick in the defensive wall around Beazley had fallen out.

In addition, Mitchell, Shanahan, and Lebovic were regularly speaking together to work out the relevant questions for the regular Newspoll survey. They decided to explore how Labor would fare under a Rudd-Gillard ticket. The results were startlingly positive, adding extra pressure on Beazley.

A politician smiles when I ask him about this. 'Any article like this will give fuel and momentum to a leadership challenge.'

The pressure that came with the final sessions of parliament in 2006 was what eventually tripped Kim up. He seemed to let down his guard. He seemed to be focused on other things. 'It was almost as if he felt he was home safe, because it was too late for anyone to challenge him,' says a person on his team.

This led to a couple of small slip-ups, and then a big one. When Kim failed to distance himself from Brian Burke at the Press Club, the insiders noticed, but it had no resonance in the wider community. He ruled out a reshuffle of his shadow cabinet, even though it was not scoring with the public and he had stars like Peter Garrett on the backbench. But by this time his position was becoming irretrievable. Every hesitation was seized upon as proof that Kim had 'lost it'.

A few on Rudd's team decided to move, apparently independently. It's not clear if they discussed tactics with Rudd beforehand. Certainly, there appeared to be no real co-ordination between two of these players. The only thing they seemed to share was a desire to replace the leader.

The journalists telephoned around again. One of Rudd's earlier backers said, 'They called to ask me if there was going to be a challenge. I said, "No, not that I know of," and then I'd immediately check back with Rudd's HQ—"that's still right?" I'd ask, and they'd say, "Yes." We were ready, but not quite yet.'

By late November, crisis speculation had built to a head. Then the team behind Beazley miscalculated. They knew that if the leadership hadn't moved by Christmas, the leader would be home safe. No plots could be carried out over the holidays, and the impending New South Wales election would intervene. No one wanted the distraction of a federal spill playing havoc with Morris Iemma's chances in March. By April the winter recess would be about to begin, and it would be too close to the election to risk a change. But they didn't know that Gillard and Rudd had reached an accommodation. They were blind-sided. They had thought that Gillard's personal ambition would mean the two aspirants would never be able to form a team.

A Labor delegation went on a visit to China in November. National secretary Tim Gartrell was on the trip, along with Rudd and some of Rudd's key supporters. 'When I got on the plane, I thought it might be a bit difficult, because I'd already worked with four leaders in three-and-a-half years,' says Gartrell. 'I didn't want to see *any* plotting going on. Occasionally, Kevin would go to his room and he probably transacted some business, but he held it close to his chest.'

'When the pressure was off and as we were travelling around, he was quite good fun. He made an extremely knowledgeable tour guide,' Gartrell laughs. 'I asked him about some earthworks near the Great Wall, and Kevin was able to explain about how students had been sent to work in the fields here during the Cultural Revolution.'

While Rudd was in China, on 21 November, Beazley's office forced him to issue a statement of support for the leader. 'Kim Beazley has had my consistent support since his return to the leadership ... my support continues for him as leader,' announced Rudd.

Journalists immediately telephoned Rudd's office and asked his spokesman to help them interpret what this meant. 'Mr Rudd has said repeatedly that Kim Beazley will lead Labor to the next election (and) that remains his position,' said the spokesman. It was like being back in Beijing, trying to interpret the meaning of words in statements issued by the Communist Party. It was obvious now that every word was being chosen with extreme care. The meaning lay in what wasn't being said, and not in the sentences in black and white on the page.

As Rudd's supporters watched Beazley they became sadly confident that a final stumble was inevitable. 'Towards the end of the year, I think most of us had come to the conclusion Kim was stuffed,' says a player. 'We showed him stuff to try and get him to realise this himself. But he was so determined. He'd say, "Well, they'll have to come and knock me off." But if you say that, then of course they will.'

A more detached observer doesn't believe this was simply his natural pessimism. 'Beazley really showed me the meaning of courage at this time,' he says. 'Deliberately blind, maybe, but you've got to admire his front. There was him, his heart, and very little else. Certainly not the numbers. Well, I'd give him points for that.'

Another person in a key position remembers, 'At this time, Kim walked in and sat down in my office. I didn't know what I'd say if he asked me if a challenge was on. Instead he just talked and talked. Then he got up and left. I breathed out a huge sigh of relief.' Nevertheless, this person did keep his faith with the leader. While one of Beazley's supporters was overseas, he received a telephone call warning him to be ready to return for a ballot at any moment.

***

There was widespread dissatisfaction along with, as yet, no catalyst to provoke change. But the feeling was growing. Then came the fatal slip. Talking to the media, Beazley meant to console television personality Rove McManus over the death of his wife from cancer, but instead mistakenly used the name of a pre-eminent American political strategist, Karl Rove.

Rove is an unusual name. It is easy to see how Beazley could get them mixed up—particularly when he was familiar with Rove's strategic genius, but probably hadn't spent a lot of time watching McManus. However, a slip was the last thing that Beazley could afford. It appeared to be symptomatic of a lack of care and attention to detail. He'd had similar problems over finding the right names in the shadow cabinet, according to a colleague.

'Rove was a trigger,' says a plotter. 'Christmas was seen as a deadline. The closer we got to Christmas, the more people started to focus on the hard decision.'

One of Beazley's supporters says, 'I think the media were particularly savage in exposing Kim. It's the trivia of daily conversation. You think of how often in daily conversation you get a name wrong, or something like that. But then again, leaders don't need to and shouldn't comment on every bloody thing, anyway. Howard's taken to doing it, but it's not seemly,' she adds.

'What are leaders doing, commenting on this sort of stuff? It's a trap,' she continues. 'Soon the prime minister and the leader of the opposition become just another part of this "celebrity club". That slips down a very dangerous slope because it degrades the whole political process, although this is something that Howard has been happy to exploit.' This is an issue that quickly touches a raw nerve in politicians. 'The media is so saturated with celebrity culture that journalists feel quite appropriate bouncing up and asking what do you think about so-and-so, but it's got nothing to do with running the country,' she continues. 'It becomes a feedback loop. It's part of the dumbing down of political discourse.'

Now the media had their event upon which they could pin the leadership discontent. 'Look,' says one of the plotters, 'it still might not have happened. Right up until that final moment, there'd been support and stability.'

A couple of people, in particular, who understood the media's need for a story, kept feeding titbits to a few journalists. It was never too much; just enough to keep the speculation on the boil. The media took the leadership-challenge story on. It was now up to Labor to provide an ending. The pressure intensified. Rudd was poised for the right moment to act.

The operation had been anticipated by some, but it wasn't planned. All of Rudd's supporters had an objective, and they were acting to achieve it—although not in concert. The awareness of a need for renewal grew.

'Others, who had not been prepared to support a change in the past, suddenly changed their view,' says an independent MP. 'Everybody was talking to everybody else about this political problem, how we were drifting, and the sort of dismal feedback that was coming from the electorate.'

Beazley had earlier hoped to nip any challenge in the bud. This explained why he had demanded the earlier expression of support from Rudd while he was in China. Although the leader had become increasingly isolated, he apparently still couldn't believe that Rudd and Gillard had reached an accommodation in which she would be prepared to accept the deputy's job. But to stave off a challenge, Beazley needed to turn events to his advantage. Unfortunately for him, every step seemed to turn into a stumble.

A timetable for a challenge was set in place almost immediately. The 'Rove' slip became the catalyst. The argument emphasised that if Kim could stuff up like this at his own news conference, he couldn't be relied on to avoid slip-ups during an election campaign. Bob McMullan quickly became aware there was movement going on. 'Once I knew that there was an agreement, and the challenge would be Rudd 1, Julia 2, I didn't have to ring round and ask anybody how they'd vote.

It was obvious the challengers were going to win.'

Carmen Lawrence was in a painful quandary. She had wanted change at the beginning of 2005, but that was before Beazley had successfully returned to lead the party. By this time she was desperately worried that it had become too late to shift. She decided to support Beazley for two reasons. First, she felt it was unfair not to give him the chance after he'd worked so hard to put the party in a competitive position. But her second reason was just as significant. 'I didn't think nine months would be long enough to do all the hard work that was still necessary before the election,' she said. 'It seemed to me that the task we were asking Kevin to perform was too massive to be achieved by anyone.'

One parliamentarian describes what happens during this lobbying process. 'Sometimes people say, "I'll vote for you," but then they end the mobile-phone call. They're lying. You need to front them, look at their eyes, and listen to how they're saying things. And after that you need to convince them.' He might have added, 'And frighten them, too.' For all the supposed factional discipline, there is always the chance of a maverick.

Four days before the vote, one of Beazley's number-crunchers told him that he didn't have the numbers to win. As soon as the news got out that Gillard had agreed to support Rudd, the result seemed a foregone conclusion to everyone who could count. But in the lead-up to the vote, Beazley was really trying to win. He was now campaigning the only way he could—publicly—and attempting to fire up support that might, somehow, convince some of the waverers to drift back into his camp. They never did.

Beazley knew he needed to do something to make up the numbers. He decided that, rather than just having a ballot for the leadership, he would spill all the positions—that is, all frontbench jobs would be up for grabs.

'It was a flawed tactic,' says one of Rudd's team, 'and another occasion where Kim was badly advised. It wasn't Beazley's idea; it came from people around him. It suggested to waverers that their best hope for a frontbench slot was not to back Kevin.'

Beazley was desperate to hang on. This was the nuclear option. It forced everyone to consider their own jobs and not just the leadership. The problem was that it looked like a reckless tactic, and Rudd was able to counter it by offering stability.

Beazley could still command a great deal of personal respect and affection amongst the caucus members. However, it was significant that most of the younger, ambitious politicians had decided to throw their support behind Rudd.

Senator George Campbell was one of Beazley's loyal supporters. He was well aware of the numbers, but wanted to do what he could for his leader. He had just flown back from New York the day before so he could be present for the caucus vote. Back in Sydney, he'd just missed a phone call from Rudd because he'd ducked out of the house for a moment. He wanted to call back before catching the plane to Canberra, but decided not to when he reached the airport lounge and saw that Beazley was waiting for the same flight.

Another Beazley supporter, Daryl Melham, joined them. Although Melham had resigned from Beazley's shadow cabinet in 2000 over a point of principle, he was now sticking with the leader. The three, now joined by Beazley's wife, discussed the challenge.

'Kim must have known what was going to happen,' says Campbell, 'but he didn't chicken out. He's a very brave man. There is no problem with his ticker.'

'There are only two possibilities,' says a politician who voted for Rudd. 'Beazley knew he was going to lose, or the people around him are very bad counters. No, my respect for Beazley grew because of his determination to see it through.'

'Maybe he did have that last little straw of hope that things were going to get better,' said one of Beazley's team just after the vote. 'He might have been hoping that someone would fold, or get the wobbles, and then he would win.' But, by the time he left his office and turned the corner to walk past the waiting journalists and cameras, and then marched down the long corridor to the caucus room, he must have known. 'I always feel that people underestimate Kim,' said one of those who didn't vote for him that day. 'He's a person of considerable integrity and courage. But, since 1998, he hasn't successfully conveyed the determination he displayed that morning to the electorate. It just wasn't getting through.'

***

The formalities of the caucus meeting were straightforward. The chairman, Melham, read out the letter from Beazley throwing open his position. Beazley moved a motion giving effect to his letter. Melham asked for nominations, and Beazley and Rudd put their names forward. There were no speeches, and the vote went ahead straight away. Counting the votes was not a long process. The result was formally announced.

There was still the deputy's position to resolve. 'Julia didn't have enough votes to topple Jenny,' insists one of her backers. 'No, Jenny definitely had the numbers to win the deputy's position, but she realised that it would have been impossible for her to work with Kevin. Not because she didn't like him, but because there had been so much publicity about the "new team". If Julia hadn't become deputy, Rudd would have been utterly crippled in the public's mind right from the start.' Macklin decided to withdraw from the contest.

When this is put to one of the numbers men, he laughs. 'You don't have to believe everything you're told. Even if there was a possibility of her winning, it would not have been in the best interests of the party.'

So who would have won if it was a contest? Senator Faulkner says, 'I think Jenny made the right decision, albeit a very difficult one. It's a clear case of someone taking a course of action that she believed was in the best interests of the party. I say full credit to her.'

First Rudd and then Gillard gave a speech. Accidentally, she forgot to thank Macklin. Rudd stood up and corrected the oversight. With tears in her eyes, Macklin came forward and embraced Rudd. It was the signal for a cathartic release of tension.

Afterwards, a couple of members retreated to their rooms to be alone with their thoughts, and, in at least one case, to cry. 'It was intelligent apprehension on their part,' said one of Rudd's supporters. 'Everyone was terribly sad.' Beazley didn't know during the caucus meeting that his brother had died; he found out only when he returned to his office. People's perspective was affected because of the combination of events. Many knew Beazley's father and mother, both in their nineties, and felt a genuine sadness for them, losing one son and watching the other's hopes, for which he'd worked so long and hard, suddenly snuffed out.

'Everyone could see that the lingering bitterness from the rivalry between Beazley and Crean could still destroy the party if it was allowed to continue,' says another MP. Whatever else happened, these tensions could not be allowed to resurface. 'There was a real resolve to draw a line under the past,' he says.

That night, Rudd and Swan had a long, emotional talk in the leader's office. Their differences were sorted out, and a working accommodation was reached. Swan remained shadow treasurer. Anthony Albanese, who had supposedly supported Beazley, retained his job as manager of opposition business, although he lost Environment to Peter Garrett. The reshuffle was about much more for Rudd than just settling differences. He understood that the real work had just begun.

'Suffice it to say,' says Fitzgibbon, 'that a lot of work went into re-establishing harmony in caucus. This was absolutely critical to the party's future success. The harmony in the party has been remarkable. We want to win.'

CHAPTER NINE

Leader

2007–?

> 'Is there such a thing as moral knowledge? Is there moral progress? These questions are not answered by science, or religion, or metaphysics, or logic. They have to be answered from within our own moral perspective.'
>
> – Simon Blackburn, *Being Good*

This is the point at which Rudd's biography intersects with the continuing story of Australia. From this point on, everything he's done has taken on a public dimension. His actions will be judged through the lens of his aspiration to become prime minister.

This is a harsh, unforgiving standard to apply to anyone. Despite an attempt to carefully craft his image to ensure that he is viewed as being up to the job, there have been slip-ups. This is only natural, and Rudd's early extended honeymoon with the voters has suggested that ordinary Australians were willing to forgive these mistakes. Nevertheless, his desire to achieve perfection has revealed previously hidden vulnerabilities.

This new phase of his life began its public play when, just after two o'clock on the fourth of December 2006, Rudd walked into a packed media conference at Parliament House. He stood behind a lectern in the opposition party room and announced to the assembled journalists that he had been elected leader of the federal parliamentary Labor Party. He then paid tribute to Beazley, wishing him the 'deepest condolences at this difficult time'—a reference to the death of his brother.

Australia, he insisted, had come to a 'fork in the road'. He was so pleased with this analogy that he repeated it nearly a dozen times. Latham had offered voters a ladder; Rudd focused instead on choice. When tackled on the detail of the alternative he was offering, he promised it would come later. By and large, people were prepared to accept this and to give him some time to elaborate the detail instead of expecting a package that could be unwrapped at once.

Rudd didn't want to alienate any of Beazley's supporters, and so at that time he was very careful not to insist that he'd be setting out on a new policy direction. He decided to focus on style, because this was one thing that every voter had an opinion about.

'John Howard has a first-class honours degree in clever politics,' Rudd told the *Sydney Morning Herald* later. He was positioning himself as somehow appealing to older, traditional values as he claimed he'd be borrowing his political style from the longest-serving conservative prime minister of them all, Sir Robert Menzies. 'There was always a set of obligations binding those in power to those who had none,' said Rudd. 'Not everything that Menzies did was bad ... I don't apologise for one bit that I am basically a fiscal conservative. Always have been, always will be.'

Right from the beginning, Howard didn't understand what Rudd was doing, or how it was being achieved. Barely an hour after Rudd had finished his first press conference as Labor leader, the prime minister walked out of his office and into his neighbouring courtyard to address the media.

John Howard thought he knew exactly what he needed to do as he walked out that sunny afternoon. The entire strategy hadn't been fully formulated, but he appeared supremely confident.

He couldn't resist a subtle dig at his new opponent. He used his ostensible congratulations to twist a stiletto into the apparition of Rudd's lack of experience. 'Leading a political party is an infinitely more challenging and difficult task than it appears,' he suggested. This was followed with a 'personal note' of sympathy for Kim Beazley, the leader he had spent the best part of the last decade attempting to destroy.

The prime minister knew quite well that neither of these comments would be reported as news, but they helped him establish a new rhetorical dynamic. Rudd had been painted, swiftly and very subtly, as inexperienced. There was also the implication of irresponsibility in overthrowing an established, competent leader. Rudd was portrayed as the new kid on the block, a theme that Howard continued to try to push over the following months. He would find it backfired very soon; the polls told him so, because it emphasised the prime minister's own age. The length of time that he'd spent in the job was quickly to turn into a negative for the prime minister.

The prime minister swiftly turned the meaning of Rudd's own words to work against the new leader when Rudd had promised a 'different style'. 'The Australian people want substance from their politicians, not style,' asserted the prime minister. By casting Rudd as just a new face carrying old policy-baggage, he tried to dismiss any prospect that the new leader would bring change. 'Labor has re-shackled itself to the past,' he proclaimed.

It was the beginning of an extraordinary attempt to cast the decade-old coalition as fresh, and Labor as tired. It was an old theme that the government had offered up before: threaten the voters that their prosperity is in danger if Labor gains office. He argued that Rudd's 'fork in the road' was a choice between an aspirational future with the coalition or a trade union-dominated past under Labor.

Howard began with an attack on policy. 'I'm a little surprised that somebody who has craved the [leader's] position is so little different policy-wise,' asserted the prime minister. But Howard was also unable to clearly get the range of his younger challenger. He claimed, 'I never underestimate my opponents,' but would not comment on the strengths and weaknesses of Rudd. In retrospect, it appears that Howard didn't understand the threat that Rudd posed.

This understanding would only come later. At that time, it looked as if Rudd would be denied a honeymoon at all. The Sydney *Daily Telegraph* was so caught-up in fury that it could barely manage to fit four vitriolic words across its front page. 'Conga line of hypocrites' screamed the paper, desperately trying to link Rudd and Latham. As readers read the report, it must have been difficult for them to work out exactly what had inspired such salivating hyperbole. But it was exactly the sort of headline that Howard desperately needed.

Ironically, although Rudd positioned himself as an insider in policy terms, he was actually something of an outsider. Except with those he knew well and closely trusted, he always retained a distance in his personal engagements with many of the people he relied on to transmit his message to the voters.

This may, in part, explain Howard's early mis-judgement of Rudd. He just didn't understand how much work would soon be put into developing a sophisticated, policy-based strategy that was targeted at tearing him from office.

Perhaps most importantly, New South Wales Labor Party polling had identified another key issue that the Liberal analysis had completely glossed over. Voters believed that it was Howard who had somehow 'changed'. Focus-group research had picked up a perception in the community that people didn't feel the prime minister was, somehow, the person that they'd voted for.

This was dynamite. It meant that voters were beginning to think that it was the government that had broken the electoral 'contract' with the voters. As a result, people were suddenly prepared to consider looking around for an alternative. In the past, under Beazley, they'd already gazed at Labor's offering but found it not up to scratch. Now they were looking again. Paradoxically, in that first week in which he was leader, Rudd didn't position himself as the 'opposite' of their prime minister. He was reassuring—different in many ways, but similar in others.

Extraordinarily, just two days after he became leader, Rudd was to find himself twice voting alongside Howard on an issue of conscience. At 6.17 p.m. and 7.29 p.m. on the sixth of December, the house divided on the issue of embryonic stem-cell research. A Bill had been put forward allowing the cloning of human embryos. Without it, there were fears that research into Parkinson's and other terrible diseases would have to stop.

Rudd claimed no moral superiority for his view. 'I realise that in taking this decision I will disappoint many,' he said. 'But I have to be true to myself, even when it may be unpopular.'

He was careful to qualify exactly why he was taking this stand. 'Some say that if you have (these) views,' he said, 'it mandates a classically conservative approach to a range of questions. I do not agree.' Using sex as an example, Rudd continued, 'These are very much matters for the individual—individual choices which should be respected, just as the privacy of people's personal relationships should be respected.'

Rudd voted with John Howard and with Peter Costello and Tony Abbott against the Bill as it slowly progressed through the parliament. A few Labor members stood with him, including Peter Garrett. Rudd was scheduled to attend drinks with the press gallery at the time, but the journalists were left nursing their beers as they waited for Rudd to appear. There was no way the new leader would take an opportunity to miss this particular conscience vote, despite the fact that his stance would be unpopular with many of those on his own side.

What many of those parliamentarians opposing the Bill had in common was their belief in a Christianity that could not accept the cloning of embryos simply for the purpose of research. This had to do with their view about when life was created. A majority of parliamentarians, however, voted to pass the Bill—including Julia Gillard, Alexander Downer, and other people with strong Christian beliefs such as Bruce Baird.

Rudd voted the way he did because of his personal principles. Nevertheless, in doing so he proved he couldn't be pushed into any confined box.

***

Rudd's new front bench reflected his need to impress business. Emerson took on the service economy and small business. This was much more than a sop for Rudd's fellow Queenslander. 'I hadn't been sitting around and thinking, oh, I hope I get small business, the service economy, and independent contractors,' he said later. His immediate reaction was one of surprise, he said, although it didn't take him long to realise the positives. 'I remember thinking almost immediately, oh, that's good, there's some real opportunity in that. It's a front-line portfolio in terms of our prospects of winning this election.'

'I think you can end up with quite important portfolios in government,' Emerson says, 'which don't offer you much opportunity to improve your chance of winning the next election. This does. I can develop policies that will appeal to a group of people who normally vote Liberal. The government's become very complacent about this constituency. After speaking to Kevin, I really got the feeling that this was not just a spot to "slip Emmo into"; it actually is a big area where we need to develop good policy.'

'It's easy to come up with ideas that sound good in opposition,' says Emerson, 'but are pretty superficial in reality. You know—let's reduce "red tape in government" by 50 per cent! It sounds good, but it's meaningless. John Howard promised that in 1996, and we're still waiting. But what does it mean?'

Bob McMullan was brought back to the front bench with a new portfolio covering federal-state relations. It had been silly to leave such an experienced player on the backbench. As Labor ran all the states, it made sense to put a former national secretary—who intimately understood the concerns of the smaller governments—into this role. It was also a smart move politically. The idea of Labor in government right across Australia represented a possible political negative. This was a cunning way of trying to turn it into a positive.

Kim Carr also had a new portfolio covering innovation, science, and research. He'd been a vital powerbroker in the relationship with Gillard and, as he was from the party's left, this new role emphasised the fact that Rudd was about much more than simply letting laissez-faire economic policy run rampant across the country. This portfolio was created to try to visualise new directions for manufacturing industry.

Peter Garrett was promoted, adding climate change to the environment portfolio as a means of strengthening opposition to the government in this vital area. Penny Wong dealt with public administration and accountability, and corporate government and responsibility. Chris Bowen took over revenue and competition policy. The line-up represented a new approach.

As always in politics, the biggest issues are the personal ones. As we have seen, the evening after Rudd became leader he met his former friend Swan for a talk in Rudd's office. After a long and emotionally charged discussion, the two decided to put an end to their past differences. Each realised they needed the other to bring Labor into government. Swan remained shadow treasurer; anything else would have been seen as a demotion. If he'd been shifted, the media would have seized on this as a clear indication that Rudd had bought his way into office by promising this plum portfolio to one of his supporters.

The pay-off for the decision to revamp the shadow ministry came when the prime minister finally announced he was shifting people in his own ministry. The *Sydney Morning Herald* greeted the new-look Liberal ministry with contempt. 'Same old age spots, same old wrinkles; for the most part, John Howard's new faces look mighty familiar,' the paper editorialised.

Over January, while Howard enjoyed the view of Sydney Harbour from Kirribilli House, Rudd was hard at work in Brisbane. Rudd was working in the Commonwealth Offices at Waterfront Place in Brisbane. There, on the 36th floor overlooking Brisbane River, the elements of the program to take to the election were put together. The building is modern; its sparkling atrium of polished steel and black marble creates reflections that turn back in on each other. The sharp sheen of the building is emphasised by the tingle of lifts racing up and down the building. It's inspiring architecture, full of possibilities: a radical contrast to the ageing Georgian façade of the Brisbane Polo Club next door.

Rudd was desperate to come up with a new agenda and to put it out in the media. But, ironically, he was to use much of the work that had earlier been completed by Beazley. Rudd simply relaunched policies after tweaking them, to a generally warm reception in the media.

Rudd was aware of a dual political problem that Labor had to resolve. He had to push out new policies, and also demonstrate that these were not simply a rehash of 'old Labor' ideas. Bob Hawke had established the model for this—the Accord—which was a coming-together of different parties that would allow them to talk through options to solve the problems and reach a resolution.

It seems that Rudd decided to do the same thing by meeting with various interest groups. In this way, he could assure them that their contributions were valued and their needs understood, and that any solution would be based on a consensus that would achieve a workable, lasting solution.

Climate change represented an obvious issue to tackle in this way. The problem loomed over the future of the economy, and yet the government had failed to directly address it. No unilateral solution would be workable, and as a result it demanded the input of different participants in the debate. In this simple way, Rudd was able to fill a political vacuum with his own ideas.

This positioned the opposition as the party of the future. Rudd was aware that, in the past, Howard had won by concentrating on the present moment. At first, Howard had promised that Australia could become 'relaxed and comfortable' rather than traumatised by continuing political debate. By 1998, voters were being told the government needed to introduce a Goods and Services Tax at once. This could no longer be put off to some indeterminate future, because the country's economic security was at risk without it. In 2001, it was the immediate security environment that supposedly mandated the return of the government. The coalition continued to push present needs to the fore at the 2004 election, although this time it was the economic threat to individual prosperity that Labor supposedly represented that was highlighted.

Until 2007, the arguments based around the present, urgent requirements of the current moment had offered a trump card that Howard had exploited with brilliance. But now he was being challenged on new ground: the future. It was here that Rudd sought to entrench himself, and Labor.

With federal-state relations, he had to arrive at some genuine proposals to put to the premiers—and they had to be ambitious ones. This required a willingness to do the hard policy 'wonking'. It also meant that in his initial period as opposition leader, Rudd would be submerged as he tackled the challenge of defining a new policy agenda, particularly in areas that weren't already part of the old Labor policy platform, such as climate change and the Murray-Darling river system.

'There was actually nothing magic about the polls, or re-releasing some policies,' says one Labor member who didn't vote for Rudd. 'But, I'll admit, people had just stopped listening to Kim. Kevin has given them the chance to view us afresh,' he adds.

'Rudd's got a consultative style,' says Lindsay Tanner, a book-writing Labor MP. 'He gets the balance right between consulting and leading. His natural style is to set out a course of action, talk to people, and then make a decision. In opposition you don't have the support to do that.'

Tanner leaps to Rudd's defence when it is suggested that the new opposition leader is socially conservative. 'Don't try to read things into the fact that he voted, as an example, against embryonic stem-cell research. I voted for that Bill—but I did so with particular reservations. The debate has gone way past the traditional spectrum of the old left-right divide. Modern political issues lie outside this framework.'

'Look at the family,' Tanner continues. 'You can argue that this is the traditional right-wing approach. But privileging human relationships moves beyond that, and beyond issues of economic distribution. This doesn't make for easy analysis.'

Rudd went to Tasmania, where he met Labor MP Dick Adams. He was photographed with timber-workers. 'I've had very easy conversations with him,' says the Tasmanian. 'Unlike Latham, he seems to understand this region.'

Michael Cooney had occasional disagreements with Rudd when he was working as Latham's senior adviser. Now heading up a Labor think-tank, he's very positive about Rudd's role as the successor to Beazley. 'Kim understood the electorate needed to be reassured,' says Cooney, 'but he also embodied that reassurance in a way that made it difficult to argue the case for changc. Kevin is naturally orientated towards thinking.'

Beazley himself is also surprisingly positive. 'Our luck has turned,' he says. 'All the hot-button issues work in our favour. Sharp differences make it very difficult for the government. The Liberals had one chance to win the election this term, and that was to switch to Costello peacefully.' The old leader is now very much behind Rudd.

Rudd proved himself adroit with his handling of the political debate. Just after Rudd's election, Howard canvassed the idea of a 'citizenship test'.

Tony Burke, who had responsibility for immigration, comments on what happened next. 'Old Labor would probably have gone straight out and called the idea ridiculous. Rudd said to me, "Hang on a minute. Let's ask for a list of the questions." Of course, the government hadn't written a single one of the questions. It was blown out of the water for the stunt that it was.'

'That's the advantage of Rudd's obsession with detail.'

***

The day before parliament first sat in 2007, Rudd called all party members in, for a four-hour seminar—something unheard of in the past. It was a warts-and-all analysis of where the party needed to make progress. Hugh McKay provided a briefing about the mood of Australia, and of the larger socio-economic picture.

'Getting us all back early was a real risk,' says Burke, 'because, historically, it's not always good. If there's ever a day where built-up tensions in the caucus might suddenly unleash themselves in a very negative way, it's when you're told you've got to go back to Canberra early on a Sunday morning.'

It was a traditional team-building exercise. The only thing lacking seemed to be the sort of game where executives are given a rope and two planks, and told to get across a river. There was no need for this sort of activity because, with just months to go until the election, everyone had become utterly focused on the need to win.

This new desire for victory demonstrated itself in unusual ways. At the church service for the opening of the new parliamentary year there was, surprisingly, a big turn-out of Labor members. 'It was unheard of,' says Quick. 'Even Anthony Albanese was there.'

The day before the service was held, an MP had stood up and addressed the Labor caucus. 'Look,' he said, 'the church service will be on early tomorrow morning. We are always embarrassed because there's only ever two or three of us there.' He finished his appeal, saying, 'Couldn't a few more of you come, please?' They did. For the first time in years, more Labor members attended the service than Liberals. It didn't represent any sudden mass-conversion, but it did have a lot to do with the new sense of unity and commitment in the party.

Early good poll-results left Rudd telling everyone to 'just take a cold shower'. After a little while, some friends suggested he needed a new scriptwriter to prepare these off-the-cuff comments, because his own natural words sounded a bit old-fashioned. Nevertheless, Rudd stuck with it, realising that this softened what could otherwise appear a hard rational edge.

Rudd adopted a different style. When promoting Labor, he didn't just preach at an audience; instead, he tried to persuade them. For example, he didn't bother appealing to the altruistic side of the business bosses. Instead, he emphasised that 'experience in Australia and other countries has shown collective-enterprise bargaining can achieve higher productivity and wage outcomes than systems based on individual contracts'.

In January, Rudd had his first dinner with the Business Council of Australia, the peak body of the top 100 companies in the nation. Mark Latham had attended a similar dinner in 2004, but it had turned into a public-relations disaster. This time, the Labor leader gave a speech carefully targeted at the audience. He stayed late into the night to answer questions and to speak individually to the business leaders.

Rudd argued that a new way of working could be achieved. 'Collective bargaining gives employers and employees the right incentives,' he said, so that they could 'work together to find ways to lift productivity and share the gains in (both) profits and pay'. It was a simple story that Rudd was telling the executives. Co-operation would pay dividends.

This was also part of a sophisticated strategy. The unions were effectively mobilising support against the Howard government's industrial-relations changes, so Rudd realised he didn't need to address this. Instead, Rudd publicly reassured bosses that, 'Despite the conventional wisdom, the government's record suggests that conservative governments are more likely to over-regulate than deregulate.'

However, sending different messages to different audiences eventually caused problems. Rudd had been desperate to tell the bosses he was focused on outcomes, and was not shackled by old shibboleths. Eventually, the union movement demanded he come out firmly on their side. When Rudd did this at Labor's national conference it caused severe ructions with employers, who felt badly let down.

Similarly, tactical manoeuvring didn't allow him to escape the past. Problems threatened Rudd whenever he sought to talk about Iraq. When he was asked on ABC Radio what the consequences of a withdrawal might be, he replied, 'I am not in the business of providing a rolling external commentary.'

The government knew that Latham's promise to bring the troops home by Christmas had been the moment from which his collapse in the polls had begun. Gleefully, conservative commentators jumped on his comments and tried to brand Rudd as adopting Latham's policy. Howard asserted that Rudd just 'didn't have the guts' to express what he really thought, with the implication that Labor would 'cut and run' from Iraq.

But the big difference now was that three long years had passed since Mark Latham had made his earlier sudden promise to bring the troops home. Today, instead of talking about 'victory', the government's rhetoric had begun to shift. There was also the extraordinary admission that the original aim of creating a viable working democracy in Iraq might not be achieved. So, although the government thought it could use this to attack Rudd, it was unable to gain any traction from the issue.

This had a startling effect in unsettling the government. By now, watching Howard destroy opposition leaders had become a spectator sport for Liberal backbenchers, who remained comfortable in the knowledge that their majorities were growing each time the prime minister launched his bruising attacks. But this was different.

Quite suddenly, Howard began to look his age. Shrilly, his attacks continued, and the government became more and more frustrated every time Rudd ducked or weaved around the assault. In the media, some columnists tried to suggest that the issue was really the opposition leader himself.

The Australian's foreign editor, Greg Sheridan, was one of those to extol what Howard had achieved. 'First, climate change completely disappeared' from the debate, he claimed—somewhat prematurely as it turned out. 'Second, Howard managed to introduce doubt about Rudd's character,' he asserted. 'Howard has a very strong point on substance. If you favour pulling coalition troops out of Iraq, you must say what you think the consequences of this would be.'

But Rudd realised this was rubbish; he didn't need to explain the consequences. That was the trap that Latham had fallen into. Instead, he continued to stand just out of Howard's reach. In *The Australian*, cartoonist Bill Leak started to picture Rudd as Tintin, shaping up to a Howard who was, by now, being shown wearing the American combat uniform.

'Drawing Kevin as Tintin was a stroke of genius,' says a political observer. 'Tintin never ages. He looks very clean, but he can emerge unscathed from all sorts of disasters. He is young, but he is not naïve because he outwits all the villains.' It's the sort of gift most politicians can only dream of.

There was no doubt that a simple message had been conveyed to the Labor faithful: Rudd could see no future in keeping troops in Iraq. Nevertheless, he had been careful to avoid giving a commitment that the government would use to tear him apart, instead keeping the focus on Howard's Iraq policy.

The dynamics of the Iraq debate had changed, and so had Australia.

Graham Morris has been one of the prime minister's inner circle of advisers since well before the 1996 campaign that vaulted the coalition into office. 'The government's job is to paint change as a risk,' he says. 'Those who decide elections do so on the basis of simple self-interest.' This is, perhaps, a venial view of the electorate, but that doesn't make it incorrect.

Morris leans forward. 'The wealthy and the academics can

tut-tut about things—but it's the worries about paying off the mortgage and buying the kids' shoes that really count.'

Morris calls these people the election-deciders, and these are the voters that Howard has appealed to in the past. By focusing on the simple, bread-and-butter issues that are vital to them, the government has been able to harness the advantage of incumbency to deal with ordinary people's immediate needs. Labor found itself, instead, talking about the future.

Rudd needed to try to find a way to bring the future into the present. He tackled this in a simple way. With climate change, he came up with a policy that empowered individuals by promising to offer subsidies to people who install rainwater tanks. The effectiveness of this has been debated, but the psychological importance cannot be underestimated. It allows those concerned about the issue to feel they are being rewarded for doing the right thing.

Another similar initiative was the promise to pay for the development of a national, fast broadband network. There was some negative publicity accruing from the use of the Future Fund to pay for this; however, it was generally welcomed by voters.

Other things worked well for Rudd. The increasing crossover between celebrity culture and politics can have a double-edged effect, as John Howard soon began to realise. Gossip moves at a much faster speed than politics. So does the gossip culture that has become so pervasive in the media. This has an effect as it takes over material, re-works it, and then sets a new agenda for public discourse. Things change fast, and this has a cascading effect.

'That picture of Howard that *The Australian* used the other day was very revealing,' says a senior Labor politician. 'It was taken very close up. You could see every wrinkle. He was clinging on to the dispatch box. He was frowning. He looked like a very cranky old man. And that's all in one photograph.'

She points out that with a picture like that, it's not necessary to tell people that Howard is looking old. It's all laid out for people to draw their own conclusions. 'The reason that that particular shot was used was to illustrate precisely this point. There are lot of photographs they could have used, but they chose to use that one to illustrate the particular error, forgetfulness, that Howard made. It *implies* exactly why he may have made those particular mistakes.'

***

Thérèse also had to make changes. She stepped down as chair of her company. 'Basically, I'm preparing to support Kevin over the next few months or whenever the next federal election is,' she said. 'We've always supported each other—he's supported me and I've supported him.'

This was not a small step for her to make. By now, her company had revenues of $175 million and employed 1,300 people in 66 offices around the world—in Australia, Britain, France, and Germany. It was also the third-largest provider of services to the government's Job Network agency.

Labour sources say she probably won't step down from running the company if Rudd becomes prime minister.

***

Rudd continued to work all the time. In fact, some Labor people became concerned that he was pushing himself beyond normal endurance levels. Others became frustrated at his intervention and what they felt was micro-management.

This dedication to work was demonstrated on 23 January 2007, when he was said to have phoned ABC Radio at 3.00 a.m. to give a news reporter an interview. Undoubtedly, Rudd works around the clock but, unfortunately, the ABC doesn't.

Only an international cable sub-editor was working at the time. It appears there may be an element of myth-making in this particular story.

Meanwhile, the rosy morning-after effect between Labor's leader and the electorate was continuing. It couldn't last, and it didn't.

There is now universal agreement that Kevin Rudd's extraordinary political honeymoon with the electorate ended at some time after 2.18 p.m. on the first day of March 2007. Later describing the moment in large headlines, both *The Australian* and the *Canberra Times* insisted that the government's attack in parliament that day had emphatically ended the honeymoon. The political editor of the *Age*, Michelle Grattan, affirmed that its dissolution had been formalised by an official pronouncement from the Labor leader's office.

The government had saved up its attack for that particular Thursday because it was the final sitting-day for nearly three weeks. Question Time normally provides an opportunity for the opposition to savage the government; a carefully crafted question can act like a rapier, slicing through anticipated defences. But this time the Liberals decided to turn the tables.

Rudd pretended to ignore what was going on in this forum that the government dominated. But, even as opposition leader, you can't control everything. The time had to come when the government would find a weak point that Rudd would have to defend. Their missile came from Western Australia in the form of one-time Labor premier Brian Burke.

The federal politicians had watched over the previous weeks as the stench from the west had spread, claiming the scalps of three state ministers as it did so. Phone taps instituted by Western Australia's Corruption and Crime Commission had put beyond any doubt the degree of highly dubious influence that Burke still wielded over politicians in that state. The former premier, Geoff Gallop, had banned his cabinet from having any contact with Burke. But Rudd, unfortunately, had decided to ignore the unsavoury stench that had surrounded Burke's activities for years when he met him in 2005.

People stopped talking as Peter Costello walked to the table. By the end of his speech, as his finger jabbed towards Labor, the house was listening—the government benches erupting in joy that someone, finally, was laying a finger on Rudd. The opposition leader himself, still pretending not to pay attention to the tirade unleashed from the other side of the dispatch box, stopped writing. The allegations themselves were not necessarily significant. Certainly, no impropriety on Rudd's part was proved. But politics is about much more than this; it's about convincing people that you can be relied on to act correctly. It was not that Rudd lost the battle; more that he did not take to the field.

Costello accused Rudd of meeting with Burke for breakfast, lunch, and dinner, and only eventually deciding to cancel a further dinner that Burke had wanted to organise because journalists would be present. Costello asserted, 'Burke never does something for nothing ... anyone who deals with (Burke) is morally and politically compromised.'

Costello approvingly quoted Stephen Smith, the Labor member for Perth, who had not had a conversation with Burke for a decade and a half. Smith had said the activities of Burke deserved 'complete and absolute condemnation'. Yet, Costello insinuated, Rudd was ready to do business with a shady character. He accused Rudd of meeting Burke for political motives, to gain more backing in the west.

An observer comments, 'Rudd's contact with Burke was just pathetic. But then you weigh it up against what Howard has done taking us to war in Iraq. There is no comparison.'

Tellingly, particular aspects of Rudd's personality seemed to hinder his ability to respond that afternoon. He'd been confronted by something new, something that was not immediately susceptible to being analysed intellectually. John Howard leant across the table, seemingly goading Rudd to reply. Howard later said he offered to let Rudd make a speech to clear his name. 'The leader of the opposition has had his back turned the whole time. I do not know why he did not have the courage to get up,' Howard said. Again, at the end of Question Time an hour later, Howard offered to let Rudd speak.

Rudd's apparently clever tactic—of turning his back on the government—had backfired badly. He appeared stunned by the assault.

As the dejected Labor MPs walked back to their rooms, glumness appeared to envelop the opposition. Perhaps this was not just the end of the beginning, but the beginning of the end. Rudd had seemed unable to answer the devastating charges that had been laid by the government.

But once he was back in the opposition leader's office, Rudd was told he needed to immediately answer the charges. He was firmly told by one adviser that he should hold a press conference and 'remain there until he had answered every question'.

He did. And he answered questions for nearly three-quarters of an hour. His leadership was resuscitated, but others noted he should have been more nimble in the house.

Ironically, it was the government that eventually seemed to be damaged as a result of all the mud-slinging. Voters had decided they liked Rudd, so the mud stuck to the government instead of its target. Casualties from the affair mounted quickly.

Ian Campbell, the minister for human services, was quickly sacked as a result of having gone to a meeting which Burke had also attended. (He's since quit politics altogether.) Labor's shadow attorney-general, Kelvin Thomson, stepped down because, years before, he had given a reference to a notorious Melbourne underworld figure. Government ageing minister

Santo Santoro quit after it became apparent he had misled Howard over his personal share trading.

The abuse only stopped when Howard himself was accused of lunching in the same room as a convicted criminal and porn king. The smears ended up leaving everyone stained. According to the polls, most people quickly decided they weren't too worried about the meetings that Rudd had had with Burke in Perth. But some insiders noticed the way he had reacted to the attack.

The wobbly response was at least in part because Rudd preferred to move deliberately, rather than quickly. He also tended to lock himself into particular methods of engagement. For example, he thought he could ignore the dynamics of parliament. This caught him completely flat-footed and unable to respond.

Some on his own side drew the conclusion that he wasn't really as clever as he thought he was. When Rudd couldn't define the debate, and when he hadn't prepared for it, he could still be outmanoeuvred. They noted a rigidity of approach, and encouraged him to take more advice and to delegate more to other people.

***

The young, sharp public servant asked about the book I was writing.

'Kevin Rudd makes such a point of his virtue,' he suddenly expostulated, 'but I wonder how fully he's really thought through some of these ethical issues.' He quickly strode over to the bookcase before pressing a thin volume into my hands.

'Here, read this,' he said. 'It's all very well to insist on the need to act as a good Christian. But where does that position sit from a moral perspective?'

He referred to the way that Rudd—like politicians from

every side—receives an allowance for the time he spends in Canberra. 'Rudd was paying rent to his wife. A public servant would be sacked if they tried to do exactly what he did, when he took money while staying in his wife's house in Canberra.'

'What he was doing may have been completely legally correct, but is it ethical? It seems to me that you can't pick and choose your ethical positions simply dependent on what's in the Bible,' he continued. 'There's no divine guidance on exactly how or when travelling allowance can be accessed.'

'And the other thing is that since this was exposed, rather than admit there may be a problem with the entire way politicians are remunerated, he's just gone to ground,' continued the earnest young man. 'There's a problem there that should concern anyone who is worried about morality. But what have we heard? Nothing.'

'The biggest enemy of being good is hypocrisy.'

There is a very real sense in which the so-called Labor-leaning public intellectuals aren't prepared to share their views about Rudd. They think Rudd is their best chance to oust Howard. Yet many seem to harbour genuine unease about different aspects of the 'Rudd Project', as members of *Team Rudd* like to refer to the task of getting their candidate into the Lodge.

'He's not really all that clever—well, certainly not as clever as he likes to think he is,' says a university academic. 'When you begin to unpick some of the detail—like, for example, his assertions about Hayek—he's failed to understand what's really going on in (this economist's) work,' she says, referring to the 1974 Nobel Prize-winning economist.

She pauses for a moment and relents. 'Yes, oh well, it's all very well me saying that, isn't it? But at least Kevin is aware of who Hayek is. So as a starting point that isn't too bad.'

Jean Curthoys is another well-known social academic who is far more positive about Rudd's grasp of the intricacies.

'He has a sound understanding of the fundamentals and the virtues of the market. But I think this is infused with a social-democratic outlook. I don't think his critics have grasped this,' she says.

***

By 2007, both sides faced serious hurdles as they contemplated the looming election. For the coalition government, it was possible to juggle particular policies to make them more electorally appealing, and it had the immense resources to do so. But that's not the same as changing the mood of the electorate. And the opinion polls, as this book went to press, continued to show a hefty lead for Labor (as they had since Rudd's ascension to the leadership) and to indicate a strong desire for change.

Nevertheless, securing victory will still be an uphill battle for Labor. 'My judgement is that, although people don't like this government and they think it's tired, they still don't hate it,' says an experienced Labor strategist. 'People don't change government lightly in Australia. Whenever we've been the incumbent, an opposition has never beaten us by saying, "Here is a better alternative." '

He reflects on two relatively recent disasters for the ALP. 'In 1975 and 1996, the opposition just had to stand there as we fell out of office. But if we want to win this time, we'll have to wrest them out.' He says that's a big ask. 'We must convince people that enough good things are going to happen if we become the government to make voters really want to change.'

For the coalition as well, achieving victory requires overcoming significant vulnerabilities. Labor now needs just 3.3 per cent of voters to change their minds to allow it to form government. In early 2007, the psephologist Malcolm Mackerras became one of the few voting analysts who was (so far out from the election) prepared to stick his neck out and announce that Rudd would spend Christmas in the Lodge. 'All the circumstances that cause governments to lose are present in spades,' he boldly announced. Not everyone agrees.

'The polls are often illusory,' says a NSW Labor member who's been analysing them all his adult life. 'They show a "feel good" attitude to Kevin. But you don't call the winner of the Melbourne Cup 200 metres after they've left the barrier, when it is a 3,200-metre race,' he says, using a sporting analogy. 'Look at that famous Melbourne Cup where everyone called Kingston Town the winner with 400 metres to go. That was when Malcolm Johnston on Gurners Lane suddenly took off, and came up on the inside rails and beat him on the post.'

'People aren't prepared to switch in the numbers the polls are showing at the moment,' he adds. 'They're saying we're interested, but it's not more than that. People use polls in a sophisticated way, and they're giving the government a message.'

Mackerras has a different view. He began his career working as a Liberal Party staffer in the Menzies years, and remembers the overweening confidence that preceded the huge shock of 1961. 'It was days before the Liberals knew they'd just scraped back,' says Mackerras, 'and was a similar complacency, even arrogance, surrounding the government when Rudd took over.'

His argument asserts that seeds of arrogance accompanied the government's last victory, and that they've now bloomed into flower. The easy victories in 2001 and 2004 have masked real underlying electoral weaknesses. Mackerras insists that the swings of the political pendulum act like an inexorable law. Even if some supposedly marginal seats don't fall, others will, cancelling out the deviations from the mean.

This is why Mackerras believes Labor can win. 'People instinctively understand Howard's insolence,' he says. The word 'deceit' recurs in our conversation.

Then there's the other issue—that voters believe he's changed for the worse. The political scientist hints that, as Howard has spent more than a decade as prime minister, he's become surrounded by people who obsequiously flatter him. 'Inevitably, this must result in a degree of detachment from reality,' he says.

And then there is Rudd. 'Since World War II, popular opposition leaders have managed to get significant swings in their first tilts at government,' says Mackerras earnestly, before reeling off statistics. 'Let's see, Menzies in '46 received 4.6 per cent, and another 5 per cent in the next election. Calwell, 4.6 per cent—well, that still wasn't enough. Whitlam, 7.1 per cent in his first election, and then 2.5 per cent the next time around to win government.'

Mackerras goes on, but his point is clear. Hayden (4.2 per cent), Hawke (3.6 per cent), and Beazley (4.6 per cent in '98) all managed to achieve the sort of swing in their first election from opposition that would be more than enough to install Rudd as the next prime minister.

The concern remains that if Labor won federally, there would be wall-to-wall Labor governments across Australia. Balancing this concern is the fact that, even if it won government, Labor wouldn't control the Senate.

One Labor strategist insists, 'Australians don't like too much power being centralised anywhere. But they can understand the difference between state and federal jurisdictions and the role of the Senate.' Even though many people were sometimes confused about which layer of government had responsibility for specific services, he also asserted that people would be prepared to give Labor government.

Giving weight to this argument are the comments of an unusually forthright Liberal senator. 'In the end,' he says, 'voters have a basic understanding that if the government doesn't control the Senate, it can't do whatever it wants to do.

In fact, it might have actually been a bit of bad luck that we got control of the Senate at the last election, because it makes that argument a little bit more difficult to stick. But it doesn't mean we won't try it.' It is a cogent point, because Australians have never elected a government of one political persuasion in every state and federally at the same time.

***

Rudd's phenomenal popularity gave Labor a dramatic boost in the polls, and he attempted to continue developing policies while carefully controlling his image. But an emerging difficulty was Rudd's inclination to favour particular journalists—people he felt he could rely on.

This was used by some to suggest Rudd hadn't yet grasped the reality that he needed to work in a new way now that he was opposition leader.

An example of this was the way that he dealt with the press. The *Weekend Australian Magazine*'s Christine Jackman profiled the 'smooth-talking ex-diplomat' who 'is not afraid to play it hard in his bid to be PM'. There was no acknowledgement of the relationship between the politician and the journalist in the article, although their friendship was mentioned in another section of the paper.

The rival Fairfax magazine, the *Good Weekend*, also attempted to profile Rudd, but he was unavailable. Rudd was also unavailable to appear on the ABC's *Lateline* for a long period after he became leader, despite repeated requests. Labor politicians found they were subject to new controls as well. Text messages were sent on the mornings of parliamentary sitting-days, telling members which entrance they should use to enter the house and what, if anything, they should say to waiting journalists.

Initially, polite excuses about Rudd's unavailability because of his 'massive work-load' were accepted by journalists, but gradually these wore thin—particularly as Rudd seems always to be available for 'soft' interviews on music stations.

The mood changed with the publication of a story by Sydney's *Sun Herald* revealing that the details of Rudd's past didn't match the story that had become widely accepted, as discussed earlier in this book. Alan Ramsey in the *Sydney Morning Herald* revealed a stream of threats and telephone calls from Rudd and his staff as they tried desperately to get the earlier story pulled.

Melbourne radio announcer John Faine was next to go public with his frustration that Rudd had refused all interview requests so far in 2007. Rudd countered these accusations with a battery of media appearances, but he was still doing things his way.

Rudd liked to control the debate. Some journalists felt that he just didn't like being questioned.

In April 2007, the *Sunrise* program attempted to stage a 'fake' dawn service at the battlefield of Long Tan in Vietnam because it would better fit into Australian television schedules. This idea was only shelved after furious opposition from the veterans, who believed the timing of the event was significant, and far more important than a photo opportunity.

At first, Rudd indignantly denied any involvement with the false-dawn plan. Then a stream of emails emerged, demonstrating that his office was fully aware of all the details. Confronted with proof, Rudd blamed his staff and promised to 'counsel' them. Shortly after telling the Sydney *Daily Telegraph* that he'd continue to appear on the *Sunrise* program, Rudd decided to ditch his involvement with it.

As the first shivers of winter spread across the Australian landscape, it was possible to glimpse potential problems residing deep within Rudd's approach to politics. Until now, he'd made all the key decisions, with any input coming from a small coterie of advisers. But you can't run a leader's office like this. Rudd found he could not determine the media's agenda, and his failure to be forthcoming with detailed interviews on policy issues was not going to be sustainable.

Postscript

Kevin Rudd's management of the media has suggested not so much hubris as excessive self-confidence. He has continued to do things his own way and this has, at times, created resentment.

Paul Keating always claimed he was able to 'throw the switch to vaudeville'; he certainly possessed a remarkable ability to charm many in the electorate, but he also alienated huge numbers of people. For his part, Rudd has been keen to extend his profile beyond the usual groups that are involved in the political debate. This has seen him cooking and dancing in daytime television appearances, and doing 'light and fluffy' interviews on FM radio. But, in doing this, Rudd has severely restricted opportunities for the serious media to question the details of his policies.

Rudd is understandably keen to control his image. As I was working on this book, I came across numerous instances of this approach. There is no point in speculating why he attempted to prevent people who knew him well from speaking to me; it was obviously not a matter of time.

I finished the final draft of this book as autumn ended. I had first requested an interview with Rudd the day after he became leader. Shortly afterwards, I spoke to him at a drinks party, but he simply smiled and placed his hand on my shoulder before moving off to join another group. Rudd was unavailable to speak to me at any time between December 2006 and May 2007.

Through sheer coincidence, half an hour after I had pressed the 'send' button to dispatch the completed manuscript to my publisher in late April, Rudd's assistant telephoned to offer an interview at 4.00 p.m. the next day. This was after I'd tried for months to secure an interview, having been told that I would be granted one. I accepted, thinking that, although some of the 78,000 words I'd already written might subsequently require some rushed re-jigging, I shouldn't pass up the opportunity to clarify some issues. Several hours later, the assistant telephoned again—this time to cancel the meeting.

The next morning, I went to the opposition leader's press office in Parliament House. 'Mate, he's too busy,' said his staffer Lachlan Harris. 'And next week we're in Washington. Are you going to travel with him so you can do it over there?' he asked.

'Off course I would, if that's a serious offer,' I replied.

At that point, the mature voice of press secretary Walt Secord abruptly cut in. 'It was a rhetorical question,' he insisted. 'Look, we will get you in to see him when we can.'

An appointment was then scheduled in Brisbane in early May. Unfortunately, when I arrived, Rudd was not there: he'd found that he needed to be in Adelaide to deal with some matters that needed his urgent attention. I didn't get to meet him before this book had to be finished.

***

One of life's lessons is that not everything can be predicted, controlled, or melded into shape. In traditional Chinese society, the concept of 'order' possesses an intrinsic virtue. In a modern democracy like Australia, sometimes the only constant appears to be chaos.

Certainly, there is no fiercer crucible of personality than exalted office. The flattering attentions of commentators and the public can't help but accentuate the slightest degree of arrogance that resides in the hearts of those who pursue and attain power. At the same time, the remorseless attacks of others will crush an individual who possesses anything less than supreme self-confidence. These tensions have be resolved satisfactorily if they are not to lead to self-destruction.

The ancient Romans knew about such things. Successful Roman generals were granted the ceremonial privilege of a 'triumph'. Wearing armour and carrying weapons from their victory, they were given the honour of being driven through the city in a chariot to the adulation of the masses. It was a heady moment. Everyone was aware of the danger that an even greater ambition might be kindled within the breast of the commander. As a result, a slave was made to stand behind him in the chariot, chanting the Latin refrain '*sic transit gloria mundi*'—'all glory is transient'.

Does Rudd need a similar reminder? Or will his personal belief protect him from becoming over-mastered by pride?

The electorate seems to want to see more of this person whose development is still, at the age of fifty, far from complete. All that can properly be said is that Rudd has made Labor competitive again. Despite all the focus groups and polling, all the pundits and predictions, all the hopes and history, no one can know the outcome of the next election until the campaign is finished and the result revealed.

Rudd's old tutor has a point to make about this. 'The first of all the Chinese classics is the book of change,' says Ryckmans. 'The situation is always fluid. There is flux and change at bewildering speed,' he says. 'And that's where I think you come back to his old reference, Sir Thomas More. He was a consummate politician and a man of skill and ability who knew how to give way. But he also knew that, at a certain point, there is no more compromise.'

Rudd's friend Alan Griffin makes another point. 'He's a good thinker. That will help him, because the situation has changed from the time when Moses came down from the mountain with his tablets and said, "This is the way it is." Politics changes, and the answers change as well.'

Will Rudd just accept change, or will he try to change the world?

Notes

INTRODUCTION

All the quotes attributed to Kevin Rudd in this book come from parliament, his own articles, or other published interviews with him, apart from the conversation referred to in Chapter 2, which was provided to me by Catherine McGrath. I have spoken to as many people as possible in the course of researching this book. Some people asked not to be quoted directly, and I have respected the wishes of those who requested anonymity. Unless otherwise indicated, all quotes come from personal interviews.

PROLOGUE

Outlined some electoral history Political aficionados can always find ways of using statistics to emphasise their political point. Paul Keating insists that the 2004 result was worse than 1996, although Latham correctly points out that he actually won more seats at the election he contested.

Confronted one of the frontbenchers Mark Latham's *The Latham Diaries* (MUP, 2005) provide a fascinating glimpse into this period.

Latham had been scheduled The best book on Latham's fall is *Loner: inside a Labor tragedy*, by Bernard Lagan (Allen & Unwin, 2005). Latham's quote comes from a personal communication with Lagan after Latham had stopped responding to enquiries from other people. Some of Latham's staff have also provided me with information on this period.

First the phones start to ring Graham Richardson earlier chronicled the difficulty of attempting to work out where leadership votes would go. 'The telephone is such an inferior method of communication,' he wrote in his book *Whatever It Takes* (Bantam, 1994). 'On the telephone you can't see people's eyes, and when you can't see their eyes don't know whether they are telling the truth.' Richardson summed up the raw brutality of leadership challenges with relish. He insisted that 'once you made up your mind that somebody had to go in order to be replaced by someone better, it didn't matter at all whether he was a decent, caring person on the verge of canonisation or an absolute arsehole completely devoid of saving graces. If the king has to be brought down for the good of the party, then so be it. Any time spent worrying about the cruelty of executing such a nice fellow is time wasted. Any time feeling guilty about what you've done is even worse.'

Rudd decided to fold Rudd made his announcement that he would not contest the leadership on 24 January.

CHAPTER ONE: **Formation**

He enlisted on 15 July Albert Rudd was given the army number NX36658. His records are held in the National Archives.

Bert took up running a farm The comments on share-farming come from the Victorian Law Foundation website. It is scathing about the practice of share-farming. 'The tenant takes all the risks in a lease', it says on its website. The big plus is that 'the fruits of their labour go to them rather than the landowner' and this requires fewer financial commitments from the tenants. But the Foundation emphasises that this 'is often regarded as the stepping stone to buying a farm'. Michael Carroll described the current tribulations of these farmers in 2005 in a presentation to the Australian Bureau of Agricultural and Resource Economics (ABARE).

Rudd said later The details of Rudd's early life come from his maiden speech in Parliament, 11 November 1998.

Bert Rudd went to Brisbane Ellen Fanning reported on the hospital story for the *Sunday* program on Channel 9 on 4 March 2007. She was the first journalist to check the circumstances surrounding Bert's death. He volunteered the details of alcohol consumption in a statement to police.

Just after he became Labor leader The *Australian Women's Weekly* on January 2007 carried the first detailed and uncritical report on Rudd's childhood after his election to the leadership.

Later, Kerry-Anne Walsh The *Sun Herald* on 11 March 2007 carried an exclusive report by Eamonn Duff and Kerry-Anne Walsh after the two journalists became aware of the inconsistencies between Rudd's account of his family leaving the farm and the story of the events according to the children of the Low family.

But it was the unprintable background Ramsey's story ran on the last day of March. It provided a devastating indictment of what appeared to be an insistence that only Rudd's version of events should be told.

It's probably no wonder that the young boy used to bury himself in books Rudd spoke about the need for children to study with Philip Clark on Sydney's Radio 2GB.

Why he chose to study Asian languages Speaking to Catherine McGrath before an interview in 2007, Rudd looked surprised when asked why he wanted to get out of Nambour. His need to escape must have appeared so obvious to a young man.

The single word 'ambitious' *A Current Affair* reported on Rudd's 'ambition' just after he became leader of the ALP.

CHAPTER TWO: **China**

The information in this chapter was obtained by personal interviews.

CHAPTER THREE: **Goss**

The trip had been The opening quote comes from page 392 of Don Watson's magnificent opus, *Recollections of a Bleeding Heart* (Knopf, 2002).

As soon as he was offered the job According to a colleague, even by this stage Rudd had not been planning a political career. 'His self-image was that of a higher-flying diplomat in foreign affairs,' he says. 'Kevin got sidetracked.'

In fact, while he was on leave from Foreign Affairs, Rudd received two further promotions: to ASO8 a month after he'd left the department and then to the Special Executive Service (Level 2) on St

Valentine's Day in 1991. The love affair lingered, but it could not last forever. Eventually, bureaucratic fashions changed and it was no longer thought desirable for diplomats to be attached elsewhere. Rudd was given the opportunity to return, but no one expected he would. More than a decade after he'd begun as a Foreign Affairs trainee, he finally left the public service.

'hmmm ... this isn't good' Taylor's article ran in the March issue of the *Australian Financial Review Magazine*.

Many nitty-gritty domestic factors The decision to build an expressway from the Gold Coast to Brisbane was one of these issues that affected a number of seats that fell to the opposition. 'I always remember Graham Richardson saying to me on the night of the election that it was a pretty bloody expensive road, if it cost us government,' says Tom Burns. His view was that it would have been cheaper to shift the koalas. 'Some of our departmental heads let us down. I think the decision-making process was bloody ratshit.'

CHAPTER FOUR: **Backbencher**

Rudd was determined to take nothing for granted As is always the case, I've relied on the brilliant statistics and analytical research provided by the Parliamentary Library. These documents provide an unparalleled tool for dissecting the results of elections.

A significant danger The response to Barry Cohen's article was printed in the *Australian Jewish News*, 10 December 2004.

CHAPTER FIVE: **Shadow**

Later, Rudd lambasted the government Rudd's quotes come from the Parliamentary censure motion, 19 October 2006.

Brereton pronounced at that time Latham quotes Brereton in his *Diaries*, page 211.

CHAPTER SIX: **Frustration**

That Rudd wanted to be shadow treasurer Latham's *Diaries*, page 253.

Mackerras arrived at a startling conclusion Malcolm Mackerras analysed the crucial role that interest-rate sensitivity played in the election. He established the link between exposure to interest-rate movements and the propensity of people to vote Liberal. After the 2001 Census, the Parliamentary Library produced an analysis which ranked electoral divisions by the proportion of dwellings being purchased. Mackerras noted that the four Labor gains in 2004 had fewer than 22.2 per cent of people paying off their mortgages. On the other hand, the nine electorates that switched to the coalition had between 26.5 and 41.9 per cent of people exposed to interest-rate movements.

The anger coalesced around Latham's decision Mark Latham later dissected the conduct of the campaign, very much from his own point of view, in his *Diaries*. Few of those mentioned in the book agree with any of his judgements. As Latham would probably reply, 'Well, they would say that, wouldn't they?' There seems to be little advantage in weighing up these competing claims to veracity. Perhaps it is best just to note that politics is rarely purely black or white. The four seats that went to Labor were Richmond, Parramatta, Hindmarsh, and Adelaide. In Richmond only 19.8 per cent of people were paying off mortgages, whereas in Adelaide it was 22.1 per cent. The seats that swung to the coalition ranged from Stirling in Western Australia, where 26.5 per cent were purchasing their dwelling, to Kingston, where 41.9 per cent were indebted to mortgage holders.

On the hot afternoon before election day The day of the election was sunny. The idea of a linkage between the weather and election results seems ridiculous. Nevertheless, in the interests of emphasising the accuracy of this book, it's worth pointing out that a paper in the *Medical Journal of Australia* investigated the issue. This suggests that, surprisingly, the 2004 election demonstrates that a tenuous link might exist. A paper by Dr Rosemary Aldrich from the University of Newcastle noted that in three of the five electorates swinging to the opposition, the 'weather was not fine and predicted to worsen during the day'. These provide a dramatic contrast with the electorates swinging to the government. In six of those eight electorates, the weather that day was fine; in the remaining two, it was forecast to clear during the day. See the *Medical Journal of Australia*, volume 181, number 11/12.

Across the island in a navy helicopter Rudd's comments on the tsunami come from the parliamentary debate on the Indian Ocean tsunami, held on 8 February 2005.

CHAPTER SEVEN: **Positioning**

The result in Griffith was one of the ten best The electorate of Griffith contained 84,105 voters on Election Day. The Liberal candidate, who obtained just 37.3 per cent of the primary vote, received the next highest proportion of the primary vote tally. After preferences were distributed, Rudd's percentage of the vote increased to 58.6 per cent.

Rudd enthusiastically engaged in parliamentary debate In particular, quotes come from the following debates in the parliament:

Private Members' Business, Human Rights in Burma, 14 February 2005;
Debate on the Asia-Pacific Region, 30 November 2004;
Questions Without Notice, 2 December 2004;
Questions in Writing, No. 304;
Debate on the National Security Information Legislation Amendment, 15 March 2005;
Private Members' Business, John Simpson Kirkpatrick, 23 May 2005;
Debate on Truth in Government, 15 February 2005;
Debate on Asylum and Protection Obligations, 15 June 2005; and
Report of the Inquiry into Certain Australian Companies in Relation to the UN Oil-for-Food Program, 29 November 2006.

Rudd appeared to positively enjoy Rudd's command of procedure to make a point was forensic. For example, in a Personal Explanation on 25 May 2005, he took the opportunity to restate his position at length, while criticising the government. This is normally a very difficult task, because the government will attempt to stop any opposition member from speaking if they diverge from strictly addressing the topic.

Rudd began by reflecting on the Christian variants The speech was at New College, University of New South Wales, October 2004, reprinted in *Online Catholics*, issue 76.

CHAPTER EIGHT: **Crisis**

I've heard the suggestion that The quotes in this chapter were all provided to me on the condition that they were not to be attributed. I have confirmed the identity of the people making the comments, and the quotes themselves, with the politicians concerned. It is not possible to further identify any sources for this account.

At the conclusion of a sitting week Dennis Shanahan had dinner with Beazley on Thursday 14 September 2006.

CHAPTER NINE: **Leader**

A first-class honours degree in clever politics The quote comes from the *Sydney Morning Herald*, 9–10 December 2006.

Tried to insist that the issue was really Greg Sheridan's article appeared on the opinion page of *The Australian* on 15 February 2007.

Had emphatically ended the honeymoon Newspapers across the nation joined in criticism of the way that Rudd had handled the government assault in parliament the day before. Even the *Strewth* column in *The Australian* newspaper included the detail of Peter Costello's attack. Making fun of what Rudd had almost insinuated could just have been a chance meeting at Perugino's restaurant in Perth, Peter Costello scoffed that it reminded him 'of the scene in *Muriel's Wedding*, when the mistress of Bill Hunter walks into the Chinese restaurant and Bill says, "Deirdre Chambers, what a coincidence!" "Brian Burke, what a coincidence, down here at Perugino's on 1 August 2005. I didn't know you were going to be here, Brian. And while I am here, I will make a speech on China." '

The force of the assault silenced the parliament, with Labor members hoping desperately that no further details of impropriety would be unleashed by the treasurer. In the event, he revealed little that was not already on the record; however, the way he stitched the facts together made a compelling case that required an answer.

Rudd's apparently clever tactic Early Chinese strategists were particularly insistent about the need to engage in the battle you wanted to win, rather than the battle the enemy wanted to force you to fight. Sun Tzu is the old and common transliteration of Sun Zi (the Pinyin transliteration). The general's aphorisms were collected in *The Art of War* some 2500 years ago. This short book still has relevance today precisely because of the general nature of many of the strategic conclusions it reached. This has enabled it to be applied to other fields of competitive endeavour, such as business and politics.

'Here, read this,' he said The quote comes from *Being Good: a short introduction to ethics* by Simon Blackburn (Oxford University Press,

2001). The philosopher wrote the book while in residence the ANU in the summer of 2000.

Melbourne radio announcer 'Is Kevin Rudd suddenly gun shy, is he media shy? We have tried every day for the last two or three weeks and every week since Christmas … (and we have) not once been able to talk to him,' said the ABC Melbourne radio announcer on 774 ABC on 29 March 2007. By the next month, Neil Mitchell was adding to this, saying, 'He's starting to look like a control freak.'